# BIG
# BUSINESS

# BIG
# BUSINESS

## A Love Letter to an
## American Anti-Hero

# TYLER COWEN

ST. MARTIN'S PRESS    NEW YORK

www.stmartins.com

Library of Congress Cataloging-in-Publication Data

Names: Cowen, Tyler, author.
Title: Big business : a love letter to an American anti-hero / Tyler Cowen.
Description: New York : St. Martin's Press, [2019] | Includes bibliographical references and index.
Identifiers: LCCN 2018045701 | ISBN 9781250110541 (hardcover) | ISBN 9781250225627
   (international, sold outside the U.S., subject to rights availability) | ISBN 9781250110558 (ebook)
Subjects: LCSH: Big business—United States. | Corporations—United States. | Industries—
   United States. | Capitalism—United States.
Classification: LCC HD2785 .C597 2019 | DDC 338.6/440973—dc23
LC record available at https://lccn.loc.gov/2018045701

Our books may be purchased in bulk for promotional, educational, or business use. Please contact your local bookseller or the Macmillan Corporate and Premium Sales Department at 1-800-221-7945, extension 5442, or by email at MacmillanSpecialMarkets@macmillan.com.

First Edition: April 2019

10  9  8  7  6  5  4  3  2  1

*To Natasha, Yana, and Kyle*

# CONTENTS

# BIG
# BUSINESS

## A NEW PRO-BUSINESS MANIFESTO

We live in an age when the reputation of business is under siege. Among Democrats, for instance, the word "socialism" now polls better than does "capitalism." But Republicans, while they pay greater lip service to some business ideals, are not in practice much better. Many of them have quite readily followed President Donald Trump into his attacks on free trade, immigration, outsourcing, and the American media (which is labeled "the enemy of the people")—all fundamentally anti-business stances.[1]

Business, quite simply, has become underrated, and thus I am writing a contrarian book that ought not to be contrarian at all. All of the criticisms one might mount against the corporate form—some of which are valid—pale in contrast to two straightforward and indeed essential virtues. First, business makes most of the stuff we enjoy and consume. Second, business is what gives most of us jobs. The two words that follow most immediately from the world of business are "prosperity" and "opportunity."

Without business we would not have:

- Ships, trains, and cars
- Electricity, lighting, and heating equipment
- Most of our food supply
- Most of our lifesaving pharmaceuticals
- Clothes for our children
- Our telephones and smartphones
- The books we love to read
- The ability to access, more or less immediately, so much of the world's online information

And let's not forget your paycheck. "Meeting payroll," to invoke a now old-fashioned phrase, is nothing less than a heroic act. Someone or some group put in the hard work and thought up the innovations required to create a company from scratch—I know it's easy enough to take this for granted if you aren't the one who did it. On top of the paycheck, jobs are among our biggest sources of pride and a significant way to meet friends and establish social networks.

By the way, when I use the word "business" I mean simply "a commercial or sometimes an industrial enterprise," to pull a quick definition from Merriam-Webster. I'll use the more legally precise word "corporation" interchangeably, even though the two concepts are not strictly the same. A kid with a lemonade stand is a business but not a corporation. That said, for the purposes of this book I will be considering institutions that are large enough and formal enough for the two words to serve as effective synonyms. I fully understand that the word "business" often sounds better to people than "corporation," so if I sometimes use the latter it is also to shock some of my readers out of an implicit anticorporate complacency.

## THE PARTICULAR VIRTUES OF AMERICAN BUSINESS

We must take a moment to appreciate the particular character of American business. By global standards, its overall performance is remarkably impressive. Stanford economist Nicholas Bloom and a group of co-authors studied and compared management practices in some of the major economies, including the United States. Their survey assessed how well a workplace uses incentives, the quality of performance measures and reviews, whether top management aims at long-term goals, whether top creators are well rewarded, and whether the firm attracts and retains quality employees, among other relevant metrics. These assessments were backed up by real-world results too, as the responses correlated with actual numbers on firm productivity, size, profitability, sales growth, market value, and firm survival.[2]

So at the end of all of these measurements of management quality, which country comes out on top? The United States is a clear first, a testament to the scope and quality of business achievement in this country, the result of the efforts of both business leaders and workers. Not coincidentally, America is the global innovation leader in a wide array of areas.

Management really matters. Let's say we take two American plants producing comparable wares, but one of those plants is in the 90th percentile in terms of productivity, while the other is in the 10th percentile. The former plant will have a productivity level four times higher than the latter plant, due to superior management practices. It has been estimated that Chinese firms could increase their productivity by 30 to 50 percent and Indian firms could do so by 40 to 60 percent merely by bringing the quality of their management practices up to American levels.[3]

And what might such improvements from the Chinese and Indians mean? America's relatively high level of workplace trust allows its companies to run with much greater efficiency. Trust allows businesses to decentralize decisions, so top managers do not become bottlenecks holding up progress. With trust, delegation to subordinates is much easier and more effective, and so businesses based on trust can scale more rapidly and have greater flexibility. In an environment with relatively high levels of trust, workers are more likely to see that rewards are based on productive contributions more than on cronyism. In these regards, the virtues of business productivity are human virtues as well, and both show up in record high levels of business output and also relatively pleasurable jobs. As human beings, we enjoy being trusted and in turn being trustworthy. So often we see that business virtues correlate with social virtues.[4]

There is another reason American business has done well: the American economy is relatively effective, compared with other countries, in weeding out the worst firms through competitive pressures. The very worst firms in the United States just aren't that bad compared with the best firms, whereas for other countries the gap is typically much larger. This is another way of saying that Americans do the "creative destruction" part of capitalism—that is, the process by which people vote with their wallets as to which is the best restaurant, car, or suitcase, and the losers go out of business—better than the rest of the world. The problem with protectionism, which at first glance looks appealing because it claims to protect our workers, is that it becomes much harder for more productive businesses to displace the less productive ones, a fundamental source of economic progress.

Compared with other major regions, the United States also does the best job of funneling labor and resources into the best-managed firms. That is, successful American businesses can grow and extend their reach. For instance, an increase in management quality of one standard deviation (a statistical measure of difference) means, for an American firm, 268 extra employees on average. A comparable increase in management quality in southern Europe is associated with only 68 more employees in the firm; similar results are found after adjusting for differences in firm size. In other words, America is especially good at matching talent to talent and getting the most out of its biggest successes.[5]

## LESS POLARIZED AND MORE VIRTUOUS THAN GOVERNMENT

We can all admit that we are a nation sorely in need of virtue, specifically in our political realm. The growing polarization of today's politics has made our government at best hopelessly sclerotic and at worst prone to unpredictable lurches. This polarization has also spurred out-of-control political correctness and censorship, rampant racism and injustice, new waves of violent marches and shootings, and an array of indictments and corruption charges. Many features of contemporary America are wonderful, including the high level of trust in the corporate sector, but the weirdness in our government has been rising.

In contrast, the world of American business has never been more productive, more tolerant, and more cooperative. It is not just a source of GDP and prosperity; it is a ray of normalcy and predictability in its steady focus on producing what can be profitably sold to customers. Successful businesses grow dynamically, but they also try to create oases of stability and tolerance in which they can perfect their production methods. These oases help to attract and retain talent and make it possible for businesses to offer consumers a steady stream of "comfort products." Business helps carve out spaces for love, friendship, creativity, and human caring by producing the resources that make our lives not just tolerable but comfortable.

American big business in particular has led the way toward making America more socially inclusive. McDonald's, General Electric, Procter & Gamble, and many of the major tech companies, among others, were defining health and other legal benefits for same-sex partners before the Supreme Court legalized gay marriage. Apple, Pfizer, Microsoft, Deutsche Bank, PayPal, and Marriott, among others, spoke out or protested the North Carolina law that sought to specify which restrooms transgender people had to use; the outcry led to the eventual repeal of that law. This push for tolerance shouldn't come as any surprise. Big business has lots of customers and relies on the value of brand names. It doesn't want any group of those customers to feel put out or discriminated against or to have cause for complaint, not least because we live in an age of social media. Profit maximization alone—not to mention the consciences of some CEOs—puts big business these days on the side of inclusion and tolerance.[6]

Larger firms, in particular, which you can think of as wildly successful businesses and thus embodiments of the logic of business, tend to be more tolerant of employee personal tastes than smaller firms. A local baker might be reluctant to make a wedding cake for a gay couple, but Sara Lee, which tries to build very broadly based national markets for its products, is happy to sell to all. The bigger companies need to protect their broader reputations and recruit large numbers of talented workers, including those from minority groups. They can't survive and grow just by cultivating a few narrow networks of local white men.

I sometimes say that if you want to understand today's world, you will do better reading the sports pages—which reflect a basic day-to-day normalcy in American life—than the front page or political section. Sports, of course, are a form of business.

## WHAT'S THE BEEF?

I have a complaint about America today, and it is simple: we don't love business enough.

It isn't just one part of the population that tends to look down on business. Here is a partial list of those segments of modern America that are often reflexively critical of business and at the very least view it with great suspicion.

## Young People

Most young Americans hold highly critical perspectives on capitalism. In one representative poll conducted by researchers at Harvard University, only 42 percent of young adults between ages eighteen and twenty-nine supported capitalism, while 51 percent said they did not support capitalism. Most of the respondents were not exactly sure what they favored instead, but a stunning 33 percent endorsed socialism as an alternative. Even if they don't mean socialism as earlier generations would have understood the concept, they are not exactly signaling their love of the corporate form. Today there is probably more anti-business sentiment, most of all among young people, than at any other time since the radicalism of the 1960s.[7]

## Bernie Sanders Supporters

Although he did not win the Democratic Party's nomination in 2016, Bernie Sanders arguably was the candidate who generated the second-highest amount of enthusiasm in that election cycle. As I write, he is one of the leading candidates to win the party's nomination in 2020, though he will be seventy-eight years of age. And as the Democratic Party responds to the excesses of the Trump administration, Sanders's progressive ideals are proving highly influential.

Bernie Sanders epitomizes the anti-business left. A self-described socialist, he has called for breaking up the big banks and for the establishment of more worker-owned cooperatives. He blames the stagnation in living standards on the rapacious nature of American business. I think you can plausibly argue that an actual Sanders presidency might not be nearly as radical as some of his rhetoric; consider, for example, that he uses the word "socialist" in varying and often pretty generic ways. Still, ask yourself a basic question: Has Bernie Sanders said much of anything good about business in general or big business in particular? If not, why is he so unwilling to appreciate one of the most beneficial and fundamental institutions in American life?

## The Media (and Social Media)

The media are perhaps the biggest villain when it comes to criticizing business, but it's not mainly about newspapers or TV stations being too left-wing. Virtually all media outlets have a significant bias toward negative news of all kinds, including news about business. So scandals, corruption, and abuse of workers all receive much more publicity than the normal, everyday massive successes of America's major corporations. "Corporations had another stellar day producing things and keeping people employed" just isn't a great news headline.

These days, it is common for major media outlets, including centrist publications such as the *Financial Times*, to run articles about the sins of the major tech companies. Rana Foroohar, for instance, stresses the negative when she writes of "the power of the big tech titans." In reality, Amazon, Google, Facebook, Apple, and others have provided Americans with some of their most amazing products, and sometimes for free or at very low prices. In terms of access to information, the world has been knit together far more tightly than almost anyone could have dreamed of two decades ago, and that may well be humankind's single greatest achievement within our generation. And yet we hear as a kind of drumbeat that these companies must be broken up, dismantled, or at least regulated much, much more stringently. If there is any good critique of business in these stories, it is that newspapers are running mediocre analyses to maximize the number of click-throughs, aided of course by the negative slant of some segments of the social media universe.

We're even seeing the reemergence of explicitly anti-capitalist media sources. Take the print and online magazine *Jacobin*, which recently published the following sentence: "In some cases, like the former Soviet Union, the failings of [top-down socialism] are nearly as deep as those of capitalism itself." This was in a piece by Mathieu Desan and Michael A. McCarthy titled "A Time to Be Bold."[8]

Social media is part of the problem too. How is this tweet, from

"Dina," for showing lack of gratitude toward business? "If you think about it. People with glasses are literally paying to use their eyes. Capitalism is a bitch." Shortly after it was posted, it had accumulated more than 257,000 likes, surely with more to come. But perhaps eyeglass companies should instead be applauded for competing against each other to make this service as cheap as possible. There is, by the way, a well-known economics literature showing that when state laws limit the advertising of eyeglasses, competition is damaged and eyeglasses become more expensive. Fortunately, the Federal Trade Commission struck down those laws, thereby helping competition to prevail and leading to lower prices.[9]

## Ordinary Americans Who Don't Trust Business Enough

Look at this 2016 Gallup poll about the relative amounts of trust Americans have in a variety of institutions:[10]

| Institution | Trust "a great deal" | Trust "quite a lot" |
| --- | --- | --- |
| The military | 41% | 32% |
| Small business | 30% | 38% |
| The police | 25% | 31% |
| The church or organized religion | 20% | 21% |
| The medical system | 17% | 22% |
| The presidency | 16% | 20% |
| The U.S. Supreme Court | 15% | 21% |
| The public schools | 14% | 16% |
| Banks | 11% | 16% |
| Organized labor | 8% | 15% |
| The criminal justice system | 9% | 14% |
| Television news | 8% | 13% |
| Newspapers | 8% | 12% |
| Big business | 6% | 12% |
| Congress | 0% | 6% |

Big business barely beats out Congress at the bottom of the trust ladder, certainly a sign that things aren't going very well on the trust scale—though our small businesses do very well indeed, coming in second only to the military. For many of us, big business suggests rapaciousness, the power to bully workers, and a cavalier attitude toward the well-being of their consumers. And yet big business on average pays much higher wages and offers superior benefits and workplace conditions compared with smaller business. In other words, arguably the biggest problem with American business is the politically incorrect truth that too often it simply isn't big enough and successful enough. It isn't ambitious enough or doing a good enough job boosting profits and growing toward gargantuan size.[11]

## Trump Supporters and the Conservative Right

Donald Trump often presents himself as a fan of big business and a representative of America's productive class. But big business also serves as his whipping boy. He is very happy to taunt businesses and business executives in his tweets (such as Carrier and Amazon). When push comes to shove, on the issues where Trump is in the wrong, do Trump supporters side with the man or with the better parts of American business? So far we've seen little evidence of a large-scale revolt against Trump's anti-business provocations.

When the topic of tech companies comes up, a lot of the conservative right identifies Facebook and Google with left-wing, politically correct cultural elites, which of course is somewhat true. The right then calls for breaking up those large technology companies or regulating them much more heavily, and more generally leads a kind of intellectual jihad against their major role in American life. The British conservative historian Niall Ferguson has become one of the ringleaders of this movement, which has made surprising inroads with a number of right-wing politicians, many of whom are convinced that the major tech companies go out of their way to censor conservative ideas and intellectuals.[12]

I am pretty critical of the media in some ways, but I would never call them "the enemy of the people," as Trump and some other Republicans have done. Do you really think Trump is so unambiguously pro-business? Don't forget that the media, too, are American corporate enterprises.

## A BRIEF ROAD MAP

I'm here to speak up for business, to persuade you that it deserves more of your love and less hate. Perhaps, like you, I am not entirely comfortable with ceding so much of the daily human realm to apparently selfish, profit-maximizing, and even sometimes corrupt entities, but on closer examination this is a better bargain than it might seem at first. Indeed, at its best, business gives our lives more scope for the heroic and the noble, as we can use the outputs of business to satisfy our own creative desires and to better our lives.

I'll argue that a lot of the most common criticisms of American business don't stand up to scrutiny. For instance, it's often claimed that American business is too focused on quarterly earnings statements, at the expense of a longer-run perspective. But in fact there is plenty of evidence that companies can think long-term when appropriate. Sometimes short-run problems are easier or more important to solve, or they are the bridge to longer-run success, and the evidence at hand indicates that American business does a pretty good job of looking to the future.

Then there's the question of American CEO pay, which Edward Luce, a *Financial Times* columnist (and a friend of mine), described on Twitter as "unconscionable."[13] American CEOs are paid much more than they used to be, but these pay hikes have pretty much moved in tandem with the size and valuations of the firms they manage. Contrary to common claims, it is hard to establish that CEOs as a whole are ripping off their shareholders with manipulated pay packages, as a look at the numbers will show that high compensation is the price of attracting top talent. Running a large corporation involves taking on more roles than ever before, including media, government, and public relations, formulating a vision, understanding consumers and communicating to them, building cross-cultural global strategies, working with governments, and keeping the company out of trouble, in addition to having a lot of sector-specific expertise. That limits the number of eligible candidates who might succeed at the job and thus it boosts their pay, according to basic principles of supply and demand. Today's CEOs are literally superachievers, and it should come as no surprise that they are compensated accordingly.

One of the most frequently cited whipping boys is the financial sector, which is portrayed as too large and out of control. The reality is that the financial sector has held to a fairly constant 2 percent share of American wealth, though of course that wealth has grown and so has finance with it. The ability of American finance to mobilize savings into riskier forms of equity and venture capital has brought Americans hundreds of billions of dollars in value each year, and those gains significantly outweigh the costs typically attributed to the financial sector. Nor is the financial sector draining the American economy of all its talent for other endeavors, as evidenced by the rise of American manufacturing output to ever higher levels.

Most of all, business is criticized for being fraudulent and ripping us off. While there is plenty of fraud in business, the commercial sector isn't any more fraudulent than individuals in other capacities, and it may even be somewhat less fraudulent. Business can make us better people—for example, by teaching us how to cooperate better—and the best evidence indicates that, on net, businesses do not make us worse compared with our participation in other institutions. A lot of us were somewhat dishonest to begin with, and if you have doubts, just look at the individual lies and misrepresentations in online dating profiles.

So many of the problems with business are in fact problems with us, and they reflect the underlying and fairly universal imperfections of human nature. Yet we respond to this truth somewhat irrationally. While we suspect business of wrongdoing, at the same time we expect corporations to give us jobs and take care of us, to give us a network of friends, to solve our social problems, and to give us risk-free consumption experiences.

This is another way of saying we judge companies as we might judge a person, sometimes even a family member: in terms of connection and standards of integrity. This is a mistake, because corporations are legal constructs and abstract entities, and they do not have purposes, goals, or feelings of their own. We would do better to think about the proper role and function of corporations in the social and legal order, and how the behavior of companies can create jobs and produce goods and services. But precisely because we tend to judge corporations by the standards we use to judge people, it is hard for us to accept the partially venal or sometimes amoral pecuniary or greedy motives operating behind the scenes, and so we moralize about companies instead of trying to understand them.

Furthermore, the common portrait of corporations as consisting entirely of selfish or greedy individuals is not the best understanding of big business. Nobel laureate Milton Friedman, a major defender of capitalism and business, published a famous but ultimately misguided article in 1970 with the title "The Social Responsibility of Business Is to Increase Its Profits." His main point was that business CEOs and managers are wrong to allocate shareholder resources for social justice or other altruistic goals. Friedman thought that ends other than profit could be valuable for society, but in his mind those ends were better pursued through charity, nonprofit institutions, or government policy, as corporations could not perform those tasks efficiently or in accordance with their basic natures.[14]

Although I am a fan of Milton Friedman and I share his skepticism about socialist solutions, I think this article reflected significant ideological blinders. Goals other than simple profit maximization often end up boosting both business profits and social benefits. For example, the people who work at SpaceX, the Elon Musk company that launches satellites using advanced and sometimes revolutionary rocket technology, often really do believe in the dream of colonizing other planets and the stars. The founders of Skype and the managers who work there seem to believe in the ideal of bringing friends, families, and business associates together. Many journalists and newspaper editors are at least trying to make the world a better place. Friedman failed to understand that the cultural, intellectual, ideological, and even *emotional* foundations of business go far beyond an attachment to profit. People care about what they do, and they seek meaning through their jobs. Profit maximization is best thought of as a convenient fiction that does a fairly good job boosting profits precisely because it rejects a sole emphasis on profits as a goal.

Particularly now in the age of social media, which allows direct connections with consumers and offers them the chance to provide direct feedback when things go wrong, the most successful businesses have a kind of messianic view of their role in society—venerating the delivery of goods and services to the consumer, or perhaps promoting a particular vision of how society ought to be. Workers wish to believe their toil is saving the environment, fighting poverty, and strengthening America as a nation. A business that instills in its workers and managers a *sincere* belief in such goals has a better chance of building a durable competitive advantage than a business that does not. It will attract more consumer loyalty and better and more cooperative partners at the business-to-business level. Think of it this way: Who wants to marry someone who is always selfishly seeking to optimize happiness from the marriage?

Ayn Rand showed a deep insight into the character of successful business when she emphasized that it can be a vehicle for the achievement of heroic goals. The character of Hank Rearden in Rand's novel *Atlas Shrugged* stressed the dignity, honor, and reason involved in good productive work, and he came to see it as the very foundation of America's greatness.

It is often those business leaders who are religious or have strong ideologies of another kind who grasp most clearly the relevance of a business having a mission above and beyond profit. They understand that the business and religious or ideological sides of their lives are by no means totally separate. They understand they can do best by their shareholders—and the broader society—by tying together the business, religious, ethical, and ideological perspectives in one bundle. Friedman's own success in building up the University of Chicago economics department, which went on to be the single biggest source of Nobel laureates, relied very much on a "corporate culture" of truth seeking and achievement, rather than a narrow focus on a single, self-oriented goal such as making the most money or publishing the most articles. When it came to business, Friedman should have drawn more on his history of institution building than on his role as slayer of socialist dragons.

In other words, business at its best is a fundamentally ethical enterprise.

So, you may be asking yourself, if business is so good, why are we so suspicious of it? This is a very good question and one I will not dodge. More on this to follow, but I'll say now that in part it's a reaction to businesses' power over us and our lack of control over them. For instance, consumers *as a group* have a great deal of control over corporations, but usually *individual* consumers do not. Indeed, many companies make conscious calculations to simply ignore individual customer complaints, as they have decided it isn't worth the time and money to deal with them. Is trying to call customer service or to get an insurance company to reevaluate an incorrectly rejected payment claim always a satisfying experience? In similar fashion, individual workers do not always have a lot of leverage over their bosses.

At times companies seem like vicious sharks, circling in the water for their next meal. This feels all the more intimidating when the companies are highly successful and efficient. Yet at other times companies seem like people, presenting themselves to us as our friends and our protectors, persuading us to judge them with our most personal and sympathetic sides. It's no wonder we can't come up with a fully square, emotionally consistent picture of the American corporation, because the system itself discourages us from doing so.

## THE RISE AND RISE AND RISE OF BUSINESS

Whether we like it or not, people are relying on corporations more and more. Almost all of our food, shelter, and pharmaceuticals are produced by corporations. More and more people meet their spouses or partners online or through apps, a process managed by, yes, businesses such as Match.com and Tinder. We use the workplace as a respite and a source of personal support if life at home is not going so well. Although they have recently faced extreme criticism and scrutiny, Facebook and Google and smartphones remain conduits for much of the information coming in and going out of our lives every day.

On the macro side, if the American government really, truly wants something done, very often it turns to business. Corporations produce most of the American military's weapons systems and most of the country's roads and infrastructure, and it was the tech companies that helped the government fix the initially malfunctioning Obamacare website.

On top of that, if it weren't for business, how easily could you get your Unicorn Frappuccino or whatever else has become the sweet caffeinated beverage du jour?

In fact, business is just getting started. In the not too distant future, we can expect business to drive our cars for us, to manage more of our lives for us through online personal assistants, and to run our homes through sophisticated appliances that connect to the internet and talk to each other. Business also gathers significant amounts of data on us, and it is possible that more aspects of our lives will be recorded and measured by some business somewhere for some commercial purpose, with that data perhaps then traded to yet another set of businesses—in most cases with our consent being more automatic and unthinking than active and conscious. As we'll see in chapter 6, on tech, the ongoing erosions of our privacy may well be the most problematic feature of American business today.

For better or worse, corporations are being asked to achieve more social goals, even social goals that we might associate with government. For instance, part of the increase in health insurance coverage that resulted from Obamacare came about because of the mandate requiring larger businesses to provide health insurance to all of their full-time workers. When the minimum wage is increased by law, as has been the case rather frequently as of late, government is ordering business to perform some kind of social welfare function by paying workers more. Americans demand more environmental protection from businesses, and often it is expected that businesses will be the ones to come up with the new technologies to fix climate change problems, albeit with governmental assistance. One of the main American programs for poverty alleviation, the Earned Income Tax Credit, is run through private employers, though with governmental funds providing the wage supplement and thus the work subsidy.

Of course, much of that deferral to business has happened by default. We are imperfect, vulnerable human beings who need lots and lots done. Because most of us don't have a vision for how we could accomplish those things on our own, or even through government, corporations end up doing many of them. "When in doubt, let it happen" has been the philosophy behind the spread of so much corporate activity in the United States, most of all in the world of tech. Did Uber even bother to ask for permission to operate its ride-share business, or request that a referendum be held on whether it should be treated as a municipal utility? In reality, we've had a tech revolution and such significant growth in American business because our companies very often solved problems first and sorted out many of the complications later.

We also rely on business to regulate speech, for better or worse. Our government usually respects the First Amendment, which protects freedom of speech, but PayPal has decided it will not process payments for extremist and hate groups. Facebook has taken to monitoring the content of ads and posts on the site, and is under increasing pressure, including from users and their own employees, to do more of this. Google fired James Damore, the author of the now-infamous "anti-diversity memo," for expressing sentiments that many believed were harmful to the recruitment and advancement of women within the company. YouTube won't let just anyone post, and Walmart recently removed *Cosmopolitan* magazine from its shelves for being insufficiently family friendly. Those have been controversial corporate decisions, but while some intellectuals complain, most of the American public accepts these arrangements or maybe even demands them. Again, that shows how many of the defaults in our system are geared toward accepting that business can have a major social impact.

Big business is a recent human creation, dating in America from the nineteenth century, and our emotions and heuristics have not evolved to evaluate it very accurately. In particular, I'd like to caution you against a kind of "whack-a-mole" argument, whereby you simply look for reasons to oppose business. You always can find such reasons, and it would be impossible for me to consider every possible anti-business argument. And, of course, there is partial validity to some of them. I do not in this book cover whether outsourcing is ravaging the American workforce, whether the major music labels have ruined rock and roll, or the potential dangers of GMOs, to name just a few of many omitted topics. Instead, I've tried to pick some focal and commonly discussed topics that are in the news today. What I am asking of you is this: if the evidence on these topics suggests a picture that might be different from your anti-business prior beliefs, don't just switch to another criticism of business to maintain your anti-business emotional equilibrium. At least consider the possibility that American business is truly underrated, including on issues I have not covered.[15]

And that means American business is deserving of higher status. But will we recognize it for its virtues, and drop enough of our exaggerated complaints? I hope so. Your ability to invest, thrive in your career, buy high-quality things for reasonable prices, travel, and care for your children—among many other aspects of life—may depend on it.

# ARE BUSINESSES MORE FRAUDULENT THAN THE REST OF US?

Let's cut right to the chase: a lot of people just don't trust business. They cite stories of companies trying to rip off customers, skirt environmental regulations, shortchange their employees, and generally put profit ahead of acting ethically. There are also plenty of recent headline cases of fraud, including Volkswagen's blatant circumvention of emissions controls, Theranos lying about its blood-testing products, and Wells Fargo employees creating phony accounts for millions of unaware and presumably unwilling customers. The conclusion often drawn from these appalling examples is that there is something inherently dishonest about corporations. It is widely understood that the profit motive can lead people to take bad actions, including within corporations. It is less commonly recognized that the incentives for honest dealing within business also can be strong, and indeed very often dominant. In this chapter, I'm going to consider what the evidence tells us about the net result of these two very different effects.

We must first acknowledge the bad news—namely, that entire sectors of our corporate economy are based primarily on ripping off consumers. The overwhelming majority of the multibillion-dollar dietary supplement industry arguably brings no benefit to its customers, other than perhaps occasionally peddling placebos. I tried to Google data on how much Americans spend each year on penis enlargement, but the thicket of ads and unreliable sources made it impossible to find a good answer. Usually I am more persistent, but I realized that if I continued, penis enlargement ads would be showing up in my Gmail. So I desisted, knowing only that the word "billions" appeared some number of times. The customers for these items spend their money to buy false hope, and profit-seeking businesses are egging them on.[1]

On top of those obvious misrepresentations, fraudulent or semi-fraudulent practices are deeply embedded within a lot of legitimate sectors. Many dentists insist you get X-rays every year, even though it's costly and there is little evidence it helps your teeth. Doctors get kickbacks for overprescribing antidepressants and other medications, and retail stockbrokers often encourage you to trade when you shouldn't or urge you to buy a higher-load fund so as to boost their commission. Retail sales reps will push that extended warranty or maintenance contract on you, whether or not it makes sense for you to buy insurance against relatively small pecuniary losses. I'm sure you have your own personal list of such abuses. To put the point simply, if I showed up at a dealership to buy a sailboat—something I know nothing about—*I would start with the assumption that the sellers are trying to rip me off.*

Or consider the food sector, which is about as mainstream as you can get. One study showed that about 33 percent of packaged fish in the supermarket was inaccurately labeled regarding type or origin. Some of that may be ignorance jointly cultivated between the supermarket and the fish supplier rather than a direct, intentional lie, but still, it would not be difficult to improve the accuracy of the labels— except the companies might sell fewer fish. Another study showed that between 15 and 75 percent of the salmon claimed as wild actually was farmed; it's funny how the error rarely runs in the opposite direction, of claiming a fish caught in the wild was farmed.[2]

At this point you might be wondering where this is going—I'm essentially conceding that businesses often behave dishonestly.

But here I'd ask you to step back and consider what standard we are measuring business against. The propensity of business to commit fraud is essentially just an extension of the propensity of *people* to commit fraud. When a manager tells his fish department to label some unknown fish as rainbow trout, it's a person making this decision. To paraphrase Cassius from Shakespeare's *Julius Caesar*, "The fault, dear Brutus, is not in our corporations, but in ourselves."

People commit fraud both in and out of businesses, and the evidence shows they are just as dishonest outside of a business context as within it. Businesses often limit fraud by creating institutional structures to constrain the worst sides of their managers and employees, if only to preserve the reputation of the business for fair and honest dealing. It turns out that is a strong means for simultaneously getting things done and limiting the extent of fraud and dishonest dealing.

Further, particularly now that digital communication has raised the price of corporate dishonesty, big business has by necessity, and despite its shortcomings, become one of the most effective institutions for *limiting* the extent of fraud. In fact, that is one significant reason big businesses became big in the first place—they evoke more trust in consumers, and rationally so. You're more likely to be ripped off by your local TV repairman, your local doctor, or maybe even your cousin than you are likely to be cheated by McDonald's or Walmart. McDonald's and Walmart, quite simply, have valuable national and international reputations to lose, and they will act to preserve their brand identities. Big businesses have more to lose from fraud, they are monitored more closely, and they are more likely to depend on the commercial value of a respected national or international brand name.

That comparison is something you won't hear often enough from most politicians or from most critics of big business.

Let's now turn to this comparative perspective in more detail.

## HOW FRAUDULENT IS BUSINESS IN A COMPARATIVE PERSPECTIVE?

To get a handle on this comparative question, we need to consider fraud and lying in some non-business contexts. The results, I am sorry to say, are often less than encouraging. Let's begin with one area rife with fraud: internet dating profiles.

According to one survey, 53 percent of people *admitted* to having lied in their online dating profiles. Of course, the true percentage is likely higher yet, as many of the liars may be lying again when they say they didn't lie. It is easy enough to see the incentive to give false information about one's age, weight, financial status, or maybe even marital status. Time-stamped photographs have been common for a long time, mostly because lying about one's age or current weight was so very frequent.

If you read the descriptions of services offered on the Match.com site itself, you'll find nothing that could plausibly be considered a lie, even though you might find the photos too glossy or the overall impression a little too cheery and positive. That's a pretty clear case where the business is itself a lot more honest than the customers are. If you think of love, romance, and sex as especially important matters—so significant to us as to cut past the genteel veneer of civilized society and to bring out our true selves—under the surface we will find massive amounts of personal lying and fraud. That 53 percent figure for lying in online profiles is the lower bound.[3]

If we look at lies in general, one major study estimates that each person tells an average of 1.96 lies per day. Very often we are most inclined to tell those lies to the people we are closest to, not to total strangers.[4]

According to a 2002 University of Massachusetts study, 60 percent of adults will lie at least once within the course of a ten-minute conversation, with the average number of lies from the liars being three. And that is only what people *admitted to*. (If you are wondering, in this study men and women lied at about the same rate.) I don't think there is any single number that captures how much people lie, as that depends greatly on context. Nonetheless, lying is rather deeply embedded in human nature.[5]

And how good should we feel about customer applications? What percentage of mortgage applications contain lies or half-truths? Are country club and other membership applications really so aboveboard in terms of their veracity? How many resumes present an accurate picture? Employees and job applicants leave blank spots on their resumes, they talk of "moving on" when they were fired, and they claim to have skills and talents they do not. A lot of these misstatements are harmless, but again they show that a tendency to stretch or violate the truth is hardly specific to business, businesspeople, and CEOs. One estimate I read, from an executive headhunter, claimed that at least 40 percent of resumes contained outright falsehoods. A more formal research study found that 31 percent of those submitting resumes fabricated information, 76 percent embellished the truth, and 59 percent omitted materially relevant information.[6]

Or compare business dishonesty with employee violations of trust. According to one estimate, retailers lost $32 billion to shoplifting and employee theft in 2014, and often it is the consumer who ultimately pays the bill, not some fat cat in a penthouse suite. That number, by the way, is not counting employee theft at wholesale levels. In 2014, 4.7 percent of American workers failed to pass their workplace drug tests, and many more simply didn't show up for the test. Other employees who use drugs go undetected because there are active markets in phony urine samples and other workarounds, or they stop using drugs sometime before the test is given. We don't know the underlying rate of lying here because we don't know how many workers are using prohibited drugs, but still, these are disquieting numbers, all the more so because many of these individuals rather desperately need a decent job. Employee drug and alcohol abuse—which of course is also dishonest and in violation of any contract—is one of the biggest problems many employers face.[7]

The reality is that businesses are swimming in a broader environment where their most important partners—their workers and their customers—are lying to them, or at least trying to lie to them, on a pretty regular basis.

Personally, I would be hard-pressed to find a big business that lies to me as much as—presumably—my friends, family, and closest associates do. (You can ask them about me.) Of course, I have to get along with those associates on a very regular basis, whereas big business remains at a distance, emotionally, physically, and otherwise. So I tend to mentally blur over the fact that my close associates lie to me so that I may continue to cooperate with them and to enjoy those interactions. Cognitive dissonance rules, but I neglect this reality most of the time, unless of course those lies prevent me from getting what I want, in which case the lies will meet with some partial but still largely nonconfrontational pushback. In contrast, it is easy enough to curse Shell but every now and then pull into one of their stations and fill my car with gas. Shell may send me misleading information on a few big things—say, about climate change—but in my regular interactions with them and their retailing agents they are telling the truth, as indeed it is usable gasoline that comes out of the pump and goes into my car. The posted price corresponds to the price I actually am charged, and so on. When it comes to Shell in their commercial interactions with consumers, they try to be very honest and straightforward, even if some of their lobbying is more problematic.

I know of one study that examined which kinds of library books are stolen most often. You might think the thieves, with perhaps their selfish commercial interests at heart, would target business manuals about how to make more profit and build large commercial empires. After all, critics of business suggest that the commercially minded are among the least honest people in American society. But no, the data tell a different story. The books that are most likely to be stolen from libraries are *books on ethics*, especially those that are likely to be read by faculty and advanced students in moral philosophy. Those books go missing at a rate 50 to 150 percent higher than comparable texts not about ethics. And if it is any consolation, books by Nietzsche are among the most likely to be snatched, and another target is Alasdair MacIntyre's *After Virtue*. Again, maybe businesspeople are not the most dishonest group after all.[8]

By the way, if you ask peers what they think of the behavior of ethicists, the common opinion is that they do not behave any better than non-ethicist philosophers. Researchers also have studied the behavior of professional philosophers and their audiences at academic conferences. The participants at the ethics sessions are just as likely to talk audibly while the speaker is presenting, let the door slam shut while entering or leaving a session, and leave behind clutter or garbage at the end of a session. The one piece of encouraging news is that participants attending sessions on environmental ethics were less likely to leave behind trash. More anecdotally, there is plenty of talk about both the philosophy profession and ethics in particular as having a culture somewhat hostile to women and being prone to incidents and scandals of sexual harassment.[9]

A study of Google searches, based on inside data from the company, also indicates that people are quite willing to lie about their actual desires and behavior, and that forms the subject of an entire book by Seth Stephens-Davidowitz: *Everybody Lies*. We lie about our sexual preferences, about the degree of our own prejudice, and about how we spend our time; we even lie about our lying. Here is just one of the sobering truths unearthed in the book. The Google search term that correlates most closely with the unemployment rate in any given American county is not any term that might be connected to job search. Instead it is "Slutload," a well-known pornographic site.[10]

Given this overall background, I thought I should delve into the literature and look for as many possible metrics as I could to measure business fraud relative to its non-business variant. The available measures are all inexact, but they do show plenty of evidence of non-business institutions being as fraudulent as businesses, and sometimes more so. Here is what I found.

## THE TAX GAP

One simple way to compare the relative prevalence of fraud across individuals and businesses is to look at tax fraud.

The Internal Revenue Service periodically measures something called the "tax gap." Quite simply, that estimates how much legally due tax people—and corporations—are not in fact paying. Another word for the tax gap is, well, cheating.

The latest estimate I have available for the tax gap is for 2008–2010, in terms of an annual average. For the category "individual income tax," the average tax gap for those years is $264 billion. Note that includes the category of business income filed on individual returns, but essentially these are decisions made by individuals rather than by businesses in the more formal institutional sense.[11]

For those same years, the corporate income tax gap averages about $41 billion, much smaller than the tax gap for individuals. In fact, the personal income gap is more than six times larger than the corporate gap.

To be sure, that comparison by itself does not prove much, because it does not consider the size of the personal income tax sector relative to the size of the corporate income tax sector, among other things. But that we can do. For instance, if we look at total revenue collected from personal income tax and from corporate income tax for 2010, the ratio is about 4.7 to 1.

So to line up this simple comparison, in revenue terms the personal income tax sector is 4.7 times greater than the corporate sector.

The relative "cheating factor" is about 6 to 1, with more of the cheating done on the personal income tax. In terms of those simple proportions, individuals would appear to cheat more on their taxes than businesses do.[12]

## CEOS IN LABORATORY GAMES

Ernst Fehr and John A. List, two of the best known economists in the field of experimental economics, set up what is called a "trust game" and compared the performance of CEOs to non-CEOs. The results were pretty straightforward: the CEOs both were more trusting of others and exhibited more trustworthiness themselves.[13]

The experiments used a modified version of the traditional trust game, which is one means of measuring how much trust exists between individuals. In the game, subjects are paired anonymously and one of the individuals receives a certain amount of money. He is then told that he can give some, all, or none of that money to the other party. For every dollar he gives to his partner, the partner will get an additional three units. A giver has the power to increase the total wealth of the two, but at a personal cost. He does have the power to request that a certain amount of money be paid back, although this request may or may not be granted.

There are a few layers of decision in this game, such as how much to hand over and also how much to ask to be paid back. The receiver, for his part, decides how much to return, given the initial request (in an alternative version of the experiment, there is also the possibility of a small fixed fine if a request for funds to be returned is not honored). Truly trusting people, of course, will hand over a lot initially, without asking for much back. There will then be some return of the funds that makes both game players better off, but that is not guaranteed. Trust*worthy* people, similarly, will give back what is requested, enough to make both players better off. At each decision point, trust and trustworthiness help to create a win-win scenario, but too much suspicion will scuttle that result.

In this context, the CEOs were both more trusting as givers and more trustworthy as receivers. They turned more money over in the first place, and as recipients they gave back more money above and beyond any consideration of facing a fine. In other words, the CEOs did a better job on both sides of the game, generating trusting, win-win interactions. Note that in this game the imposition of the fine often was counterproductive— recipients gave less back when faced with that threat—and this meant that the CEOs received higher overall monetary returns. The CEOs were more likely than the non-CEOs to rely on trust rather than on the threat of fines. This game was played in a number of variants, but consistently the CEOs exhibited better behavior with respect to trust.

To be sure, this evidence is not even close to decisive. This was a laboratory-based game setting rather than the real world, and the monetary prizes were small and segregated from the participants' life outcomes. Furthermore, the experiment was conducted in Costa Rica, so the non-CEOs, who were students, were Costa Ricans, and the CEOs were taken from the Costa Rican coffee sector. Similar results might not hold for other groups. Still, when all is said and done, this is the clearest experimental study we have on the trust and trustworthiness of CEOs relative to some subset of the general population. In this case, anyway, the CEOs passed the test with flying colors.

## CROSS-CULTURAL GAME THEORY

Another body of evidence considers how people from different cultures behave in economic games based on the choice to cooperate or not. Harvard anthropologist Joseph Henrich, for instance, has made progress on understanding the cross-cultural variation in the ultimatum game. In this two-player game, one player proposes the distribution of a sum of money between the two participants, such as by specifying 50-50. Yet if the initial offer is perceived as too unfair, the responder has the option of declining it, leading to no reward for either party.

Henrich conducted an extensive study of the ultimatum game among the Machiguenga, a people who live in the Peruvian Amazon. They have relatively little market activity, not much in the way of formal business, and a low level of political complexity. They live in small, somewhat isolated groups, and Henrich writes that "cooperation above the family level is almost unknown, except for cooperative fish poisoning," which is their method of catching fish.[14]

Henrich and his collaborators have extended this research to look at game-playing behavior across a broader number of societies and also with a broader number of games. His basic conclusion is that well-developed market societies have the strongest norms for fairness and sharing, and a greater willingness to punish those who do not internalize such norms in their initial offers. Overall, the people from the more commercialized societies are much more willing to cooperate outside of narrow kinship circles. The core message is that commerce and advanced market societies tend to breed trust and reciprocal cooperation. It is no accident that such hypotheses were common among eighteenth-century Enlightenment thinkers, such as the Frenchman Montesquieu, and others who were observing the rise of commercial society on a massive scale for the very first time.[15]

It is important to understand why business might lead to so much trust. As I mentioned in chapter 1, the most effective way to boost profits in a business is to have employees who believe in working toward something other than pure profit maximization. They have to believe in other human values, they have to believe in making the world a better place, and they have to believe in their loyalty to each other. This kind of paradox is pretty common in human affairs. If you deliberately set out to be happy, you'll probably end up less happy than if you focus on concrete achievements and building human connections. If you try to relax, or try too hard to fall asleep, or try too hard to fall in love, you may find those ends harder to accomplish. In human affairs and also in business, most optimization is done indirectly, and that means a lot of American businesses will invest very heavily in building up trust and cooperation, and making sure their employees have an intrinsic belief in those same values.[16]

When business puts some social goals ahead of profit, at least for some particular decisions, business itself is often the biggest beneficiary. There is growing evidence that corporate *culture* is a major driver of corporate *success* (or failure). By corporate culture I mean the values, norms, and formal and informal institutions embedded in individual firms, including those related to trust and trustworthiness. It can be said that corporate culture is what employees do when no one is watching. This includes what kind of behavior workers expect from others, how they frame their work tasks, and what workers view as the true mission of the organization. When I talk to CEOs or company founders, I am struck by how often they cite corporate culture as the ultimate source of competitive advantage or persistent profits. Many companies prosper early on because they have a new product or idea that their competitors have not yet developed, but over time other suppliers catch up and work on creating comparable offerings. To keep, sustain, and maybe even increase competitive advantage, truly successful companies take that initial product or service and use it to build a compelling vision, a set of cultural practices for their employees, and a select group of talented people within the company who share a special cooperative fervor, based on the belief that they are doing something really important. If done well (whether deliberately or, more likely, as the result of not-so-closely-planned evolution), those norms and institutions can keep a company above the fray for a long time.

Responses from a survey of senior executives at 1,348 North

American firms reaffirm the importance of corporate culture. More than half of the executives surveyed cited corporate culture as one of the top three drivers of firm value, and of that sample 92 percent expressed the view that a better corporate culture would make their companies more valuable. Only 16 percent of the sample believed that their current corporate cultures were satisfactory. More than half of these executives claimed they would walk away from a proposed acquisition if the corporate culture of the company to be acquired was not a good match. In other words, business leaders are working very hard to produce something other than just a rip-off culture in their enterprises.[17]

When a new fast-food chain opens, say Shake Shack, and advertises some kind of better food experience, people by the millions are willing to try it. Not many people would feel they had to wait a year to see if other consumers were harmed by the product. The same consumer expectations of trust in big business are brought to bear on new cars, new social media services, and most items put on the market. I'm not saying consumers always like or prefer these new products, but rather that trust doesn't seem to be the major problem. Americans are for the most part remarkably willing to try new products, especially from big business. Remember when the iPhone first came out? Did many people refuse to buy one on the grounds it might be recording their conversations or tracking their movements in ways that would be used against them? Well, a few hesitated on these grounds—perhaps with some foresight, I might add—but again, Americans en masse were remarkably willing to trust Apple and also its associated data and service providers.

## DOES TRUST RISE WITH WEALTH?

There is yet further evidence that wealthier, more business-oriented nations are more likely to induce higher levels of trust. Two economists, Paul J. Zak and Stephen Knack, set out to study this connection.

They began by measuring which nations' citizens demonstrate the most trust, using questionnaire answers from the World Values Survey. For instance, one question asks respondents to check one of two statements: either "most people can be trusted" or "you can't be too careful dealing with people." There is a remarkable variance in the answers, with Peru getting the lowest score at a 5.5 percent positive response and Norway getting the highest score at a 61.2 percent positive response. In other words, there seems to be a lot more trust in Norway than in Peru (note that the questions date from 1981, 1990–1991, and 1995–1996, times when things in Peru were going much worse than they are today). There are data, intended to be nationally representative, for forty-one market economies.[18]

Zak and Knack's study shows a clear relationship between levels of trust and per capita income. For instance, Norway, Sweden, South Korea, and much of the Anglo-American world are relatively high-trust countries, and also fairly rich, while the two lowest-trust countries are Peru and the Philippines, which are much poorer. Overall, the countries with the best developed commercial environments also tend to have higher levels of trust.

In such studies, it is typically difficult to disentangle cause and effect. To some extent, businesses thrive because trust is common, yet repeated commercial interactions in turn tend to boost trust. Most likely, both effects operate in a mutually reinforcing fashion, indicating that business and trust really do grow and thrive together.

## NONPROFITS VS. FOR-PROFITS

Another possible way to test the honesty of business would be to compare nonprofit and for-profit organizations. If you think profits induce corruption, you might then conclude that nonprofits should be especially trustworthy. The evidence, however, will show that for-profits and nonprofits, at least if we are comparing enterprises in the same basic economic sector, usually operate in pretty similar ways (with exceptions, which I will consider).

This is a tricky test because very often nonprofits and businesses are engaged in quite different and sometimes noncomparable activities. It's not right to criticize business by noting that the March of Dimes is more altruistic than U.S. Steel. For one thing, charities typically are funded by wealth earned through business and donated by businesspeople. It's not right to say the charity is altruistic; rather, the donors are altruistic. And charities typically cannot extend their reach further than the donations from business-created wealth will allow.

Furthermore, dishonesty and fraud are rife at nonprofits. In addition to headline-worthy cases of outright fraud, it is well known within the sector that many nonprofits manipulate metrics so that the resources devoted to fundraising or to overhead appear lower than they really are. Plenty of charities and nonprofits don't actually change or improve the world or deliver any useful product at all, but rather simply continue as lost causes with no impact. The same cannot be said for most commercial businesses, at least not over extended periods of time. If I think "nonprofit sushi," my first instinct is to run away, not to embrace it.

If we look at hospitals, we see that for-profits and nonprofits just aren't that different, in terms of either how they operate or their final results. One study in California, for instance, found that when nonprofit hospitals had some market power, and thus some room to operate free of commercial constraint, they did not supply any more charity care or offer any more non-profit-producing services (which typically include psychiatric care, rehab, emergency room services, trauma services, burn care, and labor and delivery) than did the for-profits. And yet nonprofit hospitals account for 58 percent of all non-federal acute-care general hospitals in the United States, and they receive a very beneficial tax exemption. But it's not just that one study. There is plenty of evidence suggesting that for-profit and nonprofit hospitals behave pretty much the same. For instance, after one set of hospitals switched to for-profit status, their mortality rates did not change, nor did their proportion of Medicaid patients or black or Hispanic patients. An older study, from 2000, shows that if anything, the for-profit hospitals provide better care. A study from 2007 found that the for-profits neither have worse health outcomes nor make less effort to treat sicker patients.[19] Again, this is all suggesting that the profit motive just doesn't corrupt behavior very much.

There is one area where the for-profits appear to be considerably more fraudulent than the nonprofits, and that is higher education. It has become increasingly clear that a lot of educational for-profits charge high fees and encourage students to run up debt without improving the job prospects of those students *at all*, or perhaps only by a small amount. So you can consider this as one piece of evidence weighing in favor of the honesty of the nonprofits. Still, the overall calculus isn't so simple. Rather than proving to be an indictment of all business practice, these data may suggest simply that for-profit enterprises are ill-suited for that particular sector of education. There are plenty of for-profit educational ventures, ranging from science book publishers to software companies to Apple, that have quite good records in terms of probity, honesty, and keeping their promises. It's just that one kind of educational for-profit seems to be too frequently a rip-off. Looking past this exception, the data indicate that the nonprofits do not in any obvious way behave more honestly.

## OUR OWN UNDERSTANDING OF BUSINESS LACKS BALANCE

I often find that discussions of research on corporate behavior tend to be unfairly critical. To give you just one example, consider British physician and science writer Ben Goldacre's well-known book *Bad Pharma*. Goldacre, an intellectual gadfly of sorts, emphasizes the need for standards of science when those around him are peddling myths and snake oil. I'm all for that. But the full title of his book, *Bad Pharma: How Drug Companies Mislead Doctors and Harm Patients*, is an example of how the current discourse is biased against corporations.

I've read Goldacre's book carefully and I find he substantiates many of the charges he makes. Pharmaceutical companies often promote drugs that in specific situations are unlikely to help; they bribe doctors, either explicitly or implicitly, to overprescribe medications; they keep trial results secret when they should not; and in recent times they haven't come up with so many new wonder drugs. Goldacre is right to be on the warpath against those abuses. Yet I would have titled the book very differently; for instance, instead of *Bad Pharma* I might have tried *Not Nearly as Good as It Could Be Pharma: How Corruption Is Diminishing One of Our Great Benefactors*.

Frank Lichtenberg of Columbia University, arguably the leading economic expert on the benefits of pharmaceuticals, has shown that the drug companies are saving human lives at remarkably low cost— roughly $12,900 per year of life gained. He has also presented evidence that two-thirds of the life expectancy boost for elderly Americans over the period 1996–2003 was due to prescription drugs (0.41–0.47 years out of 0.6 years total increase). Furthermore, there is also good evidence, again from Lichtenberg's work, that pharmaceuticals are among the most effective of all medical treatments. This research has not been seriously contested, least of all by Goldacre, who ignores it. You won't find Lichtenberg's name in the index of Goldacre's book, nor will you find the word "innovation." You will find a lot of one-sided moralizing about the shortcomings of pharmaceutical companies. Just ask the HIV-positive people who were preparing to die in the early 1990s when a new class of drugs allowed those receiving timely treatment a life expectancy close to the average for all people.[20]

I'm picking on Goldacre not because his work is shoddy but rather because it tends to be very good, with the exception of this lack of a balanced perspective. When it comes to corporations, his biases show through and he is himself sometimes a practitioner of bad economic science, or at least unbalanced economic science. Goldacre did, by the way, respond to me numerous times on my blog after I wrote up some of these points. He offered various arguments, perhaps correct ones, as to why drug companies should never keep trial results secret. He didn't have any defense as to why he called the book *Bad Pharma*; that was likely because his Bad Publishing Company wanted to sell more copies of it and thus needed a catchy title. Might Goldacre, like the pharmaceutical companies he criticizes, be a do-gooder but have a profit motive too?

The media, too, can share this lack of balance when reporting on business. A recent study indicates that CEOs and other senior executives are more likely to exhibit psychopathic traits than the population at large. According to an article published by researchers Nathan Brooks and Katarina Fritzon, rates of psychopathy among business leaders may range from 4 to 20 percent compared with a possible estimate of about 1 percent for the population as a whole. Of course, a moment of common sense indicates we should be cautious in interpreting that result. For instance, by the researchers' standards, a business leader can be put into the diagnostic category of psychopath without being harmful or dangerous in any way. It suffices, for instance, for a business leader to show signs of "grandiosity, glibness, and entitlement." Also by the researchers' standards, self-reporting "I am not afraid to make bold business decisions" contributes to such an impression— namely, as a sign of fearlessness and ruthless determination, in the manner one finds in a psychopath. Really? It is amazing how much the media swallowed and indeed publicized this and related research findings. By the way, this article was later retracted, although the retraction of course didn't receive the publicity of the initial claim.[21]

It is in the nature of media incentives that media outlets are looking to report eye-catching news and thus also bad news, including about business. "American business kept up its miracle record producing lots of stuff and employing many millions of people" doesn't make for a headline-grabbing story.

## THE GOOD NEWS

Even if you worry that corporations have a predilection for untrustworthy behavior, with the rise of the internet and social media they have had an increasing incentive to behave honestly. This is because unscrupulous business practices can result in high reputational penalties. If a restaurant tries to rip off a customer by overcharging on the bill, there is a good chance that will be reported on social media, and in a durable form. More generally, businesses are rated on many aspects of product quality on the internet, and this information is, for the most part, widely available for everyone to see. Such information steers consumers away from the worst businesses and induces most businesses to be more honest and forthright in the first place. This mechanism works even when businesses are selling to tourists, because of the possibility of online reviews. If there is any lesson that today's big businesses have learned, it is that they need to apologize rather quickly for their mistakes, lest a storm against them swell on social media.

As for professional services, the spread of information previously only available to experts has made it harder for dentists to push unneeded treatments. If you Google "Do I really need that root canal?" you will find some pretty credible sources suggesting that maybe you don't. Doctors receive more questions from their patients, and in general expectations for quality service seem to have become higher. And if you are wondering if those really were termites you found in the basement, just compare what you saw with photos and descriptions online before spending a lot of money on termite removal.

Consumer information is wonderful for constraining business, especially when competition gives individuals the chance to take their patronage elsewhere. In most sectors of the economy, the internet has brought a great deal more choice and information.

Finally, any assessment of business is inevitably somewhat comparative. We've already taken a look at nonprofits, so let's turn to government, also a large and focal institution and a potential regulator of business, and ask whether government has become more honest in recent times. I think there is a fair amount of evidence that it has not, at least not from the point of view of voters. Approval ratings for Congress have been at all-time lows, often below 10 percent. The election of Donald Trump as president and the choice of Brexit in the United Kingdom are often interpreted as protests against the corruption, lies, and smug, complacent, business-as-usual attitudes of our political elites. Or at least that is how things are viewed by numerous critics of the status quo.

Does that sound like a world where trust in government and its honesty is increasing? Overall, I see that the trustworthiness of mainstream business is going up and that of government is going down. And that distinction is pretty fundamental to the case for relying on commercial businesses to supply a lot of our needs and desires. Trustworthiness is an essential component of what makes lives worthwhile, what makes relationships work, and what makes some countries more desirable places to live than others. Given the higher trustworthiness of business and the lower trustworthiness of politics, I find it strange how many people look at the data and think it is a good idea to bring business more and more in thrall to government.

America just doesn't always understand how well its own companies are doing.

# ARE CEOS PAID TOO MUCH?

One of these trust issues concerning business has to do with the pay of top executives. Many intellectuals and journalists allege that CEOs are paid too much (or paid too much relative to workers), that CEOs rig pay systems, and that CEO pay is not closely related enough to positive outcomes. Not long ago, Eleanor Bloxham, writing in *Fortune* magazine of all places, described high CEO pay as "a silent killer wreaking havoc on our economy." Charles M. Elson, writing in *Harvard Business Review*, alleged that CEOs are treating their companies like ATMs.[1]

The more likely truth, however, is that CEO pay largely has to do with competition, in this case the chase for talent. Why might it be worth it for a business to shell out big bucks for top leadership? Well, as we will see, it is in the best interests of the board and shareholders to drive a business to be a creator, and high CEO salaries are part of that mix. We're all used to the idea of businesses competing to serve consumers, but the other side of that coin is businesses competing to hire the best people, and that is going to mean high salaries and also compensation tied to the profits and performance of the firm.

As you might expect from any system that awards both money and status points in such a concentrated manner, many more people are aggrieved by this process than are pleased by it. We respond by turning CEOs into victims of a kind of public ritual sacrifice, dissecting their every move, imputing malign motives, criticizing their pay, and treating them as personifications of all that bothers us about capitalism.

CEO pay is both a practical issue (how to give incentives to top performers to do a good job) and a moral issue (whether people are being paid in some way that's related to the value they add). The debates around CEO pay reflect how we deal with the excellence around us, how well we deal with cases in which rewards go to those who have failed, and how we deal with the fact that some people in life have done much better than we have.

So many of our symbolic judgments about the American corporation come to a head when we consider the pay of the most highly rewarded people. As you might expect at this point, I think this system is working pretty well. Indeed, it deserves a lot more praise than criticism, despite its imperfections, and it is part of the engine that has helped America develop so many world-class companies.

I'd like to move beyond anecdote and ask some simple questions about America's CEOs, *looking at the data as a whole.* It is true that their pay has gone up—top CEOs may make 300 times the pay of typical workers, and since the mid-1970s CEO pay for large publicly traded American corporations has gone up by about 500 percent, with the 1990s seeing many of the biggest pay hikes, mostly through equity-based compensation. In the most recent data, the typical CEO of a top American corporation—from the 350 largest such companies—made about $18.7 million a year.[2]

So why has their pay gone up so much? Is that high compensation the result of normal supply and demand—that is, there aren't actually many people capable of leading large companies? Or are many of America's top CEOs somehow ripping off their own companies? What we'll see is actually a pretty positive picture about America's corporate leaders. In particular, CEO pay *mostly*—not entirely— reflects the productive contributions of talented individuals to very important companies, rather than corruption, rent-seeking, and personal enrichment.

The best model for understanding the growth of CEO pay is that of limited CEO talent in a world where business opportunities for the top firms are growing rapidly. The scarcity of top-rate candidates sometimes causes corporate boards to make or stick with hiring mistakes, but overall the process has worked pretty well in allocating talent to important jobs and keeping that talent motivated. In other words, when it comes to CEO pay we can (mostly) trust business.[3]

The efforts of America's highest-earning 1 percent have been one of the more dynamic elements of the global economy. There's plenty of evidence that American CEOs are the best in the world for supporting productivity gains, and they work with tougher and better corporate governance than ever before. They have integrated tech into their organizations at a world-beating pace, making them more competitive and thus producing better wages for their employees.

Economists sometimes speak of CEOs as arbitrary beneficiaries of a variable called "skill-biased technical change." That phrase refers to new technologies that boost the return to skilled labor. For instance, email and smartphones allow for easier management of global supply chains at a distance, and that in turn increases the influence and eventually the compensation of many of the best managers in multinational enterprises. But skill-biased technical change does not fall from the sky; rather, it comes about because it was the vision, deeply held and tenaciously enacted, of a number of CEOs. Steve Jobs *saw* and *decided* that an iPhone could be produced in a globally integrated supply chain, finished in China, and sold to the whole world, and then he figured out the process and made it happen—with the help of a lot of workers and other CEOs, of course. It's not a popular thing to say, but one reason CEO pay has gone up so much is that the CEOs themselves really have upped their game relative to the performance of many other workers in the American economy.

## CEOS ARE PAID FOR CREATING VALUE

Let's consider a simple picture. One of the most striking features of CEO pay growth is just how much it is tied to the overall performance of U.S. stocks. While individual cases of overpayment definitely exist, in general, the determinants of CEO pay are not so mysterious and not so mired in corruption. In fact, overall CEO compensation for the top companies rises pretty much in lockstep with the value of those companies on the stock market, largely because of the use of equity holdings and options as part of CEO compensation packages.[4]

Two economists, Xavier Gabaix and Augustin Landier, have studied this connection between firm market value and CEO pay more systematically. Gabaix and Landier show that CEO pay in a simple supply-and-demand model should move roughly in step with changes in the market value of the typical firm. As firms grow larger in market value (and there are more of them), they are willing to pay more to attract CEO talent. Under some fairly general assumptions, this can lead to increases in CEO pay in rough proportion to the increase in market value for the firms. If you pay CEOs to add value to their companies and added value goes up, those same CEOs will earn more. In the period 2000–2005, for the fifty largest American companies, the typical top-three executive (among the three most important in the company) held more than $31 million in effective equity ownership.[5]

So the sixfold increase in average CEO pay over the 1980–2003 period can be explained in large part by the roughly sixfold increase in average market capitalization over those same years. Gabaix and Landier, in a later study with Julien Sauvagnat, also showed that in bad times CEO pay goes down, and roughly in proportion to the loss in firm value. There is also a growing trend for boards to vote down, or at least question, proposed pay hikes for CEOs. In other words, it isn't just an upward ratchet, as the system has checks and balances built in, most of all from the market itself.[6]

I've found, by the way, that successful American CEOs are some of the biggest critics of CEO compensation *for the leaders of other companies*. It's remarkable how many of them think the "other CEOs" don't deserve it. I find this a bit like how readily some top athletes are willing to bad-mouth other top athletes, such as when former Lakers center Kareem Abdul-Jabbar, in my interview with him, referred to Dallas Mavericks forward Dirk Nowitzki as a "one-trick pony" for taking (and making!) so many jump shots. Such barbs are especially common if both players have made the Hall of Fame, or will make the Hall, or if they are rivals of sorts. Recently Charles Barkley and LeBron James have been taunting each other. In some cases these criticisms are valid—for instance, Larry Bird of the Boston Celtics did not always play conscientious defense or exhibit the proper lateral mobility. Still, in the corporate realm, the close movement between equity prices and CEO compensation suggests such criticisms are not valid for the system as a whole, no matter how justified some individual digs may be.

The parallel with top NBA athletes is a useful one. If you look at the top-performing teams in NBA history, they are almost always based around (at least) one player who is one of the top few in the NBA and playing at or near the top of his game. Bill Russell, Magic Johnson, Larry Bird, Michael Jordan, LeBron James, and Stephen Curry are some of the better-known examples of that phenomenon. That is a major reason teams pay so much for such players—they are hard to come by and they can add so much value in the right circumstances.

At the same time, not every gamble on a big star—or supposed big star—is going to succeed. The New York Knicks poured many millions of dollars into Carmelo Anthony, who is now well over thirty, and they remain a mediocre team and ended up trading him to Oklahoma for relatively little in return. Arguably Anthony has been paid much more than his performance has justified (don't forget to blame the rest of the team too, though, and the coach and general manager). But how did Anthony get that money? By manipulating the shareholders and board of the company that owns the New York Knicks? No. Anthony offered the promise of something—a highly productive big-time star in the prime of his career—that is very hard to come by and also potentially highly value-enhancing. *He was overpaid so much precisely because such deals often work out, and pay off big-time when they do.*

And so it runs with CEOs at the top. A good one is worth so much, and they are so hard to find and keep, that some companies end up overpaying for the Carmelo Anthonys of the corporate world. That's actually a symptom of the importance and scarcity of top CEO talent, and of the fact that humans, including those on company boards, sometimes make mistakes. It's not a sign that the system is morally bankrupt. That may be the hardest truth about CEO pay for the critics to grasp because they are falling into a case-by-case judgment of merit, rather than asking whether the rules of the game are delivering good practical results. The other side of the coin, of course, is that the very best CEOs, including start-up founders, can get locked into contracts where they are underpaid relative to the value they create for their company.

Basically, you need to think of overpaid CEOs as being like the Carmelo Anthonys of their world. They are paid so much precisely because everyone is looking so hard for the next Michael Jordan or LeBron James, and that kind of truly world-class talent is very hard to find. The end result will be some pay practices that ex post do not appear entirely meritocratic.

To pursue this analogy with basketball stars a little bit further, consider the following fact: since 1926, the *entire* rise in the U.S. stock market can be attributed to the top 4 percent of corporate performers. That is a sign of how important it is to have the right kind of operation in place. Corporate leadership is hardly the only factor behind those successes, but big gains come from the interaction of many different positive factors, including the quality of the CEO. Another recent study, more subjective to be sure, polled 113 corporate directors of large companies. On average, these directors believed that fewer than four people in the entire world had the knowledge and expertise to do as good a job as their current CEO. In other words, whether or not you agree with that exact estimate, really good CEOs are very, very hard to come by.[7] And if you have a scarce resource that is exceptionally valuable, the cost of that resource is going to be high.

## THE SKILL SET OF THE MODERN CEO

Today's CEO, at least for major American firms, must have many more skills than simply being able to "run the company," as that term might have been used in older times—that is, how to operate its core business, whether that be setting up oil rigs or manufacturing furniture. As the world has become more financialized, a CEO must have a good sense of financial markets and how to use them, and maybe even how the company should trade in them. It is common these days, for instance, for a large oil company to play a significant role in commodities and derivatives trading, so understanding a Texas oil rig is no longer enough. Outsiders need to trust that the CEO has enough understanding of financial markets that the firm will not lose its shirt through trading and speculation.[8]

Today's CEOs also must have better regulatory and public relations skills than their predecessors, as media scrutiny is more intense, and the costs of even a minor public relations slipup can be significant. If a major company is reputed to be racist or sexist or homophobic, the CEO and other company leaders must act very quickly to counter this impression. Increasingly CEOs must have expertise in social media and public relations, and they need the ability to communicate in a wide variety of settings—on social media, on TV, in press conferences, and perhaps in testifying in front of Congress or trying to persuade regulators and legislators, including at the state, county, and city levels. Not surprisingly, it's hard to find someone who can both run the day-to-day operations of a company and do these other things.

And then there's the fact that large American companies are much more globalized than ever before, and their supply chains are spread across a larger number of countries. Apple's iPhone, for instance, relies on components and assembly from the United States, South Korea, Thailand, Malaysia, the Philippines, Taiwan, India, and China. A lot of Apple's key innovation was not the technology behind the iPhone, much of which already was in place, but rather new ideas about how to build up and maintain such a supply chain. Steve Jobs and Tim Cook had to develop a great deal of knowledge about trade patterns, foreign direct investment, and the global economy more generally. In each of the countries in which it does business, Apple has faced unique institutional and regulatory obstacles. It's not that any CEO comes to the job already having such knowledge inside his or her head; rather, a CEO must know which questions to ask and how to put the answers in the proper context. That skill requires a knowledge of the global economy that is actually fairly mind-boggling. Compared with earlier times, CEOs therefore must have a much better understanding of other countries and the global and cultural environments in which they work—a pretty tall order.[9]

There is yet another trend: virtually all major American companies are becoming tech companies, one way or another. An agribusiness company, for instance, may use drones to monitor its fields, may utilize online business-to-business auctions to buy some of its materials, and may focus on R&D in highly IT-intensive areas such as genome sequencing. Thus, when we talk about our farmers, we must put aside simple notions of a company that produces corn or soybeans and instead conceive of a company very much at the heart of information technology. Similarly, it is hard to do a good job running the Walt Disney Company just by picking good movie scripts and courting stars; you also need to build a firm capable of creating significant CGI products for animated movies at the highest levels of technical sophistication and with many frontier innovations along the way. All of a sudden you need to know how to recruit and retain top programming talent, not a skill that was common in the Hollywood of earlier times.

On top of all of this, major CEOs still have to do the job they have always done—which includes motivating employees, serving as an internal role model, helping to define and extend a corporate culture, understanding the internal accounting, and presenting budgets and business plans to the board.

The CEO is the modern world's equivalent of a successful philosopher, as a good CEO must have a reasonably well-rounded sense of nearly the entirety of the contemporary human experience, whether as worker, consumer, funder, media communicator, or political activist. In reality, there is no other job that is as—yes, I will stick with that word—*philosophical*. Good CEOs are some of the world's most potent creators and have some of the very deepest skills of understanding.

Consistent with these arguments, there is additional evidence that the most important CEO skills have shifted from being company specific to being those of a generalist, and that can make searching for an effective CEO harder. To the extent a CEO must have the skills of a generalist, companies will hire more CEOs from outside markets and be less likely to choose the inside candidates who are "next in line." CEOs will have shorter tenures and change jobs more often because they are more mobile across a variety of companies or even sectors. And indeed, those are the features we see in the data on CEO hires. For instance, outside hires of CEOs were only 14.9 percent in the 1970s, but by the end of the 1990s, the main period for the rise in executive pay, they had risen to 26.5 percent.[10]

In short, the exact skill set required for the CEO of a given company will depend on the company, the sector, and the situation, but all CEOs require a basic set of finely honed character traits to succeed at the very top of the corporate world.

Again, the data show high returns to important general skills. For instance, all other things being equal, CEOs start with higher initial salaries if they come to the new company with a history of good press, a career history that fits a "fast track" pattern, and an education from a selective undergraduate college. To make that more concrete, CEOs who are one decile higher in the distribution of these credentials earn about 5 percent higher pay, or about an extra $280,000 a year.[11]

Another factor is that, on average, top CEO talent helps larger firms proportionally more than smaller firms, and high salaries can be useful as a means of allocating the best talent to their most important uses. If Mark Zuckerberg had been running a midsized financial services company rather than Facebook, that would have been a waste of his talents, and likely Facebook would not have taken off as it did. A study found that when we take such "matching" factors into account, the optimal highest marginal tax rate on CEOs probably should be in the range of 27 to 34 percent. If the tax is much higher, the returns on making the right CEO-to-firm match will be smaller and productivity will be lower, and some of the star performers will end up at insufficiently important firms. If you are curious, some other economists who do not take this factor into account recommend marginal tax rates as high as 70 to 80 percent—they're focusing on the fact that wealthy people may not always enjoy their marginal consumption very much. But once you see that market prices play an important role in allocating talent to the most important firms, the more reasonable conclusion is that we should not tax away CEO salaries into oblivion.[12]

The practices of private equity investment also help show that high CEO pay is not mainly about corrupt business leaders extracting more money from sluggish or corrupt public corporations. Think of a private equity firm as a concentrated vehicle for making major investments in other enterprises, either buying private companies (or parts of them) or taking public companies private, often as part of a broader restructuring process. The individuals who are the major players in private equity firms are very often potential or former CEOs themselves, and the firms they acquire are tightly held, so those individuals are not likely to be ripped off by the CEO of a firm they acquire. And in the private equity domain, the fees that accrue to the major investors—which are usually tied to the performance of the company they're investing in—have gone up by a factor of five to eight since 1993, which is a bigger average gain than what CEOs of major corporations have seen. That suggests there are large and growing returns to managing significant business enterprises well—a task that demands the best CEO talent available.[13]

It is common to see private equity investors pop up in lists of the wealthiest Americans. That is a pretty clear sign that high pay for CEOs of large public corporations is not fundamentally the result of agency problems or corruption, but rather is the consequence of sophisticated, well-informed investors deciding they must pay top dollar for a shot at getting the very best corporate talent.[14]

Another way to put CEO compensation growth in a broader perspective is to consider lawyers, who cannot squeeze compensation out of loyal boards but rather must court and keep clients in order to be paid well. If law partners do not as a group bring profitable new clients to a firm, they cannot keep on paying themselves more, because at some point the money will run out. And if we look at the numbers over the period when CEO pay rose so rapidly, we see that law partner compensation rose at roughly the same rate. In 1994 the average profit per law firm partner was about $0.7 million, but by 2010 it was almost $1.6 million, increasing from about ten times median household income to about thirty times median household income. Again, the lesson is that the returns to skilled talent have been rising fairly generally, and higher pay packages for CEOs are one symptom of that broader process.[15]

Let's turn again to those athletes. From 1993 to 2010, the pay of top baseball players went up 2.5 times, the pay of top basketball players rose 3.3 times, and for football the multiple was 5.8. In other words, in percentage terms the CEOs gained about as much as the baseball players, with baseball arguably being the relatively most stagnant sport in terms of popularity. Michael Jordan and other NBA stars elevated the pace of basketball pay raises over that of CEOs, and top performers such as John Elway and Jerry Rice, in addition to some blockbuster teams such as the Dallas Cowboys, made higher salaries even more the case in football. (That's not counting endorsement income.) Once more, these high returns are representing some very general features of the American economy, and not the ability of the athletes or CEOs to systematically defraud either consumers or the system more generally.[16]

The idea that high CEO pay is mainly about ripping people off— or extracting rents, as economists put it—also doesn't explain history very well. By most measures, corporate governance has become a lot tighter and more rigorous since the 1970s. The 1950s and 1960s were much more of a "good ol' boy" era in corporations, as you see reflected in such TV shows as *Mad Men*. Yet it was during this period of weak governance that CEO pay was relatively low, while during the more recent periods of stronger governance CEO pay has been high and rising. That suggests it is in the broader corporate interest to recruit top candidates for increasingly tough jobs. Furthermore, as we've seen, the highest salaries are paid to outside candidates, not to the cozy insider picks, another sign that high CEO pay is not some kind of depredation at the expense of the rest of the company. One more piece of evidence: the stock market reacts positively when companies announce compensation plans tying CEO pay to stock prices or other long-term indicators of the company's prosperity, a sign that those practices build up corporate value more broadly and not just for the CEO.[17]

Yet from the press you receive a very different impression of what is going on, one that focuses much more on issues of economic inequality. In fact, high CEO pay has less to do with income inequality than it might seem at first glance.

Note that CEOs have generated a lot of their high pay by creating new superstar firms or by significantly upgrading old firms into corporate superstars, as happened with Apple, Facebook, and many other "unicorn" examples. These are the cases where it is easiest to see that very high senior management returns stem from value creation, at least on average if not in every individual case.

In general, within business firms, returns to higher-tier workers have not risen relative to the pay of the lower-tier workers, contrary to a common impression. The main exception to that claim is workers at the very top, which of course does include CEOs, whose pay has risen at high rates over at least parts of the last few decades. But changing pay scales within firms are not major drivers of income inequality.[18]

But wait, how can that be? Doesn't it contradict so many of the articles published on income inequality? In fact, the main driver of income inequality has been the blossoming of superstar firms that sell an innovative product and have global reach, as well as productivity shifts that benefit those companies especially. These firms include Google, Facebook, Boeing, and Verizon, as I'll discuss in chapter 5. Typically, everyone in these companies—from senior managers to personal assistants and janitors—is paid more than workers at their older, more traditional counterparts.[19]

That is one of the truths about American business that you are least likely to read about in a major media outlet: income inequality is mostly about the differences between the superstar companies and the others. But that reality makes for a less juicy narrative than stories of CEOs taking money from their workers. And to tie this back to CEO pay, the overall value of superstar firms is yet another reason a first-rate

CEO can be so very, very valuable. Building a superstar firm helps those firms raise wages for just about everyone. So the real question, looking forward, is what we might do to get more of those superstar companies, so that more people's pay can go up.

## WHEN GREAT CEOS DIE

Looking at the deaths of entrepreneurs and CEOs is another way of establishing how much corporate leadership matters. Economics does not always have the luxury of running controlled experiments, but when it comes to CEOs there are some cases that come close to satisfying this description—namely, when CEOs pass away suddenly. A database of 149 sudden deaths of top executives in the United States found that changes in leadership directly affect firm values; that is, when good leaders die, companies tend to lose value. So by studying death events and measuring how much company values change in response, it is possible to measure the differences in quality across corporate leaders. It turns out that leader quality accounts for about 5 to 6 percent of the value of the company. In another study, the sudden death of a CEO causes a firm to lose, on average, 2.32 percent of its value over the succeeding three-day window. That is likely the best measure we have of how the long-run prospects of the company have changed. If it is a young, founder CEO who dies, the share price decline is 8.82 percent.[20]

A big study of CEO deaths from Norway reveals the power of leadership, most of all when it comes to corporate founders. Sascha O. Becker and Hans K. Hvide looked at CEOs deaths in companies where the founding entrepreneur owned at least 50 percent of the company shares initially (in general, those companies are smaller than the companies in the American study mentioned in the previous paragraph). When those companies are compared with similar "control" firms, on average their sales fell by about 60 percent after the death of the leader. Employment within the firm fell by about 17 percent. Two years after the CEO's death, the survival rate for those firms was about 20 percent lower than the rate for the controls.[21]

Hospitalizations are more frequent events than deaths, and the data from hospitalizations tell a pretty similar story about the value of good corporate leadership. A study based on Danish data shows that a company whose CEO is hospitalized for more than five days underperforms its peers by about 1.2 percent in terms of corporate equity value.[22]

I wish we had more direct studies for American companies. Still, the numbers above suggest that entrepreneurs and CEOs add great value.[23] In the larger American marketplace, the value of CEO leadership may be higher yet.

There is another lesson from the numbers: CEOs are paid less than the value they bring to their companies. More concretely, CEOs capture only about 68 to 73 percent of the value they bring to their firms. For purposes of comparison, one recent estimate suggests that workers in general are paid no more than 85 percent of their marginal product on average; that difference is attributed largely to costs of searching for workers and training them to become valuable contributors. In other words, workers actually seem to be underpaid by somewhat less than CEOs are, at least when both are judged in percentage terms. Both of those are inexact estimates, but in fact these results are what economic reasoning would lead us to expect. It may be easier to bargain the CEO down below his or her marginal product a bit more, given that the talents of the CEO would be worth much less in non-CEO endeavors.[24]

I find the most convincing estimate of the gap between pay and marginal product to be that of Lucian A. Taylor, at the Wharton School of Business. He finds that a typical major CEO captures somewhere between 44 and 68 percent of the value he or she brings to the firm, with the additional qualification that the CEO's contract offers some insurance value—that is, in bad times for the firm the pay of the CEO won't be cut in proportion, but the CEO shares to a lesser degree on the upside. That 44 to 68 percent is therefore a better deal for the CEOs than it may appear at first glance. Still, you won't find credible estimates suggesting that major CEOs, taken as a group, are capturing more than 100 percent of their value added. Here too, that is what you would expect from a competitive bidding process.[25]

By far the most volatile component of pay for top executives is their stock options, most of all at the very top of the income distribution. In other words, the way to get paid a lot more is for your company to do well. It's quite common for 60 to 80 percent of a top executive's pay to come in the form of bonuses, options, and other forms of compensation that are directly dependent on how well the firm does. That's not how it works in every case, but that's how it works on average. So when American business earnings take a turn for the better, CEO pay usually goes up as well.[26]

One source of outrage is when failed CEOs walk away with very large "golden parachutes"—severance packages that can sometimes run into tens of millions of dollars. A lot of times this payout comes about because of entrenched special interests and rapacious senior managers, but such practices also have two efficiency justifications. First, throwing out the CEO can involve a destructive battle. A golden parachute can help ensure that a bad corporate leader will abandon the mess he or she has created and will do so in a relatively constructive manner, rather than just trying to dig in. The resulting payments (cue the word "exorbitant") are probably unjust, but still they help solve a very real problem, even though we hate the idea of paying wrongdoers to go away. Second, in some cases the shareholders wish to encourage a CEO to explore risky new strategies that may fail. Generous severance payments make such risk taking more likely. I do think that a lot of supercharged severance payments are just manipulation of the system, but still, it would be quite wrong to think the practice has no efficiency justifications whatsoever. Consumers probably end up with a better mix of goods and services in a world where large severance payments are allowed than in a world where they are banned.[27]

## ARE COMPANIES TOO FOCUSED ON THE SHORT TERM?

Another common complaint is that we live in a world of "quarterly capitalism," or "short-termism," as it is sometimes called. In this view, corporations focus on short-term earnings and neglect various forms of long-term investment, including in their workers, in research and development, and in cultivating their future capabilities. In reality, this is usually another complaint about CEO pay. Often the critics charge that equity- and options-based pay for CEOs helps drive this phenomenon, as the company's leaders manipulate quarterly earnings statements to drive up the price of the company today and boost their own compensation at the expense of longer-term corporate prospects. After all, most CEOs won't be with their companies twenty years down the road. So why not pump up your share price in the short term, even if it means neglecting longer-term prospects?

These criticisms, like many others, are overblown. To be sure, there are many anecdotal examples of corporate leaders having a vision that's too focused on the short term. Mainstream media companies were fine-tuning their mostly mediocre television programs while Netflix was developing a new delivery model and ramping up the funding for a new kind of TV show.

It can be very difficult to distinguish between short-termism and an inability to see into the future. The failed Netflix competitors were mainly not venal rip-off artists; rather, most of them genuinely did not see that providing massive amounts of streaming content would prove to be a winning strategy. If half of the time businesses think too short-term and the other half of the time too long-term, there will be thousands of valid examples and anecdotes about excessive short-term thinking and planning, and they aren't necessarily related to CEO dishonesty. But that's seeing only half of the bigger picture. Furthermore, many of these stories of short-termism are often also accounts of how, overall, the market *did* arrive at a better long-term situation, thanks to the strategic thinking of (in this case) Netflix and other innovative companies. Usually the short-termism behind the failures isn't fully revealed until someone with a better long-term vision comes along. So be careful when you hear "short-termism" anecdotes: very often they are success stories—for some other company—in disguise.

It is not hard to think of examples where companies made big mistakes because they were thinking too long-term. For example, various tech companies have committed to major expansions in China, feeling that sooner or later its 1.3 billion citizens would pay off for them. In part because of ongoing hostility from the Chinese government, profits have not materialized, and many of those companies, including a number of major American tech and financial services companies, have pulled out. As another example, many recent tech start-ups have high valuations, even though their revenue is zero or near zero. A great many of these may end up being cases in which investors were lured by dreams of the long run and failed to be hardheaded enough about the short-term limitations. Tesla in 2017 achieved a higher market value than either Ford or General Motors, even though there are no visible signs that the company is capable of selling electric cars at an affordable price at a profit. Maybe they'll pull a rabbit out of their hat, or maybe not (as I write, their prospects seem to be deteriorating). You can see the same kind of price spikes with a lot of biotech stocks, often before the companies have brought their products to market.

From where I sit right now in 2018, I don't know which of these high valuations are mistakes, and that is part of the point—most critics don't either. But for sure, in many of these cases the market is thinking *too* long-term and should be more worried about the lack of revenue today. More generally, price-to-earnings ratios are historically high at the moment, and they have been so since the recovery from the 2008 financial crisis (that may or may not still be true by the time you are reading this). My point is that these currently high P/E ratios are directly inconsistent with the charge of excess short-termism. In essence, the price has been high because the market is expecting high forthcoming earnings, not because earnings are high enough today to justify those valuations.

Of course, markets also think long-term when it comes to successes, and that long-term mentality is encouraged through CEO pay structures. Consider Amazon, which has a stratospherically high share price, even though the quarterly earnings reports usually fail to show a sizable profit. Whether you think that valuation has been justified or not, it is a clear example of how markets can consider the broader, longer-term picture. Circa 2018, Jeff Bezos ended up as the richest man in the world, and he achieved that status by sticking with some long-run goals. Amazon does keep investing its profits in the future of the company. That suggests markets are striking a pretty decent balance between short-term and long-term considerations. There is even some research from two top finance researchers, Kenneth French and Nobel laureate Eugene Fama, suggesting that companies with high current cash flow are relatively *undervalued* by the market and subsequently earn above-par returns. Maybe their work isn't the final word on this question, but it makes it much tougher to establish the charge that investors have excessively short-term time horizons.[28]

To cite a simpler point yet, consider what is going on when so many investors lend billions to governments for thirty years, looking to reap a somewhat higher return. That too is an instance of long-term thinking, and it is exceedingly common. Even if you sell before the thirty years are up, the market has no problem valuing the thirty-year payoff stream embodied in these assets.

If we look at the CEOs of major corporations, they seem to have pretty long time horizons. If we look at bosses who left S&P

500 companies in 2015, their average tenure in office was eleven years—the longest it has been over the past thirteen years.[29]

More generally, short-termism does not have to be bad, if only because the short term is easier to manage. Companies very often see their short-term problems staring them in the face, such as the need to fire an incompetent manager or fix a broken machine. It is much more difficult to know what the overall market will look like twenty years hence, especially in sectors where information technology is a significant input, which of course is most sectors today. Planning for twenty years out can involve a lot of expense and a lot of risk, and it is not clear those plans will end up being useful anyway. In other words, it is often short-termism that is underrated.

In information technology the average life of a corporate asset is measured at about six years, in health care it is about eleven years, and for consumer products it runs from twelve to fifteen years. So, for instance, if you run a health care company, you might need to be commissioning very different medical tests or using different kinds of medical scanners eleven years from now. In the meantime, the new tool or device you will need hasn't even been invented yet, much less approved. So exactly what type of specific planning are you supposed to do, above and beyond a general awareness that some significant changes will be coming? That logic limits the planning horizon of companies more than any managerial short-term bias does.[30]

Note also that the American economy is shifting toward sectors with relatively short asset lives, many of them being service sectors. As a result, what we might need in many cases are more CEOs who are able to make the shift toward a shorter-term orientation.[31]

In some industries you simply might *have* to be short-term because there is no real long-run planning available. Perhaps the world is too uncertain, or maybe the company just doesn't have enough variables at its disposal that it can control in a useful way. In that scenario, it might very well be true that the companies in sectors that allow for more long-run planning *are* better run or more profitable. But that doesn't mean there is necessarily anything wrong with the short-run-oriented companies; they might simply be doing the best they can, relative to all the constraints they are facing.[32]

What the data show is that in the U.S. economy, R&D expenditure relative to GDP has been roughly constant for about thirty years. That's hardly ideal, but it also is not consistent with a picture of increasing short-termism. In fact, since services have been growing as a percentage of the American economy, and services R&D is harder to pull off with success, the trend can be read as a signal of a slightly positive overall trend.[33]

If shareholders in a public company are placing too much short-term pressure on a firm for a good quarterly earnings report, there is always the option of becoming a privately held firm. Start-ups are almost always privately held during their early critical growth period, in part because it may be impossible to signal to potential shareholders early on that the company really does have a great idea. Venture capital can step in to fill the funding gap. In the longer run, the company can choose structures that give founders enduring control, even after public trading of shares has commenced—as, for instance, Facebook and Amazon have done.

In this context, note that venture capital typically is considered one of America's big success stories, as I will discuss in chapter 7. American venture capital is highly sophisticated and skilled at taking risks for the prospect of a big payoff. But it is also, in some regards, oriented toward the short term. A venture capital round very often will be capped at ten years. By the time that ten-year period is up (or, more commonly, well before that time), the company is expected to be self-sustaining. In the meantime, there will be successive mid-period rounds of additional venture capital that are contingent upon signs of progress, thereby enforcing discipline. I would not say "short-termism" is the right word here, because venture capitalists are in fact willing to assume big risks for some longer-term payoffs. Still, this process has at least some of the superficial signs of demanding short-term progress, and yet it has operated very well, most of all by benefiting the United States across longer-term horizons.

A related claim about American companies is that they have a financial short-termism problem because all of the earnings are drained out in the form of dividends. Sometimes I've heard or read claims that payouts to shareholders represent more than 90 percent of net income for firms in the S&P 500. But on closer examination, once you consider new capital raised by those companies, that turns out to be a misestimate. The reality is that major companies are paying out to shareholders about 22 percent of their net income, which is not an unusual or unhealthy figure. This is another example of people latching on to and publicizing a negative figure about American corporations simply because it fits their preconceptions. The reality is that CEOs are not somehow sucking their companies dry. And money paid out to wealthy shareholders typically ends up invested in some other part of the economy.[34]

If I were grading practices and institutions on a 1-to-10 scale in terms of how much they've contributed to what's either good or bad about the United States, with 10 as the best influences and 1 as the worst influences, I might put assault weapons and opioid abuse as a 1.0 and Silicon Valley and NBA playoff action as a 9.0. CEO pay I would give a 7.5. It could be better, but it works much more effectively than many people think. There's a natural tendency to find something wrong whenever rich people are being paid a lot of money and have a lot of status, but on the whole our CEOs are providing good value for the money they earn.

# 4.

## IS WORK FUN?

Yes, running a business is rewarding for the CEO, but what about the workers? Worker exploitation is one of the oldest charges levied at capitalism, and it persists through the current day. For instance, in a recent *Times Literary Supplement* review of books about work, Joe Moran summed it up bluntly: "These books are about the misery." David Graeber, in his recent highly popular book, says it all in the title: *Bullshit Jobs: A Theory*. Jeffrey Pfeffer, from the Stanford School of Business, calls his latest book *Dying for a Paycheck*, even though there is established evidence that unemployment is worse for your health than working.[1]

I'd like to suggest that productive work is one of the most fulfilling sides of our lives. For the most part, it makes us happier, better adjusted, and better connected to the social world. It gives balance to our home lives. It helps us realize who we are as human beings. This is one of the subtler ways in which capitalism is a creator—namely, a creator of our better selves.

I'll get back to those points, but in the meantime I do need to put some bad news on the table. It's called "work"; it's also called "labor." Those are not in every way positive words. If you said to a friend (or, rather, an ex-friend), "Being with you is work," it would not be an entirely positive comment. Or it might be said that you labor under a delusion, but no one would say that you labor under a happy or ecstatic feeling.

To oversimplify by only a bit, *they have to pay you to do it*. And that suggests work is not in every way fun. Furthermore, for most people work is the main way that they interact with business on a daily basis, which means that business is associated with the activities that take some of the fun out of our lives. Bits of fun are drained on a very regular basis, often five days a week, but the paychecks arrive less frequently in most cases and often by the less visible means of direct deposit. So the stresses and tedium of the work are for many people more vivid than the wages they earn. And that in sum is one reason business is not entirely popular with the American public—or, indeed, with the public elsewhere in the world. Business is like the parent who tells you that you can't have everything you want all the time.

Some recent studies and surveys illustrate the potential burden of work. Nobel laureate Daniel Kahneman and economist Alan Krueger measure our "daily affective experiences" by having people wear beepers that go off at irregular intervals, at which time the people record what they are doing and their feelings. You can think of this as a technique for measuring moods. But the researchers ask about more than just the subjects' feelings at a given point in time; they also ask how happy people are with various aspects of their lives. The study thus considers both momentary pleasure and the overall feeling of satisfaction from a life well spent, because happiness isn't just a single thing with a unidimensional scale. For this study, the researchers recruited 909 employed women with an average age of thirty-eight and an average household income of $54,700.[2]

And what did the researchers find? The highest-rated activities, from most favored to less favored, were intimate relations, socializing, relaxing, and prayer/worship/meditation. In the middle of the list were watching TV, preparing food, and talking on the phone, among other mundane activities. The bottom five were childcare, computer/email/internet, housework, working, and—dead last—commuting.

So working is next to last in terms of producing a positive mood, and that is sad news. But that doesn't mean we don't like work; it only means we like other things better. And in fact, when you drill down, the ratio of people who have positive feelings about work to those who have negative feelings is just over 3.5 to 1. (That's not as good as the 5.10 to 0.36 positive-to-negative ratio for intimate relations, but sex always was going to beat out work anyway.)

Consider also that the same data set shows people spending 6.9 hours a day working, whereas prayer/worship/meditation is done only about 24 minutes a day. Presumably that is because you are paid to work but not paid to pray. If people prayed 6.9 hours a day, most of them probably would find it less intrinsically rewarding, and arguably it would have a much lower score. (If you are wondering, intimate relations averages 12 minutes a day, and that too might be less popular if it were at 6.9 hours a day.) In that regard, work doesn't do nearly as badly as those numbers at first seem to indicate. People are doing so much of it precisely because it has a high *net* reward, even if not all of that reward is direct fun in the moment. Furthermore, work is often an important pathway toward both intimate relations and socializing, the two highest-rated activities on the list; that induces many people to work more than would otherwise be the case.

Do note an important caveat: namely, that the women in this study were polled only on workdays. Had they been polled on weekends, perhaps work would seem a bit more welcome and a little less burdensome. How would children have done as a source of pleasure if the queries had been posed on the weekends too? We just don't know.

It is interesting to see what the authors find about work as a source of lifetime satisfaction compared with immediate mood. Some of what we do, such as caring for our children, seems more important for lifetime satisfaction than for fun in the moment, as having kids can be pretty stressful. When it comes to work, the same is true: a good job boosts overall feelings of satisfaction more than it helps our immediate mood. On this measure, the benefits of work are again higher than they may look at first.

I am not trying to whitewash the burdens of the workday and the workplace. Nonetheless, a lot of the other evidence points us toward the more positive side of work. Work provides us with a lot of what we value in life, including affirmation of our social worth, a structure for problem solving combined with rewards, and an important source of social interactions with (sometimes) sympathetic or like-minded others. Many jobs are creative: 82 percent of all workers report that their jobs consist mainly of "solving unforeseen problems on their own."[3] Plus there is always the paycheck. It's not just the food and rent; the money from work often gives us the means to make, keep, and stay in touch with some of those friends we value so much. In this regard, the value of work and the value of friends are by no means so separate.

Of course, these benefits from work are no accident; in large part they are created by employers to try to lure more talented workers. That is exactly what competition requires. Even if the bosses do not explicitly plan all of the social benefits of work, they allow them to persist and grow, for the purposes of worker morale, recruitment, and retention.

Another way to think about the non-pay-related benefits of having a job is to consider the well-known and indeed sky-high personal costs of unemployment. Not having a job when you want to be working damages happiness and health well beyond what the lost income alone would account for. For instance, the unemployed are more likely to have mental health problems, are more likely to commit suicide, and are significantly less happy. Sometimes there is a causality problem behind any inference—for instance, do people kill themselves because they are unemployed, or are they unemployed because possible suicidal tendencies make them less well suited to do well in a job interview? Still, as best we can tell, unemployment makes a lot of individual lives much, much worse. In the well-known study by economists Andrew E. Clark and Andrew J. Oswald, involuntary unemployment is worse for individual happiness than divorce or separation.[4]

Often it is more valuable to watch what people do rather than what they say or how they report their momentary moods. The aggregate data on work hours are striking, and they show that Americans have fairly positive attitudes toward work. For instance, if we consider weekly work hours per American, that number rose from 22.34 in 1950 to 23.94 in 2000, hardly a sign of work falling out of fashion. Over this period, too, large numbers of women came into the workforce, many because they wanted to work and earn their own incomes. The reality is that preferences for work haven't declined nearly as much as commentators had been predicting earlier in the twentieth century. Earning and spending money is fun, and many jobs are more rewarding, more social, and safer than they used to be. Even with much higher living standards now than in the immediate postwar era, Americans still basically want to stay on the job.[5]

The economist John Maynard Keynes, writing in 1930, famously predicted that by 2030 most individuals would be working no more than fifteen hours a week. He thought most human wants and needs would be satisfied, work was mainly a drag, and at the relevant margins people would be seeking more leisure time. But he underestimated the pull of more money and the pleasures of work. A well-to-do Cambridge scholar, he overestimated the value of leisure, at least for the American public.

The data on stress also put work in a pretty favorable light. A study by Sarah Damaske, Joshua M. Smyth, and Matthew J. Zawadzki asked 122 adults in a midsize American city in the Northeast to swab their cheeks six times a day to measure their levels of cortisol, which is considered to be a hormonal marker of stress levels. Those measurements were to be taken both at work and at home.[6] The results were pretty clear: a majority of these individuals seemed to experience higher levels of stress at home than at work. Furthermore, women were more likely to report feeling happier at work, quite possibly because so many women are responsible for childcare. (That said, the likelihood of experiencing lower stress at work actually was greater for individuals who did not have children at home, so perhaps in many cases the spouse was the bigger problem.)

Another surprising feature of these results is that the "work as a safe haven" effect was stronger for poorer people. We don't know if that is true more generally across larger samples of people, but it points to a potentially neglected and egalitarian feature of life in the workplace. In contemporary American society, poorer individuals are more likely to have problems with divorce, spousal abuse, drug addiction in the family, children dropping out of school, and a variety of other fairly common social problems. These problems plague rich and poor alike, but they are more frequent in poorer families and, furthermore, very often wreak greater devastation on poorer families, which have fewer resources to cope with them. The workplace, however, is a partial equalizer here. At least in this sample, the poorer individuals found relatively greater solace in the workplace than did the richer individuals. The poorer individuals, of course, were paid less at work. But in terms of psychological stresses, a lot of corporations are creating "safe spaces" for individuals who otherwise are facing some pretty seriously bad situations.

Indeed, when we look at the actual measurements, there was a negative correlation between stress as measured by cortisol levels and the socioeconomic status of the worker. Here too we should be cautious about how grand a conclusion we draw from a single study, but this is suggestive evidence that the workplace often serves a significant protective and equalizing function when it comes to personal stress. Furthermore, the Kahneman and Krueger research generates a broadly similar result. The positive affect associated with the workday is not closely related to the features we usually associate with a "good" job. (For instance, the correlation coefficient of positive affect in the workplace with "excellent benefits" is only about 0.10.) People with lower-quality jobs still get a lot of the benefits from the positive affect associated with work.

Here's a simple and probably familiar story from Elizabeth Bernstein, writing in the *Wall Street Journal*. This narrative reflects how important work can be as a refuge and a hiding place:

> Tara Kennedy-Kline, a family advocate and owner of a toy-distribution company, says on an evening or weekend she has been known to go to her warehouse and rearrange 1,500 boxes in a shipping container just to get away from her family's requests of "What's for dinner?" and "Where is my uniform?"
>
> "I love my home and family, but there is just something about being able to walk away from the homework, dinner, karate, football, piano lessons, roller-skating transport and laundry folding, and retreat to my cold concrete warehouse," says the 43-year-old, who lives in Shoemakersville, Pa.[7]

Another way to consider the pleasurable nature of a lot of work activity is to measure how much work time is associated with a feeling of "flow." The flow concept, which has been developed and promoted by the Hungarian American psychologist Mihaly Csikszentmihalyi, refers to an integrated, dynamic feeling resulting from processing stimuli, responding to changes in a developing situation, and solving problems with some measure of success. Think of those times when you are playing tennis well, cracking that programming problem, or delivering that perfect presentation at work. It seems as if your whole mind (and sometimes body too) is being brought to bear on something that really matters, and then you ace it. Doesn't it feel great?

Indeed, the sensation of flow is correlated with higher levels of motivation, cognitive efficiency, activation, and satisfaction. I've found the flow concept to be very popular with a lot of highly successful people; one of its biggest promoters has been John Mackey, who founded and built up Whole Foods. Presumably that was a lot of flow for him, but a lot of hard work too. I can recall my own days working in a supermarket as a produce clerk. A lot of it was hard, tiring, or frustrating, but almost every night I felt real joy at wrapping a package of plums with great speed and efficiency, or putting the bananas away and giving the cart that little extra push into the refrigerator, with more speed than perhaps my manager would have found appropriate. It's true I knew I wouldn't be doing that forever, and that made it easier, but nonetheless a lot of the time the work was pleasurable for its own sake and I was able to slide into that state of flow.[8]

The data show that work tends to promote a state of flow. One study looked at workers from five large companies in Chicago. About 27 percent of these individuals had management and engineering jobs, 29 percent had clerical jobs, and 44 percent had assembly-line jobs (so the study was not primarily of top-of-the-line CEOs); 37 percent of the sample were male, and 75 percent were white. The respondents carried beeping devices, and seven times a day they were asked to provide short reports on the challenges and skills of the activities they were engaged in, including the quality of their experiences. These same individuals also were asked to report on their leisure activities.

The results were pretty positive toward work. First, the individuals spent more time in the flow state while they were working than when they were doing leisure activities. A lot of leisure activities, such as reading, talking, and watching TV, did not seem conducive to the mental flow state. Furthermore, most dimensions of experience were higher during the flow state, including motivation, activation, concentration, creativity, and satisfaction. This is just one particular psychological approach, to be sure, but these results are consistent with the view that individuals derive a considerable deal of satisfaction and enrichment from the time they spend working. A second study, by Mihaly Csikszentmihalyi himself (co-authored with Judith LeFevre), concluded that "the great majority of flow experiences are reported while working, not when in leisure."[9]

Upon reflection, it should not come as a shock that work makes so many of us feel happy, satisfied, or just less stressed. For one thing, work often provides a significant amount of social validation. At home the number of possible appreciators is fairly small, although they are important validators ("Daddy, you're a great teacher"). That said, the spouse and children and extended family are not always and in every way entirely grateful. In fact, arguments over household chores are pretty common, and often those who work—especially women— have to emphasize to other family members how much they have already contributed outside the home. Work in some ways offers more approbation. The number of appreciators at work varies with the job, but many Americans work with dozens or even hundreds of people, and they may have contact with a large number of customers or suppliers from outside their immediate business. Some jobs, such as those in journalism, the arts, and politics, raise the possibility of having many thousands or perhaps even millions of potential appreciators.

Work also can be satisfying because you're paid to do it. Yes, you're paid because it isn't always fun, and also because employers need to be sure you'll show up when scheduled, if only for purposes of coordination. Still, a lot of people very much enjoy the notion that their efforts are worth money to the broader world. Some of that may be greed or an uncomfortable kind of egomania, but a lot of it is a very healthy desire for reward and recognition, and the points system created by money is an important one. The pay validates the work, and the work in turns validates the pay. That can be a fun virtuous circle, and it is corporations that are the ultimate creators and source of that pleasure.

If there is one thing we should have learned from Donald Trump's 2016 campaign, it is that Americans want jobs. Trump's rhetoric was directed toward jobs, jobs, jobs, and he didn't talk much at all about redistribution or welfare. Nor did he talk much about "the economy" or "inequality." As the economist Mike Konczal (a Trump opponent) put it: "Trump talked about jobs. All the time." Whatever you may think of President Trump, middle America responded to this rhetoric because deep down most people know that having a decent job is a major source of happiness, satisfaction, and social standing. That is also one reason I have moved away from the idea of a guaranteed annual income; if it is set at a decently high level, too many people will use it as a reason not to work, to their own long-run detriment in many cases.[10]

Work provides us with a tangible sense of progress, of improving. Each time we get raises and bonuses, promotions, and moves into better offices, to more successful companies, and into positions of greater social visibility, we receive external validation for our labors. And at times when we're not moving up, we have something to aspire to. For all the talk of wage stagnation, that phenomenon describes pay for the aggregate of all jobs, and it means that the new set of jobs for a later cohort of workers don't, as a whole, pay more in inflation-adjusted dollars than the old set of jobs for the earlier cohort of workers. It is fully compatible with ongoing raises over the course of a career trajectory for those people who do have jobs. Even in a slow-growing economy, individuals typically get raises and promotions throughout the course of their work life, at least typically up through some point in their fifties (depending on the nature of the profession— mathematicians and basketball players tend to experience age-related frustration and retrogression before novelists, caregivers, and philosophers).

Work also provides people with access to human relationships. You have the opportunity to interact with other intelligent human beings in a fairly structured environment, and those individuals typically share a common mission with you. That creates opportunities for a lot of meaningful human interaction, camaraderie, and sometimes a healthy sense of competition against other companies, or a healthy sense of mission against some significant social problem, such as working in an ICU to patch up gunshot wounds or working for a charity to help feed the homeless. More than one-half of American workers reported having very good friends on the job.[11]

So companies are actually responsible for some of our most important relationships. Further, they produce different kinds of relationships than we tend to find in other parts of life. For the norms of work set boundaries on the kinds of interactions deemed acceptable there. For instance, your work colleagues are not supposed to get too angry at you in public, they are not supposed to cry, and they are not supposed to burden you with all of their deepest or darkest desires, demanding that you clear up the mysteries of the universe for them. To be sure, a great number of workplace relationships do cross over these boundaries, sometimes in rather extreme or unsettling ways. We've all heard tales of the boss having a disastrous affair with a senior partner, or the coworker who turns into a stalker. Still, on the whole, workplace constraints hold, and for the better. That offers us the graceful option of a lot of human relationships based on fun and cooperation, with many of the emotional stresses minimized or left at home. Sometimes the work relationship acquires a depth of its own, based on shared interests and appreciation, precisely because it is insulated from some of the more terrible or corrosive emotional stresses of life. Other times the work relationship may be superficial, but keep in mind that superficial but positive connections often cheer us up and motivate us. In fact, a lot of cultural critics underrate superficiality. There is a lot to be said for inauthenticity, especially since we have limited emotional bandwidth and sometimes just want the normal, routine pleasures of human interaction in the workplace.[12]

Pay and prestige aside, work also can be an important vehicle for helping others. Let's say you wish to be a great benefactor of humankind. It is really hard to do this without using the vehicle of work. One path is to earn millions or billions and give it away; of course, that has to run through the workplace. More typically, people choose jobs that help other people: being a brain surgeon, doing medical research, being a fireman, teaching kindergarten, running and financing a suicide help line, providing good advice to the government, or being a first-rate president of the United States, among many other options. Work is one of the main vehicles for our altruism, and unlike altruism within the family, when things go well it can help many hundreds, thousands, or even millions of people.

This connection between work and altruism isn't just an accident. Many employers go out of their way to make their companies *sources* of worker dignity and satisfaction, most of all because workers and potential workers, especially among the relatively young, value such things. The more a company is viewed positively, the easier it is to recruit talented workers. The desire to attract and keep talent is the single biggest reason companies try to create pleasant, tolerant, stimulating atmospheres. That is yet another example of how Adam Smith's invisible hand leads greedy corporations to take costly actions in the social interest.

## ALL IS NOT PERFECT

As I have been writing this book, sexual harassment in the workplace has emerged as one of the major issues in the public eye, and I am seeing an increasing number of appalling scandals being brought to light, including in the corporate arena. Many women have reported that harassment in the workplace (and elsewhere) has damaged their self-confidence or led them to think a particular profession or institution was not for them. The full extent of this terrible behavior remains to be seen, but for now I would like to make two very general but important comparative points.

First, the possibility of working outside the home has given women many more options for greater independence and reduced the net harassment they face in their lives overall, including from partners and spouses. A job and a paycheck mean that a woman (or a man, for that matter) has the option of leaving an abusive, harassing, or otherwise undesirable partner. Just ask a simple question: Is a woman more likely to be hit at work or at home? I think we know the answer is at home, unless of course she is a professional boxer.

Second, harassment appears to be at least as common outside the corporate sector as in it. For instance, harassment scandals are hitting academia and politics too. It is striking that the first harassers to have to resign or otherwise cede power have been in the corporate world, not in politics. And quite a few famous media harassers have had to resign or give up their movie projects more or less immediately upon the revelations becoming public. By contrast, so much of politics is set up so that the perpetrators are relatively invulnerable. If we take the very centerpiece of American politics, the U.S. Congress, as a counterpoint to corporations, effective complaints are hard to lodge. As an employer, Congress is exempt from most of the laws governing employee relations; furthermore, any accusers who wish to file a lawsuit first must go through a lengthy series of counseling and mediation experiences. There is also a special congressional office that tries to resolve cases out of court. And if a settlement is ordered, the specified congressional office does not have to pay the settlement; rather, confidential payments come out of a special fund from the U.S. Treasury. As another example, a senator or president has a lot of power, often over the entire U.S. economy and legal system. In a case where a male leader is accused of abuse, many other people in the system will take the word of the man, even if deep down they probably know better. How can any of that be a disincentive for sexual harassment?[13]

But it's not just about the law. The culture of Washington also creates a worse environment for harassment whistleblowers than in the corporate world. Politics has a tribal nature, so that if you speak against a member of your own "team"—maybe a congressman or staffer who employed you—you are seen as handing a public relations gift to the other side. It can be career suicide in Washington, the ultimate company town, to speak out in this way. "Don't talk to the press" is one of the most important commandments for virtually anyone who works in government or on government-related issues. Unlike in Hollywood, the women in Washington with power tend to be older, and the younger women just don't have much of a voice or ability to command the attention of the media or to speak with credibility. Very often their strategy is simply to keep their mouths shut and endure.[14]

What I've seen so far is that companies have acted much more quickly to address harassment problems than the public sector has. Although companies have been out to lunch on this issue for far too long, competition nonetheless seems to be more of a constraining incentive within business than outside it. For instance, a company with a history of harassing female employees has to pay a wage premium— what economists call a "compensating differential"—to continue to hire women. Clearly, that is not enough of an incentive, and the legal penalties for bad behavior need to be applied much more consistently, but it is at least one competitive, commercial pressure for better treatment of women. As for further incentives to solve the problem, the notion of fiduciary responsibility constrains the behavior of company leaders (or at least ought to), and corporations are vulnerable to boycotts, bad publicity, and consumer dissatisfaction, all factors that have induced many companies to pursue best business practices and thus fire harassers who work for them. I am hopeful that we will see further progress in this area, with business leading the way, just as it often has done for gay rights. The evidence we have to date is that jobs for women have become more rewarding and less stressful over the decades.[15]

In sum, harassment is a big, big problem of human nature. To date I haven't seen evidence that corporations are making it worse, relative to behavior elsewhere, and to some extent I see within corporate structures the potential for redress and reform. We've already seen in chapter 2 that a lot of the most telling criticisms of corporations in fact reflect broader limitations of human nature, and in some cases corporations actually meliorate our underlying moral flaws.

## DO COMPANIES OPPRESS WORKERS THROUGH THEIR ECONOMIC MARKET POWER?

What about the economic power of bosses over their workers? Many critics, such as the philosopher Elizabeth Anderson, argue that workplace relations are fundamentally those of power and coercion, but I see strong competitive pressures to treat workers better. There is a lot that can be wrong with jobs, including long hours, so-so or lousy pay, and unjust treatment or firings. But the data are showing that on the whole, work in contemporary America is largely a positive experience, not just financially but emotionally.

One recent trend among economists is to stress a concept known as "monopsony," a term used to describe when a single company has a good deal of market power over the workers it employs. Think "monopoly" but inverted to be a problem for the worker rather than the customers. However, this has not yet been demonstrated to be a major problem or a significant force behind lower wages. The major reason wage growth has been so slow for decades is relatively slow productivity growth, not the power of employers. One study concludes that even Walmart—for a long time the largest private-sector employer in America—does not have significant monopsony power except in some parts of rural America. Without significant monopsony, the threat of workers leaving—and, more important, the desire to attract new and better workers—can enable and enforce a lot of worker freedoms. In other cases, monopsony may be present but not a problem. For instance, I much prefer to teach at George Mason University than at many competing universities. But that is because George Mason treats me well (so far!), and if many other workers are in a similar position, it is because they are relatively well matched to their current employers. In other words, although the word sounds a little sinister, monopsony does not have to represent a kind of exploitation.[16]

Many workers grow attached to their current firms, as they may have friends there, a good relationship with the boss, and a preferred commute or maybe that comfortable corner office with the nice sofa. Ex post, that gives many companies some power over their workers, in the sense that it raises the perceived cost of leaving. But the companies only got that bargaining position by giving workers a big chunk of what they wanted to begin with.

The tax system is yet another nonsinister reason worker mobility is not as high as might be ideal. We all know that wages are taxed, sometimes at pretty high rates, but workplace perks generally are not. If the boss buys a comfy chair for you or gives you a flexible schedule, those are in essence forms of compensation, but you are not paying any income or Social Security taxes on them. So, at the margin, bosses will pay workers more in terms of perks than in terms of money. The perks-to-salary ratio will be relatively high, and distorted to the side of perks, relative to what would prevail if salaries and perks were taxed at the same rate. An economist would say that there are too many perks relative to base pay, given the overall level of compensation, because some of the perks are in essence a kind of tax avoidance. The cruder way of putting this economic point is that bosses treat workers too well and pay them too little. Keep that in mind the next time you hear that markets don't give workers enough liberty or enough fun in the workplace.

Before closing this chapter, I'd like to note that at least some of the inequities of the employment relationship are not the fault of business. In many cases it is truly difficult for workers to exit jobs, but better public policy could lower those costs. The particularities of health insurance, retirement benefits, and immigration status are often too closely tied to particular jobs, largely as artifacts of regulation and tax law. A specific company supplies something valuable to a worker, and the worker is therefore reluctant or afraid to leave that company. A lot of work visas, for instance, are tied to continuing employment at the original sponsor of the visa. We allow too many noncompete agreements, which forbid workers from moving to a competing company; that limits mobility and makes it harder for workers to get a raise. It would be easy enough to change these laws for the better, thereby improving the lives of many Americans.

Other times it is *the other workers* who are at fault. Along these lines, I hear many criticisms that companies do not give workers enough personal or intellectual freedom. For instance, critics have noted that companies have the right to fire workers for their Facebook or other social media postings. Surely that sounds like an unjustified infringement on freedom of speech. But on closer inspection, the stance of the companies is often quite defensible. Unfortunately, a lot of workers put racist, sexist, or otherwise discomfiting comments and photos on their Facebook pages, on Twitter, or elsewhere. When employers fire them, very often it is to protect *the freedom of the other workers*—namely, the ability of those other workers to enjoy the workplace environment free of harassment and threats. It's not always or even usually a question of the employer versus the workers, or the old story of a struggle between worker and boss. Rather, the boss is trying, sometimes in vain, to adjudicate conflicting notions of workplace freedom among the workers. In other words, the firings are in part an employer attempt to take the overall preferences of the workers into account. Questions of "workplace freedom" are often not worker versus boss but rather one set of workers against another. And workers often hold their greatest resentments against their peers rather than against their boss. Yes, very often bosses do get particular decisions wrong, but still, the corporate side of these workplace dilemmas is not always well enough understood.

The frank reality is this: most people don't want their coworkers ultimately in charge of the company, for they place greater trust in their boss. They might in fact trust the boss more than they trust themselves, as many workers require some degree of external control, and often themselves recognize as much.[17]

There is a pretty simple reason employer discretion is required in a lot of workplace situations: many employee transgressions and misbehaviors simply cannot be handled by written contracts in advance, and so the boss has to make decisions on a case-by-case basis. Or not every troublemaking worker can be fired right away for legal reasons. In the meantime, the boss might want to restrict the expressions of those workers to protect the other employees. At the margins, the deployment of employer discretion can lead to abuses, and indeed you can find many examples of such abuses in the media, ranging from workers who are screamed at unjustly to workers who are fired for their contributions to particular political campaigns, even if the stated reason is something different. Still, the evidence indicates that *the gains for workers and customers from a fairly high degree of firing discretion*—not just the gains for bosses—outweigh those costs.[18]

Also consider the comparative perspective. You can look at co-ops owned and run by their workers, or worker-managed firms, because those organizational forms are sometimes feasible in competitive markets. But those structures do not in fact offer significantly greater freedom for their workers. One problem is that these organizations simply are often less profitable and less efficient, and that makes it harder for them to help their workers with higher pay or better conditions. Another issue is that when workers are ostensibly in control, they can be consumed with the problem of trying to get the other workers to do the work, much as a traditional employer would be so concerned. The logic of capitalism is not so easy to replace, and different organizational forms, while they may sound better, usually do not improve the basic trade-offs that rule the workplace. Very often they actually make those trade-offs worse or harder to skillfully manage.

To consider another example, labor-managed partnerships often give their workers *less* personal freedom. The old-style investment banking and legal partnerships expected their owner-members to adhere to some fairly strict social and professional codes, including outside the workplace. Those were codes of dress, behavior, and public manners. More generally, when workers are motivated to monitor each other through the holding of equity shares, monitoring becomes easier and so corporations engage in more of it. Again, the main issue is not control-seeking bosses versus freedom-seeking workers; very often the person most likely to restrict the workplace freedom of one worker is another worker.[19]

In other words, we can put the workers in charge, but they cannot escape the basic constraints of running a productive and successful business, which are enforced by marketplace competition.

# HOW MONOPOLISTIC IS AMERICAN BIG BUSINESS?

One of the most common recent criticisms of American business is that it is monopolistic and growing more so all the time. I think this claim is true in some ways, though it is also overstated by the critics, and in particular the harms are greatly overstated. Some of the rise in market concentration has benefited consumers, while in sectors such as health care and schooling, monopolies have resulted from regulation rather than from business itself. In this chapter I'll go through some basic facts about monopoly and market power in America. (Tech is a paradigmatic example of what is going on in American business—namely, higher concentration levels but relatively few harms to consumers and some very real benefits. A separate chapter on tech companies follows.)

Let's first consider the broader history of monopoly. Most monopolies just don't last that long, even if they have some government assistance or entry restrictions supporting them. For instance, well within my adult lifetime the following companies have been called monopolies or impregnable franchises in some way: Kodak, IBM, Microsoft,

Palm, BlackBerry, Yahoo, AOL, Digital Equipment Corporation (DEC), General Motors, and Ford. General Motors and Ford are still major companies, but they face more competition all the time; for instance, Toyota long has been a more significant domestic car producer. I am pleased to hear talk that maybe GM will "disrupt" Tesla, but that mainly reflects what an underdog the company has become. On that list, only Microsoft remains a dominant entity, yet these days it is hardly feared or considered a major source of monopoly. It is a very large and sometimes bureaucratic software company that provides useful services to many Americans.

Keep in mind that all companies, even the largest and longest-standing, have some degree of vulnerability. They become more bureaucratic, they fail to foresee new and important products, market conditions turn against them, foreign competitors enter the market, disruptive technologies can "change everything," or their costs rise as they lose their dynamism. Most of all, the long-run story of capitalism is one of market churn. Not long ago it was feared that Nokia would dominate cell phone markets for a long time to come, and now the company is not even a major player. Myspace too was considered by many to have a dominant "first mover" advantage. In other words, the costs of monopoly dissipate more quickly than a lot of people realize. Incipient competition is powerful even when it is not always immediately visible.

Later in this chapter I'll consider some of the cases where monopoly has gone up, but let's start with the good news. In most sectors of the American economy, consumers have significantly greater choice than in the past, at least where a market is allowed to operate. Even when concentration indices have risen, as is the case for much of the retail sector, it is far easier to go outside of established institutions. Let's say, for instance, that I wish to purchase a book. My former favorite Borders is gone, and my part of the country, northern Virginia, doesn't have many vital independent stores for new books. Still, I can buy from a large number of suppliers on Amazon, new or used; I can buy from eBay; or I can just Google the book title and find numerous other sellers. If I still end up going through Amazon, that is because it has kept low prices, and also provides good service, in part because of all this competition at the fringes. Even though Amazon may appear to "dominate the market," my options as a book consumer have never been better. I don't engage in the practice myself, or condone it, but illegal downloads of free PDFs are yet another competitive pressure on the market.

Information technology is also reshaping the market for clothing. There seems to be less turnover in the retail clothing sector than in the past, as particular brands and chains last longer, probably because they have invested effectively in information technology. Rather than "falling out of touch," as major clothing chains tended to do in the past, they can track demand very closely, and some have lower-cost outlet stores that help keep them in the less expensive parts of the market too. That means more choice for consumers, even though market concentration has gone up. Furthermore, it has never been easier to use the internet, or for that matter travel, to buy clothing from other locales. By no means does everyone do this, but again the potential competition and contestability of the market imply that the dominant incumbents have to match consumer preferences for both price and quality pretty closely. This is another case where, because of potential competition, you shouldn't worry too much about rising concentration ratios.

More generally, large numbers of Americans have been traveling more than ever before, whether within this country or abroad. That exposes them to a greater number of products than ever before, and this ability to make on-site purchases in more areas is yet another (unmeasured) way in which our economy is more competitive than it might at first appear. You can wait until your Texas trips to order barbecue, for instance, if you don't like what is in your local area. Or order some new suits during your next trip to Hong Kong. This kind of cross-border arbitrage was much harder a few decades ago.

The current domestic retail environment does seem to involve more price discrimination than in the past, largely because companies have become more adept with data. So the same company will sell some pretty similar clothes to varying classes of buyers at differing prices, sometimes wildly differing prices. That means greater bargains for those who take the time to search at the local Neiman Marcus outlet or who have the facility for effective, well-informed web searches, and perhaps higher prices for individuals who just go to the mall and automatically buy the first item they see that fits their needs (that is me, if you are wondering). That state of affairs does not benefit everyone, but it is hardly rampant monopolization. Furthermore, a disproportionate share of the gains accrues to the people who have more time and inclination to search, the people who take greater care to patronize outlet malls and cheap clothing stores, and the people who don't just walk into Nordstrom and pick up a suit off the rack. Price discrimination is usually an egalitarian development.

I do also see that in the core of retail markets, the winner-take-all phenomenon may be going up; for instance, the top four brands on average accounted for 15 percent of the market in 1982 but 30 percent of the market in 2012. Some leading firms have the ability and intent to launch well-known national brands backed by extensive marketing and product development, and the other, smaller firms cannot match their pace. I don't consider that to be an ideal development, but still, those suppliers are constrained by increasing competition on the fringes of retail, again in part from online sources. When it comes to prices and product selection, the reality is much more positive than if you look at concentration indices alone.[1]

For very ordinary, cheap goods, consider Dollar General and Dollar Tree, the two biggest chains of dollar stores. As of 2017 they had 27,465 outlets between them. That is more than the total number of CVS, Rite Aid, and Walgreens stores combined. One lesson is that there is too much super-low price competition for American retail to engage in much price gouging. A subtler point is that the dollar store sector itself shows a reasonable degree of concentration across the top performers. But of course that is yet another way of seeing why concentration indices can be misleading: "They've taken over a big chunk of the nation's dollar stores!" isn't exactly a recipe for sustained high prices.[2]

When it comes to retail, keep in mind that there used to be an entire branch of antitrust law devoted to what are called vertical restrictions. One example of a vertical restriction would be resale price maintenance (RPM), or when a manufacturer sells a product to retailers with the stipulation that it be sold at a fixed or minimum price (note that sometimes it is *the retailers* demanding this practice, in a desire to collude and keep prices high). There are classic RPM cases about toothpaste in drugstores, books in bookstores, and canned goods in the supermarket, among many other areas. These days, it is hard to find cases where retail prices truly are binding. They might be binding for a particular brand or title or line, but there is almost always a way to get a close substitute for a different price and often a much cheaper price. Walmart, eBay, and Amazon sell their amazing number of items by lowering prices, not by keeping prices high. Or use Google to find a bargain elsewhere, or if all else fails, order from Alibaba in China. Most of these vertical restrictions just don't matter anymore, as they can be circumvented by a minimum of consumer effort.

I submit that most of the law and most of the enforcement on resale price maintenance is now obsolete. The laws are still there and are still studied by academics, but they are mostly a quaint curiosity, reflecting concerns from times past.

More generally, you can think of Amazon and Walmart as two big reasons a lot of collusive and price-fixing schemes don't work anymore or don't have a major impact on consumers. Amazon and Walmart are the two biggest retailers in America, and both compete by keeping prices low—permanently, it seems. Their goal is to become dominant platforms for a wide variety of goods and to use low prices to boost their reputation and their focal status as the place to go shopping. By now both companies are old news, and it is increasingly difficult to argue that their strategies are eventual market domination and then someday super-high monopoly prices. Instead, their strategies seem to be perpetually low prices, followed by taking in insanely large amounts of business and using data collection to outcompete their rivals on the basis of cost and quality service. That's right, low $p$ (price), high $q$ (quantity), and high quality as well—the opposite of the strategy a classic price-gouging monopolist would follow. It's not just that these companies offer you great deals, but their very presence strikes fear in the hearts of many would-be monopolists who think they can dominate a market with high prices. Who wants to go up against the price competition from Amazon and Walmart?

There is another big reason monopoly power is less fear-producing these days: a new and near-universal competitor with a multitude of products—namely, new and improved leisure time. In the old days, when I observed people waiting in line, so often they did nothing. They simply waited. These days, people waiting in line check their smartphones, text, and spend time on Facebook, among other mobile-internet-enabled activities. Furthermore, they don't really seem to tire of these activities. I sometimes call the mobile web "the universal substitute," to invoke some economics lingo.

Given that context, what happens if some supplier were to monopolize the market for, say, apples, movies, or ski boots? Well, consumers could just sit back and spend more time on Facebook, if need be, and for them that would constitute a good enough outcome. Keep in mind that the switch to "Facebook time" doesn't actually have to happen; rather, it is an implicit threat constraining many would-be monopolists. Texting and social media aren't a good substitute for everything; they can't fill in for a needed heart transplant, or if you are on the verge of not having enough food to eat. But it's remarkable how many of our daily activities they can substitute for, as evidenced by the big time shift to those activities in so many of our daily lives. And that is the great unheralded virtue of the mobile internet. It's not only fun but also a kind of near-universal consumption substitute that constrains monopoly power in many invisible ways. You call it addiction; I call it trust-busting. These days, virtually all suppliers, whether they know it or not, are competing with Facebook, social media, and texting. That's a hard battle to win.

There are further figures suggesting that overall concentration in the American economy is rising, but we need to give those numbers more critical scrutiny. According to one set of figures, going up through 2007, the four largest firms then controlled half or more of the market in about 40 percent of U.S. manufacturing sectors, up from 30 percent in 1992. But are there really signs of manufacturing monopolies or oligopolies becoming major problems? The broader evidence shows that American manufacturing output has gone up at a steady pace, manufactured items at the retail level have become remarkably cheap, there is a flood of recent news about cost-saving automation in manufacturing, and there is much more competition from abroad for manufactured goods. If there is one sector of the American economy where I am not worried about monopoly, it is manufacturing. If there really were rising monopolization in American manufacturing, we would have to discard all of those stories and studies of automation and Chinese manufacturing imports taking away American jobs. Keep in mind that not all complaints can be true at the same time, a point that is all too often forgotten when it comes to American business. The actual reality has been rising output, falling (inflation-adjusted) prices, and falling returns to labor in some parts of the sector.[3]

There is some evidence, by the way, that observed increases in concentration ratios are correlated with rising government regulation of business. As government regulates business more, that favors corporations large enough to have substantial legal and compliance departments. Regulation serves as a kind of fixed cost of doing business, discouraging market entry. Not only do higher rates of regulatory growth correlate with increases in market concentration ratios, but the period during which regulation increased significantly, 1990–2000, was followed by increases in market concentration. None of those correlations prove causality, but at the very least it is possible that government regulation is a major force behind the rise of market power.[4]

## WHERE ARE THE REAL MONOPOLY PROBLEMS?

Given that manufacturing and retailing seem to be doing OK or maybe even fine in terms of competition and monopoly, where are the real centers of market power in the United States?

As I've noted, the American economy today does have some pretty notable superstar firms. At the time of writing the list would include Google, Facebook, Amazon, Walmart, Apple, Exxon, the major auto companies, UnitedHealth, CVS, and AT&T, to name just a few.

But most of those companies are not best understood by invoking the traditional theory of monopoly. Rather, they are dynamic organizations that track markets and innovate repeatedly, and end up offering a wide variety of old and new products. These businesses build on the advances of others and are extraordinarily talented at learning from other companies; in more technical language, you could say these organizations are receiving a lot of intangible capital at very low expense, often in the form of expertise about information technology, but also in the form of pretty healthy corporate cultures. For that reason, these businesses often make high profits without charging high prices; furthermore, it will be hard for competitors to copy them. Individual products perhaps can be copied, but the idea of superstar firms as potent learning organizations indicates that the underlying formula is quite complex and involves a lot of expertise in finding, hiring, cultivating, and then retaining talent. Those are not skills that an aspiring competitor can easily learn overnight. So America's superstar firms are most of all institutions that have mastered some very impressive elements of the human dimensions of production.[5]

Given that background, what we really need are more superstar firms. Arguably, a lot of particular businesses have not been sufficiently true to their business nature; rather, they have been too content to let matters slide instead of ambitiously innovating and cultivating talent along more margins.

If we consider the biggest real market power problems in the American economy today, I would start with the health care sector. For instance, mergers have brought the number of major health insurance companies down from five to three. In many parts of the country there is only one insurer selling policies on the exchanges, maybe two, and overall the exchanges have not developed into the thickly competitive markets many people had hoped for. Perhaps more important, hospitals have been undergoing significant consolidation as well, with a long-run trend toward much greater concentration and higher prices. Many parts of America have one hospital chain selling to most of the local market. In addition to causing higher prices, this makes it harder to go elsewhere if you are frustrated by the quality of hospital service, as many Americans are.[6]

These developments, to me, are the single greatest market concentration issue in the United States today, and I think the critics are on the right track there. I would suggest, however, that to some extent this market concentration is the result of heavy regulation rather than a natural development from the nature of business. Observers differ on whether we should blame Obamacare or blame Republicans for not supporting Obamacare properly (or a bit of both), but still there is no market-based reason health insurance should have become so concentrated in this fashion. Insurance companies have consolidated to deal with costly regulations, which is easier for large companies to do, and because of economies of scale in lobbying government, an increasingly important activity in America's politicized health care sector. Insurance company consolidation is also a partial response to hospital consolidation, as an attempt to gain some countervailing pricing power when it comes to reimbursement rates. On top of that, the number of doctors and assistants to doctors is significantly limited by regulation and also by restrictive immigration policies. I'd also consider a new policy that would allow elderly Americans to take their government-supported health care to Mexico and let them keep half of the savings.

Hospital consolidation is driven partly by economies of scale in new information technologies but also by the need to deal with heavy regulation and liability risk, both of which raise the cost of starting new hospitals and also favor large companies with fully built-out legal and compliance departments. The point here is not to argue for zero regulation but to note that we get the level of hospital concentration that we have in essence chosen through politics and the law. The safer we want our hospital system to appear, the fewer providers our institutions will end up supporting. But given the power of competition to lower prices and improve quality, I leave it as a question for open debate whether such a hospital system is in fact actually safer and more efficacious in the long run.

When it comes to health care suppliers that stand outside the most heavily regulated parts of the sector, it is remarkable how much less concentrated provision has become. Retail health clinics once were rare, but now they are found in many shopping malls and strip malls across the country, including in many drugstores and Walmarts. Retail health has been one of the major growth trends of the sector; it is now much easier than before to simply walk into a clinic or pharmacy and receive immediate service. For the most part, these clinics have lowered prices, eased access, and relieved stress on many patients who require some kind of medical attention but who either find it hard to get a doctor's appointment or consider a full doctor's appointment too costly, or who would otherwise burden an emergency room. It's a big advance in the direction of less consolidation, and it is the direct result of competitive market forces. Medical supply could be more competitive yet if Medicare would allow reimbursements for medical tourism, which could lower prices and boost choice—and give the patient some percentage of the savings to provide the appropriate incentive to shop around. Again, you may or may not favor this policy, but it shows that if concentration is going up on the supply side, that is the result of some deliberate policy decisions.

Where else do we find significant signals of monopoly and pricing power? Cell phone service and cable television are two other areas where the United States has higher prices and higher consolidation than many other developed nations. As for cell phone service, it would be better if American regulators took additional steps to encourage more entrants into the market. As I write, Verizon and AT&T are the two dominant providers, with T-Mobile and Sprint present too, though on a smaller scale. Perhaps these companies do not explicitly collude, but they may at times have coordinated on relatively high price points and then stood their ground, enjoying relatively high levels of profit at consumer expense.

In part, I expect these prices to fall further through the natural spread of market competition. In the meantime, a good set of policies might consist of antitrust vigilance, such as when the Justice Department blocked the merger of AT&T and T-Mobile in 2011. The government also should sell off more government-owned spectrum to the private sector, which would lead to greater capacity and eventually lower prices. A relaxation of NIMBY (not in my backyard) regulations at the local level would make it easier to build cell towers, lowering costs and also easing market entry for new competitors. In fairness to the cell phone service companies, some of the problem springs from the size of this country: a national network has to cover great distances and many rural areas, thereby raising cost and ultimately price. Still, there is a general sense that cell phone connections in this country could and should be cheaper.

The good news is that cell phone prices have been falling significantly as of late. For instance, from April 2016 to April 2017, wireless service prices fell by 12.9 percent, the result of a price war and the spread of unlimited data plans. This trend may or may not continue, but we should not think of high wireless prices in the United States as an intrinsic feature of the economic landscape. Most likely, suppliers will continue to find ways to give consumers a better deal—for competitive reasons, of course.[7]

When it comes to cable, which is also a conduit of broadband and sometimes home phone service, the United States should adopt a common carrier system, as is done in many countries. In essence, that reform requires the owner or controller of the "pipes," in this case cable, to open them up to competing companies on more or less equal terms. That reform, a version of what is called "local loop unbundling," enhances competition, lowers price, and improves quality for consumers. Unfortunately, the United States has not done that, in part because the cable companies have lobbied local governments to keep competition restricted. This is one case where the influence of business on government has been directly pernicious.

Even for cable, however, we have to place the market concentration in perspective. Subscribing to cable service seems pretty expensive, and that is why millions of Americans have been "cutting the cord." But when I was growing up, viewers depended heavily on a few major network channels, receiving a pretty dismal range and quality of programs. High-speed internet wasn't even a dream. You could say that back in the 1970s the price of quality cable television, for all practical purposes, was infinite, as was the price of high-speed internet. Today, you can buy access to hundreds of channels and a fairly rapid internet connection for a price much, much lower than that. When there is lots of innovation, looking at the level of a currently high price is misleading because, though still relatively high, it will have been coming down a great deal over time relative to quality. So any critique of cable monopolies should be tempered with the broader recognition that over a thirty-year perspective this has been an area of truly massive progress in terms of quality and diversity.

Another area that might seem to demonstrate more economic concentration is the airline industry. From 2005 to 2017, America has gone from nine major airlines to four. That might sound terribly monopolistic, but the classic economic sign of monopoly is a restriction of output. In fact, the total number of miles flown in the United States has risen steadily, and for the most part flying has continued to become cheaper, after adjusting for general inflation. In part this is because of a new class of much smaller, super-cheap airlines competing at the fringes to force down the prices of the major carriers. Yet again, just looking at the aggregate concentration ratios does not tell the real story; in fact, across individual markets concentration does not seem to have gone up at all. If there is any problem, it is the discontinuation of many air routes to some of America's small and midsize cities, but that is not a monopoly issue; rather, it is simply unprofitable to fly those connections.[8]

Furthermore, one of the big problems with the domestic airline market is that foreign carriers, by law, are not allowed to serve domestic routes. Repealing that law would usher in much more competition and a new era of low-fare flights. So often when there is monopoly or partial monopoly, it is actually regulation that is at fault. Note that the entry of foreign carriers also could help lower costs through innovation, and that in turn could increase flights to those smaller and mid-tier cities that are currently underserved.

OK, so on the negative side of monopoly I've already mentioned hospitals, cable TV, and cell phone contracts. Those we could and should remedy with better policy. What else?

One way to make progress on this question is to approach it from the perspective of a typical citizen's household budget. Obviously, if we look at entertainment, information, most retail goods, and electronics, prices have been falling rapidly and diversity of choice has been increasing. What, then, are the major problematic expenses, and how do they relate to market power?

Health care for sure is a problem, as covered earlier.

Rent, or housing expense, is also a problem, but this is not primarily a matter of monopoly of a single seller or small number of sellers. There are plenty of homes to buy and plenty of apartments to rent, and we do not have to pay an exorbitant price to a monopolist. Instead, we pay an exorbitant price in a competitive, albeit highly restricted, market. Legally imposed restrictions on building make rents and home prices much higher, and that is a serious economic and social problem. Still, it is not a market power problem, and most of the villains are local homeowners who push for NIMBYism and building restrictions, not big businesses. It ought to be much easier to put more high-density, lower-rent housing into America's major cities and suburbs, since San Francisco, Oakland, Boston, and New York City are by no means entirely built out.

Next is higher education, which also has risen dramatically in posted price in recent decades. This too is an economic and social problem, though beyond the scope of this book. In any case, as with real estate, the problem is expense rather than monopoly. There are plenty of higher ed providers, and they compete against each other vigorously. You might think there is some collusion and restricted access at the level of the Ivy League and other very selective colleges, and indeed there was once a successful antitrust suit brought against top universities on the basis that they restricted scholarships to top students. Still, when it comes to viewing higher education as an affordability problem for the average American household, those institutions are not the culprit, if only because most students do not go to them or even consider applying. The major affordability problem, for most people, is at the mid-tier institutions and large state schools, and most students attend state institutions with deliberately subsidized prices relative to cost. If you want, complain about the decline in the subsidy, or maybe cost bloat, but not monopoly per se, because probably your state school is serving you at below-market prices relative to the quality of what you get. (And say there is only one major state school in your state. No, it is not a monopoly if only one provider is willing to sell to you at, say, 50 percent below going rates.) Furthermore, at the community college level tuition prices have been pretty stable, at least once you adjust for financial aid and tuition breaks. In fact, if you take all benefits into account, community college tuition in real net terms has declined since 1992.[9]

K-12 education arguably is an example of a big monopoly problem, but of course that isn't the fault of business; it is the result of government provision and some deliberate policy decisions.

In sum, the business-driven monopoly problems in the American economy are pretty easily identified and are fairly few in number. We could and should fix them. I am somewhat worried that market concentration ratios in many parts of the American economy are rising, but most of those markets seem pretty contestable and offer consumers lots of choice. The upshot is that the analysts who raise this issue usually are exaggerating the problem, harm to consumers is hard to find, and American competition remains alive and well.

# 6.

## ARE THE BIG TECH COMPANIES EVIL?

Google's original motto, which endeared it to many geeks, was "Don't be evil." And indeed, for a long time it seemed the company realized this aspiration. People under thirty may not know how hit-or-miss it was to search the web prior to Google. It has greatly enhanced our ability to find the right restaurant reviews, look up medical information, research dating or business partners, and track down old friends, not to mention that it provides the means for good, link-based blogging, among many other advances. Google changed our lives, and very much for the better, even if we sometimes misuse it, such as consulting it as a substitute for serious medical advice. And for a long time we held the company in high esteem for supplying these services without charging us any dollars whatsoever.

But somewhere along the way, the story changed. Google still supplies high-quality search for free, but a growing number of people believe that Google and many of the other major tech companies are evil. They describe a company that has invested so heavily in superior data that no competitor can come near it, thereby giving the company a dominant position in the online advertising market. And they say that its supposedly free offerings come at the cost of our privacy and vulnerability to the surveillance state. (By the way, since often I am referring to the slightly distant past, most of the time I will use the word "Google" to refer to what is now Google and its parent company Alphabet combined, with Google as a subsidiary of Alphabet since 2015.)

Coming from another direction, Nicholas Carr wrote a book arguing that Google is partly responsible for the decline in our memories—why remember facts when you can just search for them? He asserted outright that Google makes us stupider. More recently, social media companies have been blamed for the ascent of Donald Trump, the renaissance of racism, "fake news," and the collapse of appropriate democratic discourse. The framing of "great stuff for free" has been replaced by "the product is us."

Hostility toward American big business is nothing new, but of course the key question is to what extent the critics are correct. For the most part, to continue my love letter to American business, I would like to speak up for the tech companies, especially the big ones. They have brought human beings into closer contact with each other than ever before, whether emotionally or intellectually, mostly through social media. They also have placed so much of the world's information at our fingertips, and more often than not it is accessible within minutes or even seconds. Whatever problems these developments may have brought in their wake, they are unparalleled achievements and arguably the greatest advances of the contemporary world. And, speaking on a purely personal basis, I find that the existence of a well-functioning, searchable, shareable, and mobile internet has given me public audiences far greater than anything I ever expected to have. The internet and the ease of use enabled by the big tech companies drove the single biggest revolution that ever has come to my career.

So what's not to love? Well, there are some drawbacks, and I'll focus the second part of this chapter on where some future and present problems might lie—namely, our privacy. I don't necessarily mind that tech companies store information about us, but the terms of that storage and its use are opaque, it is not always easy to opt out, and the companies do not always keep that information sufficiently private and secure, as evidenced by multiple hacking episodes, including a major information hack of Yahoo emails in 2013 and a hack of Equifax, a credit bureau (and not really a tech company), in 2017, not to mention various illegitimate drains of information from Facebook. I'll lay out these criticisms in more detail, but for now I'll just say that I think the benefits of the tech companies still far outweigh their costs, as evidenced by how few Americans are trying very hard to opt out.

In any case, first I'd like to turn to the charges of monopoly and the disappearance of competition. It is easy enough to see that the contemporary tech industry has plenty of firms that seem to dominate a particular area—just consider Google, Facebook, eBay, Netflix, Apple, Snapchat, Twitter, and Microsoft, among others. But what are we to make of this? Are these new tech monopolies as bad as the price-gouging monopolies of yore? At least so far, it hardly seems so.

Many of these "monopolists," if that is even the right word, charge either nothing or much lower fees than their pre-internet counterparts. eBay takes a commission and never has been connected to a zero-charge model, but typically it is much cheaper to put a lot of items on eBay than to cart them around to resale or antique stores and arrange for their disposition by consignment or outright sale. Microsoft charges for its software, but once you take multiple copies, educational discounts, and piracy into account, the company hardly seems like an extortionist. For each copy of Microsoft Word that is sold, other copies are pirated or otherwise reproduced in a way that does not result in a traditional fee for sale at the price set by Microsoft. Apple is the company on this list that charges luxury prices, at least for its hardware. But before the iPhone, you couldn't buy something like that at any price. And within a few years after the debut of the iPhone, there were plenty of cheaper smartphone models on the market, and since that time those models have gained most of the market share. As of this writing, smartphones are becoming cheaper yet, due to imports from China, and the quality of those products is likely to improve rapidly. Apple helped enable these cheaper products, whether it wanted to or not, and all along the company knew it would end up creating competitors. So it is inaccurate and unjust to attack the big tech companies on the grounds of price, most of all compared to the counterfactual in which those tech companies did not exist.

A new set of charges, however, comes from another direction: that the major tech companies dominate their platforms and therefore may be stifling innovation. For instance, if Google controls search and Facebook dominates one segment of social networking, maybe those companies won't work so hard to introduce new services. Furthermore, those large and successful companies may be evolving into stultifying bureaucracies, afraid that new ideas might transform the market and threaten their dominance. To cite a possible example, if social networking becomes the primary means for accessing artificial intelligence (AI), maybe Facebook would lose its dominant market position to some other company better at AI, and in turn Facebook might steer the market away from AI to protect its current position. A related fear is that large, monopolizing tech companies will buy up potential upstart competitors, with the foreclosing of potential competition. Indeed, we've seen Google buy over 190 companies, including Deja-News, YouTube, Android, Motorola Mobile, and Waze, while Facebook has bought up Instagram, Spool, Threadsy, and WhatsApp, among numerous others, and purchased intellectual property from former rival Friendster.

In theory, you can imagine how those arguments might carry some weight. Yet in practice the major tech companies have proven to be vigorous innovators. Furthermore, the prospect of being bought up by Google or one of the other tech giants has boosted the incentive for others to innovate, and it has given struggling companies access to capital and expertise when they otherwise might have folded or never started in the first place.

## HAS COMPETITION REALLY DISAPPEARED?

First, I'd like to challenge the premise that competition has disappeared from tech markets, as has been suggested by numerous commentators. Recently, Alex Shephard wrote in the *New Republic*, "Giants like Google and Facebook and Amazon don't have meaningful competitors." *New York Times* tech columnist Farhad Manjoo told us that "smartphones and social networks might be ruining the world," which of course requires the presumption that we have no easy way to get away from their influences. I won't cover every possible example or complaint, but let's consider what are sometimes nominated as the two most egregious tech monopolies, Google and Facebook, with Google coming first.[1]

One rating of the top eight search engines goes as follows:

Google
Bing
Yahoo
Ask.com
AOL
Baidu
WolframAlpha
DuckDuckGo

That's actually plenty of choice, and even includes DuckDuckGo, whose chief selling point is that it attempts to offer complete confidentiality and doesn't store or sell data on your browsing history.[2]

You might argue that Google is the best of the lot and that the company holds a kind of natural monopoly due to the data it has accumulated over the years. That is a plausible argument, but still, a natural monopoly based on higher quality of service is the way a lot of markets are supposed to work. Google keeps that leading position only by having, at least in the minds of most users, the best product, and indeed the best overall suite of associated products, such as its email, chat, and Google Docs services.

Furthermore, a natural monopoly through data is unlikely to last forever. As the years pass, search engines will compete across new and hitherto unforeseen dimensions, just as Apple and many other competitors knocked out Nokia cell phones. There is no particular reason to think Google will dominate those new dimensions, and in fact Google's success may stop it from seeing the new paradigms when they come along. I don't pretend I am the one who can name those new dimensions of competition, but what about search through virtual or augmented reality? Search through the Internet of Things? Search through the offline "real world" in some manner? Search through an assemblage of AI capabilities, or perhaps in some longer-run brain implants or genetic information? I genuinely don't know. What I do know is that new dimensions of product quality arise all the time, and supposed natural monopolies find out their monopolies are not so natural after all. The internet is still in its early years, and whatever is required to succeed ten or twenty years from now likely will be quite different from what is required now. In the meantime, Google is doing a great job with search and advertising, and that is why the company is leading those markets.

Alternatively, you might ask whether Google (or for that matter Facebook) has some kind of monopoly power over advertising markets. While Google offers search for free, of course advertising on its platform costs money. As we know, advertising is a major source of the company's income, and if you sell something to a searcher clicking on your Google ad, Google gets a share of the proceeds. In 2017, for instance, Alphabet took in $95 billion from its advertisements and search advertising services. And other than Facebook, Google doesn't have a close, comparably scaled competitor in the online advertising market.[3]

Nonetheless, I'm not very worried about monopoly in this context. First, Google still competes with Facebook, television, radio, circulars, direct mail, and many other sources of information, and if you wish, you can throw email and word of mouth onto that list; instead of searching for where to buy something, very often I email one of my friends and ask. Second, insofar as Google has taken on a big share of the market, it is because its ads are cheaper and better targeted than alternatives. In the longer run, Google cannot charge higher prices than the status quo ex ante, because users would go back to previous methods of advertising, such as television or radio, or maybe try something better yet. That limits Google's monopoly power and constrains Google's ads to be a price-lowering institution. In other words, when it comes to advertising, the main source of the company's revenue, Google has to offer a better deal than what went before it, and indeed it has consistently done so, thus accounting for most of the company's revenue.

So what about Facebook? Doesn't the company have a kind of monopoly on social networks?

Well, I belong to or have considered belonging to the following social networks: LinkedIn, Twitter, Snapchat, email, various chat services, contacts lists in my cell phone, Pinterest, Instagram, and WhatsApp, the last two owned by Facebook (I'll come back to that). Facebook's main personal page has to compete with all of those. I also use my blog as a means of social networking, and believe it or not, sometimes I circulate in the physical world as well.

Facebook is the biggest player on that list, but one lesson is simply that it is possible to start new social media services, provided they offer something useful to users. Another lesson is that a lot of the communication that is now on Facebook could jump to another social network, even if users could not take their photos and old posts with them. People seem to feel quite comfortable using multiple social networks, and in their minds those networks compete against each other for usefulness and convenience. It's actually not that hard to imagine Facebook becoming less of a major player on some future list of the major social networks that people use. Users still could keep access to their old Facebook photos, just as people might use Linked In for some concrete purposes, including some purely friendly purposes, yet without necessarily making it their major means of social networking. Again, there is plenty of competition and rivalry for the market.

For a moment, I'd like to consider both Instagram and WhatsApp, both of which are owned by Facebook. Both compete against Facebook's main service in a way that improves the quality of that main service. Facebook has not turned either of these services into appendages of the Facebook page proper, in part because the company realizes that users value some version of those services in their current form. To make them too Facebook-like would invite potential entrants to in some way copy or improve upon what Instagram and WhatsApp have been, and a new and growing upstart rival social network is the last thing Facebook wants. So those services continue to exist as alternatives to the main Facebook page, and thus they are indirect competition for that page, *even though they are owned by Facebook.* My ability to have a multiperson chat with geographically dispersed friends on WhatsApp, for instance, limits how many ads or other forms of clutter the company is willing to place on my main Facebook page. And while I would not be shocked if, over time, Facebook lowered the quality of my Instagram and WhatsApp services, doing so would in essence be inviting new competition in those service areas. I would in fact be quite happy to use a better version of WhatsApp, and I don't care whether or not it is connected to Facebook the company.

I really do get that Facebook is the elephant in the room. If I ask the more practical question of whether I can choose from a lot of high-quality services—usually free—doing some pretty nifty things, the answer clearly is yes. That too is the result of competition.

## HAVE THE BIG TECH COMPANIES STOPPED INNOVATING?

Other than giving me the best free search in the world, what does Google do for me? Well, I use Gmail, one of the best and biggest email services in the world, and it is completely free. Anyone can set up a Gmail account and begin using it immediately. That possibility would have astonished us as recently as the 1980s.

Google also has taken a lead role in developing self-driving vehicles. While I don't expect Google to become a major manufacturer of such cars, they put in key work on the underlying artificial intelligence, scanners, road mapping, programs, and other features of the service. They also helped make the idea publicly acceptable, in part by having driverless Google cars take people to work for years. While it is debated exactly when driverless cars, trucks, and buses will be ready for regular use, by now it is a debate over when rather than whether. Twenty years ago, or maybe even ten years ago, very few people expected that, and Google has helped pave the way for this progress.

Self-driving vehicles arguably will be the biggest and most important technological breakthrough since the internet. They hold out the promise of seriously limiting the number of car deaths, easing commutes, and making many of the elderly, the disabled, and the young far more mobile across space.

Another innovation, still a work in progress and from Alphabet rather than Google more narrowly, is the use of hot-air balloons to give an area internet access, also known as Project Loon. This was used after Hurricane Maria in 2017 to restore internet access in Puerto

Rico and may end up being important in remote areas of Africa as well. Perhaps the value proposition here remains uncertain, but it is a bold attempt to create a better and more connected living situation for some of the world's more vulnerable people. It does seem that the technology works, though at what cost or sustainability we do not yet know. The work of Google and Alphabet on robotics also has not yet shown a real payoff, as far as outsiders can tell.

Even some of Google's failures will likely prove to be of use. Google Glass, the wearable device intended to integrate a goggles experience with internet access and viewing, failed. Still, this was a learning step in the broader development of wearable devices and a stepping-stone for others, or maybe Google/Alphabet itself, to build on.

Google significantly upgraded YouTube after buying the company. At the time, it was considered a very risky purchase, and many commentators suggested that Google was crazy to pay $1.65 billion for a company that, at the time, had very little revenue. Furthermore, YouTube appeared to be a cesspool for comments and a bottomless pit for copyright violation suits.

What did Google do? They cleaned up the legal issues, using their advanced software capabilities to spot potential copyright violations, and they enforced takedown requests. They also improved search on YouTube. Perhaps most important, Google invested heavily in the technology that made video so widely used on the internet today. When Google bought YouTube, video on the internet often was slow, interruptions were frequent, and you had to engage in a process of buffering, which meant you either had to preload the video or put up with starts and stops in your watching experience. By figuring out and investing in ways of shortening the path of video transmission, Google made video watching on the internet far more efficient. Many different parts of the internet benefited from these advances.

Today YouTube is also a leader for academic video and online education, far beyond what it was before the Google purchase. When Alex Tabarrok and I started our online economics education site,

Marginal Revolution University (MRUniversity.com), do you know where we decided to place the content? You probably can guess: You-Tube. How much did Google charge us for this service? Absolutely nothing, nor does it charge the users anything, nor is our product connected with advertisements, either for Google, for us, or for any third party. This means that users around the world, in any non-censoring country, can access all kinds of video-based educational resources for free.

Google and cell phones for a long time did not seem to be an obvious combination. Yet in 2005 Google purchased Android and elevated the company's open-source system to the most commonly used cell phone software in the entire world. Other companies have since modified and arguably improved this software, so Google probably has not been the major beneficiary of its own actions. Because of the Google-Android combination, hundreds of millions of people have enjoyed better and cheaper smartphones. More generally, Google has made most of their software open-source, enabling others to build upon it with additional advances; there are entire companies devoted to helping other companies build upon Google's open-source software.

And all that from a company that is just twenty years old. The astonishing thing, to my mind, is how many people attack and condemn Google. After I wrote that the antitrust authorities should not go after Google, one commentator on my blog, *Marginal Revolution*, had the following gripe: "They show zero interest in calendar innovation, for instance, and have a half-broken to-do list product, but both are protected by Gmail integration." *That's* your complaint? Those are some pretty high standards.

OK, so Google looks pretty strong as an innovator. What about Facebook?

Facebook has consistently upgraded the quality and diversity of its product since its inception. In 2006, Yahoo offered to buy out Facebook for $1 billion, and at the time many commentators thought this was a no-brainer offer for Mark Zuckerberg. Of course, he declined it and proceeded to invest further, making the company worth many times more than that—more than $50 billion as of 2017. Arguably Zuckerberg has done a better job allocating capital within his company than any other recent American CEO. Most of those increases in value have sprung from service and quality upgrades, innovations at the time they were instituted.

The idea of the News Feed, for instance, was introduced in 2006, and now it is seen as a standard and indeed central feature of Facebook. Facebook also has been a leader in the development of targeted advertising, and now the company and Google command the two largest shares (by a wide margin) of the advertising market. The big advantage of Facebook is that you can reach demographics or individuals with particular interests. For instance, do you wish to advertise a product or service and target individuals with interests in economics? In the old days that was hard to do, but Facebook has made it cheap and easy. You place the ad and Facebook ensures it is sent to individuals whose feed reflects an interest in economics. This has revolutionized how companies communicate information about their products to individuals. Furthermore, Facebook has made the advertising market work for mobile. When the company went public it was not doing mobile ads, and many industry observers wondered whether mobile ads ever could succeed. These days, mobile ads are by far the biggest part of their revenue stream.

Facebook also has revolutionized how media companies deliver stories to their readers, and the reality is that Facebook became the world's largest and most important media company within a small number of years. I have some reservations about that development, and I will get to those, but if we are looking for innovation, this is unquestionably a significant example. Finally, Facebook is seeking to improve the quality of AI services and integrate those into its pages. It remains to be seen how well they will succeed in this endeavor, but at the very least they are helping to drive this highly competitive race.

Just to be up-front, I should note that, in my own personal life, I am not a fan of Facebook in the same way that I am a fan of Google. I consider it to be an amazing company and believe that Mark Zuckerberg has been one of the most impressive CEOs of our time. Still, I have two complaints. The first is mostly personal and subjective: I find their page confusing to look at and use, and their changes in page organization over time have confused me as well (too much innovation, from my point of view). That said, I recognize that the Facebook page seems to be working very well for most users.

My second complaint about Facebook is my belief that the company is not elevating the quality of news consumed by the American public. More and more people use Facebook as a means of accessing news items and sharing those items with their friends. The net incentive is that news producers come much closer to "giving the people what they want," which in this context means many pieces that are partisan, personality driven, cutesy, glib, or some mix of those qualities. The news organizations have in a rather undignified fashion run after this traffic as rapidly as possible, obliging market demand. One observer described the archetypical social media sharing story as being titled "What Could Possibly Even Happen, My Goodness. Baby Ducks See Water for the First Time, Can You BELIEVE What They Do?" In fact what they do is sip water from the pool, but I suppose you have to click to find that out.

To put it bluntly, it is quite easy to waste time on Facebook. The services of Google, in contrast, are more tailored for specific uses, such as querying for information, looking for how to buy a movie ticket, or maybe using Google Maps to get from one place to another. There is a clearer beginning and ending of tasks, which is one reason I think Google does more social good than cultural harm.

When it comes to Facebook news stories, Russian-manipulated content has received a lot of attention in recent times. I view that as a minor problem; the amount of money spent on such ads seems to have been quite small, at the time about 0.1 percent of Facebook's *daily* advertising revenue. Many of the reports of "fake news" following the 2016 election strike me as misrepresentations. Most of us probably saw the clickbait headlines about how many people clicked on or liked totally false stories on Facebook, but as a share of total interactions with Facebook, under generous assumptions, that was only about 0.0006 percent of user actions. That's bad, but there are also plenty of misrepresentations on television, in tabloids, in forwarded emails, in dinner table conversations, and in personal gossip. There simply hasn't been serious evidence presented that Russian activity on Facebook influenced election outcomes.[4]

The "more serious" mainstream media sources ran innumerable stories about the Hillary Clinton email scandal, even when there wasn't much there, and that probably hurt her chances more than anything on Facebook. Maybe each story was factually accurate, but the overall impression was more negative than was appropriate. Very often, misleading frequencies for reporting (or not reporting) true news are a bigger problem in the media than outright lies and falsehoods. By one estimate from *Columbia Journalism Review*, over a six-day period near the end of the campaign, the *New York Times* ran as many front-page stories about Clinton's emails as it did about all policy issues over the sixty-nine days immediately preceding the election.[5]

I don't think we ever will have a fully clear idea of the impact of "fake news" during the last presidential election, but keep in mind that only 14 percent of Americans reported that social media was their main source of electoral news. When it comes to opinions about elections, Facebook has nothing close to a monopoly, as it competes with family influences, private conversations, cable news, talk radio, email, books, and many other sources. Or look at the broader electoral picture. The Democratic Party did quite poorly with respect to governorships and state legislatures, and it does not seem that Facebook fake news or Russian-bought propaganda played a major role in those races. A recent study shows that the most politically polarized Americans are the elderly, the group least likely to be getting its reporting from social media and the most frequent watchers of cable television news. The problems of media bias and polarization—in various directions— are real, but they are not mainly about Russian-bought content on Facebook.[6]

For all the criticism Facebook has been receiving on this issue, keep in mind that for-profit publishing houses have a long history of publishing the works of Marx, Mao, Hitler, and Stalin, thinkers whose ideas have led to the deaths of many millions. These books hardly had a neutral impact in the West, as they commanded the imaginations and loyalties of a big chunk of several generations of the Western intelligentsia. These books continue to be sold on the open market, and I am happy about this, as much as I disapprove of the embodied ideas. I save my criticisms for the bad ideas, not for, say, Penguin Random House or the owners of the printing presses. Yet Facebook has become the whipping boy du jour, perhaps because it is such a visible part of our lives. The truth is simply that an open publishing environment is going to lead to the communication of a lot of bad ideas; that is part of free speech, and there is nothing new about this dilemma. This time around it is supposed to be "really different" because Facebook is a kind of monopoly, or because Facebook uses algorithms to order articles, or for whatever reason. From my naive, long-term historical perspective, Facebook hasn't come anywhere near to doing the damage that the printing press (and radio) did by helping to communicate the ideas of fascism, Marxism, communism, and so on.

I should add that I have personal experience buying "propagandistic" ads on Facebook—namely, for my free online education program MRUniversity.com, mentioned earlier in connection with YouTube. The purpose of these ads was to target Facebook users who showed an interest in economics or were connected to universities and to encourage those individuals to click on the videos. I can't say I was unhappy with these expenditures, as they did drive some traffic to our site. But it was hardly possible to manipulate people like zombies, and we have moved away from buying the ads, even though they helped give us an early boost. That is a much more typical Facebook advertising story than what you might hear about these days.

The idea of a "filter bubble" is another criticism of Facebook, but it is not supported by the facts. So many times I have heard that Facebook or other social media put us in worlds where conservatives listen only to conservatives and progressives only to progressives, or some such similar complaint about echo chambers. Maybe at times that feels true, but the numbers just don't support the fear, at least not so far. As far as we can tell, ideological segregation in online news is relatively low, inasmuch as conservatives visit a lot of fairly left-wing news sources and those on the left consume a reasonable degree of conservative media. For instance, the best available data show that the average conservative on the internet is exposed to about 60 percent conservative sources, hardly an overwhelming number. Liberals are exposed to about 53 percent relatively conservative sites. Those same data also show that there is far more ideological segregation in our face-to-face interactions with family, friends, and coworkers than happens online.[7]

I do have a very specific concern about Facebook: I worry that it is making us a little too sociable—in the online sense, of course—and taking scarce time away from other things we might be doing, like talking to our spouse or children. I don't doubt the sociability is what the users want, but the ability of Facebook to command our attention so effectively may pull human attention away from other endeavors—in my view, not always for the better.[8]

This concern is related to some broader problems with relatively open online media. Facebook is a medium, and therefore it will channel user preferences in many regards. That will include nasty notes to friends, racist sentiments, and organizing for harmful or inefficient political causes. Any highly successful medium will carry along a lot of the bad along with the good, and Facebook is no exception. Most of the blame I put on Facebook's users, and to some extent on the media companies that, in a shortsighted manner, decided to chase Facebook traffic too intently. Still, I don't think we should be entirely happy about a medium that allows so many base or simply banal instincts to be channeled so effectively. I understand that fixing this problem would require Facebook to be much more paternalistic and big brotherish, and the cure could be worse than the disease.

As I am writing this chapter, the big controversy is whether Facebook and YouTube will too heavily censor controversial sources of news and information. Overall, this is a stronger concern on the right than on the left. I frequently hear right-wing, conservative, and Republican thinkers and analysts worry that so many of the employees in the big tech companies are left-wing and one way or another will put the other side's ideas at a disadvantage.

This issue is developing as I write, and my discussion might be out of date by the time you are reading this, but I'd still like to make a few points. First, the major tech companies for the most part have not wanted to censor content. It is expensive for them, and they know better than anyone how hard it is to find clear lines in this area. To the extent that censorship has arisen as an issue, it is because the public and some politicians have demanded a response (with tech company employees exercising some pressure as well). So maybe our beef should be with the intrinsic difficulty of the problem, and not with the tech companies per se.

Second, Facebook and YouTube carry so much content we should not be surprised if some number of their take-down decisions turn out to be mistakes. As I write, their overall record seems remarkably good, no matter how much some people may howl over anecdotal evidence of mistakes. With the exception of some small number of overt fascists and racists who have been banned from some social networks, the rest of us are free to post our opinions as we see fit.

Finally, we have to compare the present to the past. Let's say that Facebook and YouTube unjustly took you off their platform and would not let you back on. That is indeed a bad development. But were you so much better off in the "good old days," when you had basically zero chance of getting on the three major networks or the big radio stations or of writing for the major newspapers? Dissident voices have more outlets than ever before, even if a few of them receive tough treatment from the big tech companies.

Overall, this is an area where we need to be careful, and I do in fact share the concerns of people who worry that public pressure will push the major tech companies into too many take-down or "no service" decisions. But it's also not an easy problem to fix. Given that we've already decided they have the right not to carry images of beheadings and child porn, we really can't deny them some discretion. And would it help to split either Facebook or YouTube into two or three entities? I don't think so. That simply means that a slightly larger number of entities would face the same public pressures and quite possibly arrive at the very same content-carry decisions. Your real options are to find corners of the internet that will be interested in your ideas, and adjust accordingly. It's still a far freer intellectual world than what we knew only a short time ago.

To consider a third major tech company: Apple too continues to be a major innovator, in spite of its reputation to the contrary. Not only does Apple have three truly major developments under its belt—personal computers, smartphones, and smart tablets—but the company continues to try to drive further advances. The future of the Apple Watch remains uncertain, but at the very least it is a major achievement along the path of developing higher-quality and more practical internet-connected wearables; its millions of users already find it a convenient way to receive messages and track and measure certain aspects of their behavior. Apple Pay is a major player in fintech, and millions of people use it to pay for goods and services with a simple swipe at a terminal. Even if that doesn't prove to be the winning technology, it is a stepping-stone for the later improvements of others.

Or look at Amazon. The company started off selling books but moved to many different sectors of retail. It innovated by showing that it made sense to allow used books to compete alongside new product, thereby lowering prices for the millions of customers wishing to buy the used copies. Amazon has constructed what is arguably the world's best logistics network ever and these days is working on the use of drones to deliver packages. Whether or not that succeeds, or is allowed by the regulators, it is a bold attempt at innovation. Amazon's work in cloud computing has driven that market and made it much easier for other innovators to rapidly scale their businesses. Amazon also pioneered home artificial intelligence with Alexa: just speak to it and it will do your bidding as well as the software allows. Expect upgrades. And Kindle—well, that was an Amazon innovation too. Amazon's cell phone didn't work out, but as with the other tech companies, Amazon's overall record shows how hard it is trying to improve our lives with better products. It's now trying to innovate, if that is the correct word, by showing that brick-and-mortar bookstores can still make good economic sense. The principles Amazon uses for choosing and displaying titles are very different from those of traditional bookstores, as they rely more on data generated through Amazon. We'll see if they succeed.

Overall, I am astonished at just how varied the innovations of the major tech companies have been. It seems they have a core capacity for assembling, motivating, and coordinating human talent above and beyond the particular business lines where they won their earliest victories.

## DOES TECH MAKE US STUPID?

Another criticism of the tech companies comes from thinkers such as Nicholas Carr, who has referred to the internet as "the shallows" and who has argued that Google is making us stupid. This criticism strikes me as a bit outside the focus of this book, as it pinpoints broader social and technological forces rather than the tech companies qua companies. Still, one feature of the current intellectual environment is that if a criticism of companies can be made, it will to some extent stick.

This criticism of the new technologies points to their effects on human beings. Supposedly the tech companies have ushered in a new world where we have a limited attention span, less memory, and a more superficial understanding of the broader world. That's a little hard to assess after only about ten to fifteen years of this new internet-focused world, but a few points deserve to be made in response.

First, if anything, interest in longer works and serials seems to be rising, not falling. The Harry Potter books have been the best sellers of their time, and *Game of Thrones* is pretty popular too, in both its book and television forms. In terms of cultural consumption, if there is a major trend it is toward serial television shows, which involve the viewer for many hours on end and require a significant commitment of time and attention. The average published book is growing longer, not shorter; one survey of best sellers and widely discussed books indicates an average length of 320 pages in 1999, rising to 400 pages in 2014. Of course, there are plenty of tweets and short Facebook posts, but it is not obvious that the net trend is away from the long. And even if it is, perhaps viewers are discarding some of the long works that were less than entirely compelling. I don't see most of the internet critics flying around the world to track down new performances of *Die Meistersinger* or reading the five-volume Penguin edition of the eighteenth-century Chinese novel *Dream of the Red Chamber*. Maybe they should, but perhaps the internet is as likely to stimulate interest in these works as to pull people away from them. Those are minority tastes, and if there is one thing the internet is great at, it is matching people to niche and obscure works they really are going to like.[9]

Second, the internet, and by a somewhat dubious extension the tech companies, really has changed the way we think and how we pay attention, or sometimes don't pay attention. I just don't believe we know the long-term consequences of this yet. It *might* be problematic, but it's also had a wonderful impact in terms of exposing people to different ideas, different cultures, new music, and the amazing quantity and quality of intellectual discourse you can find in blogs, on YouTube, and in many other corners of online life. It is far too early to conclude this has been a disaster, and in fact, over the broader span of history, having more information and more diverse information usually has worked out well for humankind.

You may know that the current criticisms of the internet were made, in varying forms, in earlier ages against the opera, the novel, the paperback book, television, and rock and roll. In the eighteenth and nineteenth centuries, for instance, the novel was tied to bad health, disobedience to parents, the breakdown of class distinctions, increased independence among women, and other "sins." One critic noted: "The reading of novels is to the mind, what *dram-drinking* is to the body." At that time, the older media did not like the competition from the newer media, and so an ideological war was fought across different media platforms. Sound familiar? Yet for most of the world, and for America particularly, life typically has gotten better and media have grown successively more useful, informative, and entertaining. Maybe *this time* it really is the cultural and intellectual apocalypse, but the evidence for those claims just isn't there. At least not yet. Is it so terrible if these days we remember fewer state capitals and phone numbers, instead relying on our electronic devices?[10]

There is a scenario for the future that is perhaps a little scary but is worth giving some thought to. It could be that the age of the internet is quite temporary, as the internet might be replaced by something more powerful and more popular—perhaps some use of virtual reality to connect us with information and entertainment, to name just one possibility. And who knows what that will be like? Furthermore, assume there is a unique internet way of thinking and presenting ideas. With the internet as a potentially endangered species of sorts, maybe it is our cultural duty to exploit, mine, and propagate that way of thinking and communicating as much as possible before it disappears. Even if you don't prefer the "internet style," this kind of intertemporal substitution could well make sense. For instance, Baroque music is not my favorite style, but still I am glad that the seventeenth and eighteenth centuries gave it their best shot before moving on to more classical modes of composition. So arguably we ought to be intensifying our efforts to immerse ourselves in "internet ways of thinking," whatever we might take that to mean.

Another very recent criticism is that Silicon Valley only specializes in the trivial. In 2017, some of the critics pointed to Juicero, a $400 Wi-Fi–enabled juicer that has been called "the absurd avatar of Silicon Valley hubris." (The company later went under.) Scott Alexander, one of my favorite bloggers (on the internet, of course), set out to rebut this charge. Here is what he found:

> I looked at the latest batch of 52 startups from legendary Silicon Valley startup incubator Y Combinator.
>
> Thirteen of them had an altruistic or international development focus, including Neema, an app to help poor people without access to banks gain financial services; Kangpe, online health services for people in Africa without access to doctors; Credy, a peer-to-peer lending service in India; Clear Genetics, an automated genetic counseling tool for at-risk parents; and Dost Education, helping to teach literacy skills in India via a $1/month course.
>
> Twelve of them seemed like really exciting cutting-edge technology, including CBAS, which describes itself as "human bionics plug-and-play"; Solugen, which has a way to manufacture hydrogen peroxide from plant sugars; AON3D, which makes 3D printers for industrial uses; Indee, a new genetic engineering system; Alem Health, applying AI to radiology, and of course the obligatory drone delivery startup.

Scott did find that nine other of the supported companies might count as "silly," and of course not all of those listed will succeed, but overall is that such a bad record? Keep in mind that as you look forward, it is not always easy to tell which "silly" innovation might, every now and then, prove to be pathbreaking.[11]

In any case, I wonder how much the internet critics really believe their own words. I recall one time debating Nicholas Carr in a television studio on whether Google makes us stupider. The first question I asked him was whether, in preparing for the debate, he had used Google to research who I am. I thought I had won right then and there. I also suspect that a book as intellectual as his sold a disproportionate share of its copies online rather than in physical stores. There is simply too strong a tendency for critics to think that the internet is mainly making "the other people" stupid. Virtually all of us consult the internet on a very regular basis, and I would say that is because it is extraordinarily useful and informative.

## THE ENDURING LOSS OF PRIVACY

When I consider all the different parts of the elephant, overall I am struck by just how much there is to admire about the tech companies. In addition to their incredible innovations, they have been leaders in expressing a vision of a new and more tolerant America, and they have helped make nerds and geeks cool. They've turned northern California into one of the world's most dynamic (and, sad to say, expensive) areas. Over the last twenty years, Silicon Valley really has become one of the major places where the history of the world is being written, and probably there is more to come.

Another nice thing about the big tech companies is how little interest they showed in lobbying Washington, at least at first. In most cases they had very small or no Washington offices early on, didn't much plead to the government, mostly wanted to be left alone, and did not request legal restrictions on their competition. As you probably know, this lack of interest in governmental affairs resulted in some negative consequences, including the antitrust suit initiated against Microsoft in 1998. Silicon Valley CEOs were some of the most frequent visitors to the Obama White House, and they are now dealing with the unorthodox presidency of Donald Trump. Yes, they liked to be feted by the president, but they also have learned the hard way that being well connected is essential to keeping their companies up and running. And if their first inclination was to thrive and prosper by offering superior products and by besting the competition—isn't there something very admirable about that?

So what, then, is the catch with the big tech companies? The downside here has been the loss of privacy, and in this regard I really do see a significant problem, or at least a potential future problem. The simple truth is that the tech companies record, store, and sometimes trade all the information about your life that they have, including what they can infer from increasingly sophisticated statistical techniques, sometimes called Big Data.

Unlike many of the critics, I don't think the privacy violations *to date* have been unacceptable or world-ending. When individuals join social networks or go shopping in an online store, they know data is being collected and stored about them, even if they do not have a full sense of how that data is being distributed and used. They make trade-offs, and most individuals have been willing to proceed with these activities. Furthermore, many Facebook users partake in the service rather enthusiastically; they do not give the impression of using the service only grudgingly, as you might, for instance, ride the bus only because you cannot afford a car. I'm not saying there is no problem here; rather, I often see the privacy critics exaggerating the dilemmas faced by internet users. If Facebook really is so horrible, why aren't more people setting up email lists as an alternative? Of course many are, and that returns to the above point that there is more competition among social networks than may at first appear.

Rather than the present, I'm more worried about possible futures. I really can imagine these privacy issues becoming significantly worse over the next ten to twenty years. It seems we are on a slippery slope of sorts, and even if matters are acceptable now, we may slide down to a much worse part of the curve. Furthermore, a lot of what the private sector knows about us, or will know about us, may fall into the hands of the government, whether through subpoena, forced information sharing, government surveillance, or hacking. So even if you trust a business with your data, you can't be guaranteed the data will stay there.

So how might the privacy landscape change for the worse?

First, facial recognition technologies are starting to spread, and they are becoming much more accurate. I've seen recent reports that such technologies are 70 to 80 percent accurate, although I don't think those numbers are so meaningful, because they raise the question of the conditions under which such accuracy might be possible. Still, it seems quite possible that in normal, controlled commercial settings, such as walking into a supermarket, within a few years facial recognition will be able to identify most of the customers. Facial recognition outdoors and in public is harder because of varying conditions and angles and the greater diversity of spaces, but again major advances have already been made and there are more to come. There is already plenty of facial recognition technology in China, and more is on the way in public spaces such as Dubai International Airport. It deters criminals, but one can't help wondering how much it is also used to track dissidents. Are you really so happy to hear that Shanghai is using facial recognition to identify and then shame jaywalkers by posting their photos at bus stops, with a fine thrown in as well, not to mention a cross-check against a national database of IDs? In the near future, if you have visited a public space, the safe assumption will be that your visit was recorded and, furthermore, that there is a searchable way to go through the data and trace many of your movements. For a start, we need a better public conversation about facial recognition and close scrutiny of the default and opt-out rules, and we should consider giving citizens greater ownership rights over their facial images, and perhaps the pattern of their gait as well.[12]

Voice recording is another worry for the future. Due to advances in technology, it is becoming easier to record private conversations from some distance—and, of course, they can be put online easily. What will it be like when recording equipment is so sensitive that only sealed rooms are truly secure? Even the classic walk in the public park might be vulnerable. Just as people are now very wary about what they will put in an email, in the future they might have to be equally careful about what they say in private conversations for fear of being recorded, even from a considerable distance or perhaps with the aid of a micro-drone disguised as an insect. It helps that many states have made such non-consensual recordings against the law; still, anonymously recorded conversations uploaded and tweeted anonymously can ruin careers, and I expect we will see more of this. We should toughen the relevant laws here and make them consistent across the states—and, in general, be careful what we say. Politeness was underrated to begin with, and all the more so in this new world to come.

Even your home spaces may not be fully secure as we move to an Internet of Things in the daily household. It will be wonderful to talk to your garage door, stereo, and television and have them respond immediately to your commands. Of course, that means they are listening all the time too—to your family arguments, to how you scold your kids, to how you talk about your colleagues at work, and to what you do in bed and how loud your orgasm is (or isn't). Now, you might say, "Ah, my home devices won't really be listening to me. They won't listen until I shout 'Abracadabra, listen to me!'" Well, maybe. But they still have to be doing some kind of background listening to know when to be turned on. And do you really know what is happening to that raw data feed? Are you *sure* it is secure and cannot be used to recon-struct your original conversations at home? And for *all* of your devices, including your car? (How many of you knew all along how much data the National Security Agency had potential access to?) Are you *sure* your Alexa has not been hacked so that the listening function is turned on? I genuinely do not know, and of course no one can know until the devices have been on the market and tested for a longer time. In the meantime, I don't want those devices, but at some point the newer generations of appliances and homes on the market may require them. When that rueful day comes, I'm going to be more careful about what I say, even in the confines of my own home. Perhaps *especially* in the confines of my own home, where it is going to be fairly clear who the main speaker is.

And this isn't just science fiction. Already there have been cases where law enforcement has subpoenaed Amazon for recordings from Echo—for instance, in connection with a murder suspect. In 2015 a man was drowned in a hot tub in Bentonville, Arkansas, and the po-lice wanted to see if background recordings might hold additional clues. The police also may have the ability to hack into the device, with or without a search warrant. (At the time of this writing, the final dis-position of these matters remained an open question, with a flurry of court rulings in process.) Probably you're not a murderer, but how many people, even fully law-abiding ones, would want an IRS agent to listen to a recording of how they talk about their taxes to their spouse?

Subpoenas aside, we live in a world where everything that can be hacked will be hacked, and perhaps that will apply to the recordings of these devices too. One of the things the hackers might do is turn on the device, even when it is supposed to be only listening passively for activation instructions and nothing else. After all, to hear your activation command some kind of microphone has to be listening to your voice and in some manner evaluating its content. It seems hard to believe that the potential for accidental recording can be eliminated altogether. What if you actually have a friend named Alexa? Or what if you use the mathematical phrase (common in microeconomics, I might add) "a lexicographic ordering"? Might an errant recording device sometimes register the opening bit there as "Alexa"? Or perhaps hackers will find ways of entering these systems.

The onset of interest in Big Data also could lead to further privacy losses, most of all what I call stochastic or probabilistic losses of privacy. Let's say that some software knows your general shopping habits, and that software starts "talking" to a facial recognition program that spotted someone buying a mattress in a store and decided there was a 0.6 probability it was you. Another piece of software then reports that you just moved house. "The system" might then decide you really did buy a mattress—at least with, say, a probability of 83 percent—and thus ads for bedding will be sent your way. In such a situation, you can't say that anyone knows as a matter of fact where you were, but odds are "the system" has a pretty good idea. Of course, a similar process already occurs when software judges whether the owner of a particular iPad, smartphone, and PC are all the same person. Usually they know it's you, and that is how they target ads to all of your devices.

It is easy to imagine extensions of such probabilistic knowledge as tracking technologies improve, more of our lives go online, and interest in Big Data increases. To put it simply, I'm worried about all of our character flaws and imperfections becoming public knowledge, if only stochastically. What if you have ordered a few too many bottles of Scotch or shown too much interest in "medical marijuana"? It's not so bad for me and others who lead staid, boring lives, but what if you are just starting a new career?

Electronic medical records are another area of concern. Although they are touted by many health care reformers, I worry about their potential for abuse. Imagine an America with fully integrated electronic medical records tracking everyone's health care history. Then consider the scenario where some individual or hostile foreign power hacks into that database and makes it available to the whole world, or perhaps only selectively. That would be a massive violation of individual privacy. Any person with any history of mental illness (not a phrase I like, but I suspect you know what I am trying to reference), misbehavior, or any number of other maladies or misfortunes would be marked for life. Statistical discrimination based on these categories would rise and the number of "second chances" in life would decline, and as a result, many more people likely would be reluctant to seek professional help at all. Some parents might keep their children away from the health care system altogether, or at the very least for ailments of mental health. The medical diagnosis of your kid might make it harder for her to get certain jobs. And keep in mind that there are plenty of false positives in any medical assessment, most of all for a variety of mental conditions that can be difficult to identify or even define.

The medical privacy situation is already worse than many people realize. For instance, in 2015 there were more than 720 medical-related data breaches, and the seven biggest of those exposed almost 200 million personal medical records to fraud and identity theft. In early 2014, 80 million or so customers of the health insurance provider Anthem had their account information stolen, mostly so the thieves could file false tax returns requesting refunds or perhaps apply for credit under false pretenses. While the available evidence indicates that so far most of these hacks are for financially relevant information, such as Social Security numbers, rather than to violate patient privacy, it is not hard to imagine a future where the medical records themselves become public or semi-public knowledge. Imagine you have a pre-existing condition related to mental illness, your records are hacked, and then you receive an email blackmailing you, threatening to release the information unless you send $10,000 in Bitcoin. By the time you are reading this book, I bet this already has happened, whether or not the story made it into the newspapers.[13]

It's not so well known that currently hackers actually *target* hospitals and electronic medical records. They get into a hospital database, pull out some medical information, store it in such a way that the hospital can't access it, prove to the hospital that they are holding sensitive information, and then ask the hospital for a ransom. On the black market, hacked medical records can pull in ten times more than hacked credit card information. Usually the hospital pays up and does not make too big a story of the hack; after all, why would a business-minded medical institution publicize its own vulnerability? Still, I don't think we should assume it always will work out so calmly. At some point the blackmailers will seek to hit up the patient too; maybe it's already happened. Or eventually some hackers might just release the information rather than ask for a ransom, or the hackers in turn will be hacked. Or some hospital might not pay up, fearing the information will be released anyway, or believing that the asking price is too high. Or the hackers might repeatedly try to extort money for the information, leading to a breakdown of the deal and the release of the information. Just as not all kidnappings of humans end with the victim being returned unharmed, we cannot expect a peaceful, consensual resolution of all kidnappings of information. Again, while right now credit card numbers and Social Security numbers are most vulnerable, it is easy to imagine a future when the medical information itself also is a valuable commodity to be bartered or held for ransom.[14]

Here too, we need to keep such problems in perspective. In many of these instances the main problem is the criminals, not the tech companies. Furthermore, better tech in the form of cybersecurity is also our most likely *protection* against such outcomes. Still, every new technology does enable new kinds of crimes, and that is a growing worry, even if the innovating companies are not themselves morally at fault.

Another potential problem could spring from genetic testing and the information embodied in those results. Right now, you can swab your cheek to get a DNA sample and send it in to a number of companies, most prominently 23andMe. They will send you back some information about yourself, including an assessment of your susceptibility to particular diseases (some legal restrictions have been placed on this), information about your ethnic background, and information about other people you are probably related to. That may involve some privacy issues, but so far it seems manageable; furthermore, the information held by the company has not (yet?) spilled into the public realm. But imagine a future where genetic testing is a more sophisticated science. Perhaps a reading of your genome could indicate your conscientiousness, your IQ, your temperament, your susceptibility to depression, and other factors of interest to prospective employers and also prospective mates. Most likely this will only be probabilistic information, but it is valuable—and potentially burdensome—nonetheless.

In that case, which is admittedly speculative, the potential for privacy violations could be severe. The pressure on individuals to allow such information to be registered could be very strong. Imagine showing up for a job interview and not volunteering to turn over your genetic information; the company might respond by refusing to hire you. Or the interviewer could offer you a cup of coffee and then get some of your DNA off the cup. If you are dating someone, it would be very hard to keep all of your genetic information to yourself. And once this genetic information is in some way "out there," expect it to be spread. Individuals with favorable genetic profiles, or profiles perceived as such, will disclose their information voluntarily to an open database. Those people who do not follow suit often may be considered "inferior," the natural inference from a failure to disclose (imagine that a disclosure of criminal records and history of involvement with the law was at stake, and apply the same logic to those who would not disclose). Or the data may be hacked and published somewhere like WikiLeaks; bribe payments probably won't keep this information a secret forever.

In 1998, David Brin published a famous book called *The Transparent Society*. He noted that individuals were losing their privacy, but wondered whether this might be a good thing overall. He stressed that there would be an attendant decline in corruption, an openness about who we really are, and a strengthening of reputational and competitive checks as reasons to welcome this development, which indeed can be described as "greater transparency" and not just "loss of privacy." At the time, I found that a pretty persuasive vision, but as the years have passed I don't think it has stood up so well. For one thing, we've learned that openness and transparency are less likely to bring out the truth than we might have thought. In a world where all or most information is on the internet, some politicians just lie a lot more, and there are plenty of individuals and institutions out there who have an interest in backing up their claims. The anticorruption effects of transparency also seem weaker than advertised. If you consider Donald Trump, for instance, when conflicts of interest are exposed, his main strategy is simply that of denial or lies, and so far he has gotten away with it. Again, in a world of full transparency there is always a competing source of "the truth," and it seems hard to settle on who the most important gatekeepers should be.

On the bright side, there is a good chance that in the future privacy-protecting technologies will outrace privacy-denying ones. Private business, including the tech sector, has already done a lot to further privacy protection. It is now easy to encrypt your messages, and encryption would have arrived sooner if not for opposition from America's national security establishment. You may or may not favor the spread of encryption, given the potential for terrorist and other criminal abuses, but it belies the notion that the tech world is only about privacy violations. Similarly, you can buy a disposable, or burner, phone or acquire a burner email address, two other examples of privacy protections offered by business.

Many privacy-enhancing technologies have been with us for a long time. You can buy tinting film for your car windows or a home on an isolated lot, and it is easier than ever before to find shopping malls, movie theaters, and restaurants where the odds are that no one there knows you and you can conduct your business or personal life in privacy. I sometimes think of today's ethnic restaurants—the spicier and dowdier and more extreme the better—as being, among other things, a source of potential privacy for people who do not belong to that ethnic group.

Just compare privacy in contemporary urban and suburban America with privacy in small rural towns. Even though people living in the more densely populated areas use the internet more, they seem to have much more privacy, in large part because of these areas' density and their very large networks of different kinds of physical spaces, whether it be restaurants, political gathering places, supermarkets, or somewhere else. For the most part, it is the density of businesses and commercial activities that is boosting your privacy in the urban and suburban areas. Or consider more extreme comparisons, such as your privacy in modern urban America compared with your privacy in an Indian village with no internet at all. Again, the answer seems pretty obvious—the net effects of commerce and business have been to increase personal privacy. That trend may someday be reversed, but for the time being, commerce and business have done more to guarantee privacy than to violate it.

Finally, it is not obvious that corporations are the major enemies of our privacy as individuals. In general, for most people gossip from friends, relatives, colleagues, and acquaintances is a bigger privacy risk than information garnered from Google or social networks. I don't know how to assess the relative scope of internet versus noninternet violations here, but gossip is an age-old problem, and even today a lot of the biggest privacy harms come through very traditional channels. And unlike false charges planted on social media, often there is no way to strike back against secretive whisperings behind one's back. In the workplace, one employee may tell the boss that another does not work hard enough, shows up late, drinks too much, is fooling around sexually with someone else in the office, and so on. Again, it is at least possible that these kinds of privacy violations and/or lies are worse than what happens over social media and the internet.

Public high schools and junior high schools are one part of American life where untold misery is caused by privacy violations, driven mostly by gossip. There is gossip about family scandals, friendships fallen apart, romantic gamesmanship, petty jealousies, sports performance, who is a "wanker," and many, many other personal matters of great concern to the individuals who attend those schools. Sometimes the parents care too, as when the gossip turns into bullying or damages a child's academic performance, as often seems to happen. Of course, these gossip problems long predate the tech companies, or for that matter electricity. The brutality of American high schools and junior high schools is first and foremost testament to the sometimes sadistic privacy-violating tendencies of ordinary human beings, often relying on technologies no more advanced than word of mouth or the telephone. Maybe tech is making some aspects of that bullying worse, but it's giving people refuges from those worlds as well.

Finally, in closing I'd like to make one more point about the tech sector. By the time you read this chapter, new issues involving tech will have come along, maybe involving hacking, antitrust, political scandal, data misuse, and other possibilities. Most likely you will be reading about those issues from the mainstream media, or watching a discussion on cable TV. Just keep in mind that a lot of those media institutions have been financially ailing, either because of cord-cutting or because they have lost ad revenue to social media, most notably Facebook and Google. Arguably *these media companies' main competitors are Facebook and Google*. And if they are covering Facebook and Google, just how much objectivity do you expect? A simple question: Do media outlets apply conflict-of-interest rules, as might be placed on one of their journalists, to their own coverage of their main competitors?

I'll stick with my core claim that America's tech sector is increasingly underrated.

## WHAT IS WALL STREET GOOD FOR, ANYWAY?

Since 2008, the financial crash, and the Great Recession, the financial sector has been a major whipping boy in American politics and rhetoric. If you're looking for a pretty typical headline, consider this one from the *Wall Street Journal*: "Elizabeth Warren Maintains a Hard Line on the Big Banks." I'd like to suggest a broader perspective. At this point you might not be surprised to hear that I think America's financial sector is very much overcriticized and underrated. Toward that end, let's first consider some history.

If we look at the rise of the West over the centuries, the rise of civilization and the rise of finance have gone hand in hand. The first sophisticated city-states of Sumer appear to have made big advances in accounting, record keeping, lending, and banking by five thousand or so years ago. That helped the major ancient civilizations get their starts, eventually transforming Europe and the Middle East. The Greek city-states had advanced systems of banking for lending and also wealth storage.

Later, the rise of the Renaissance, as well as the patronage of art, was closely connected to advanced systems of banking that tied together many parts of Europe through lending, capital accumulation, and bills of exchange. The medieval money fairs turned into more systematic and far-ranging institutions that were major drivers of economic growth. Accounting technologies advanced accordingly, and many of the prerequisites for the modern state were put into place, most of all through the record-keeping techniques of financial institutions. Later, banking and public credit helped Britain rise as a leading power and gave the country the ability to protect itself from European invasion and depredation, thereby enabling the later Industrial Revolution. In fact, the rise of banking and finance was essential to civilizational development, the rise of Europe, and the best parts of Western civilization.

In other words, the growth of banking and finance has usually been very good for economies, and thus good for most citizens too. It can be debated to what extent banking and finance were causes or effects of earlier economic growth, but probably they were both. It is hard to imagine sustained economic growth without an ongoing and concomitant growth of banking and finance to allocate the capital that goes along with that new wealth. Banking and finance take society's saved resources and convert them into higher-yielding investments, and without that function, economic growth won't take off.

Consistent with this truth, banking and finance are important for the building of the American republic, the settling of the nation, and the rise of New York as a major global city. To side with banking and finance was to embrace these processes of development and to be on the right side of the debate. The more radical Jeffersonians, who were skeptical of banking in quite general terms, also were skeptical about the broader industrialization of the United States. Indeed, throughout the nineteenth century, anti-banking rhetoric was common in the United States and also quite similar to a lot of the current charges. The banks were supposedly parasites, sucking dry the body politic, rife with corruption and abuse, and using the patronage of Washington to win legal privilege and extract profits from the broader citizenry. Yet at the end of this entire process it turned out that American banks, for all of their imperfections at the time, had helped build an extensive network of roads, canals, waterworks, and ports, and a bit later railways and electrification facilities, all of which served to knit America together and make this country one of the wealthiest and freest in the world. The anti-banking vision of the critics was oddly consistent, but it reflected how a world without much banking is also an agrarian world, a world without powerful uses of energy, a world without much social or geographic mobility. Note also that the superior banking systems and finance of the North were essential to winning the Civil War, and thus for freeing the slaves.[1]

To be sure, along the way this process saw many excesses of finance, many bubbles, and many regulatory mistakes. The point is not that everything was so ideal, whether during the Renaissance or the history of the United States. Still, in the broader historical view, siding with banking and finance has meant siding with economic development and with the unfolding of the glories of civilization more broadly, be it the arts, philosophy, or the growth of the modern nation-state. Yale finance professor William N. Goetzmann makes this point in his book *Money Changes Everything: How Finance Made Civilization Possible*. Had banking and financial innovation not been allowed to proceed, the Western world would be a far less developed, creative, and indeed happy place. A few hundred years from now, our descendants probably will look back and say the same.

But since the financial crisis of 2007–2008, attitudes have swung in the other direction and critics have hit the financial sector with virulent attacks. The 2016 campaign of Bernie Sanders, which got much further than almost anyone expected, focused like a laser on banking and finance, as has Senator Elizabeth Warren. It's remarkable how many intellectuals, internet forum contributors, and even working-class Americans profess a strong dislike for the banks, or at least for what they think the banks stand for.

And it's not just the left wing anymore. Even the Republican 2016 presidential platform endorsed a new version of the Glass-Steagall Act as a way of breaking up the big banks. Neel Kashkari, who ran the TARP bailout program for President Bush during the financial crisis, has called for bank breakups more directly. Some other conservative and libertarian voices, including Thomas Koenig and Arnold Kling, have wondered whether America shouldn't apply antitrust law radically and move to a greater number of much smaller banks. In particular, if a bank is "too big to fail," doesn't that mean the bank is too big, period?

On top of that, there are so many (true) stories about the financial sector ripping off customers and clients. In 2007, the five biggest Wall Street firms paid executives $39 billion in bonuses, even though shareholders lost over $80 billion in value. Angelo Mozilo, the former CEO of Countrywide, realized $121 million in stock options in 2007 though his company lost $704 million that year and he became a stand-in figure for irresponsible lending behavior during the bubble period. Moving beyond the financial crisis, payday lenders appear to charge exorbitant fees, and numerous brokerage houses have recommended stocks to their customers in order to get commissions or kickbacks, even when they knew the stocks were bad investments. And the list of misdeeds is growing.[2]

It is also suggested that finance drains away American talent. Prior to the financial crisis, most of the Harvard graduating class set its eyes on financial jobs, but that is no longer the case. In 2007, right before the financial crisis, 47 percent of the Harvard graduating class went into finance, but by 2013 this was only 15 percent, still high but a more reasonable number. If nothing else, finance is an area where a smart person can get up to speed quickly and make a big splash without the benefit of experience accumulated over decades. Like tech, it plays to the cognitive strengths of the young: speed, stamina, and the ability to master (or invent) new products and trading techniques very quickly.[3]

These days Silicon Valley has risen in relative stature and, perhaps more important, wage and bonus opportunities, and some of the earlier interest in finance has dwindled. Banking and finance just aren't so cool anymore. Who wants to grow up to be a "bankster"? The diminishing interest in financial careers is a sign that the system is adjusting toward more balance, but the critics allege that the lust to go to Wall Street still mirrors a partial disconnect between the size of the rewards possible there and a person's overall contribution to society.

Indeed, there is something problematic about banking and finance that is not true of every other business activity. One of the central features of finance, broadly construed, is to take a lower-yielding asset and in some way try to turn it into a higher-yielding asset. On one hand, that's great—who doesn't want a higher-yielding asset? It's no wonder that fortunes are made in finance. On the other hand, this is an activity fraught with risk. It may lead to bubbles, attract fraudsters, or induce financial structures that try to stretch the underlying lower-yielding assets too thin by relying too heavily on the alchemy of debt and illiquidity and just plain flat-out irresponsibility.

The rest of this chapter will focus on how finance can indeed bring modern American society higher returns and some rather significant benefits. I'll also conclude that many of the downsides of banking and finance are not as significant as many people claim. So again, American business is underrated, and, as we will see, finance is one of the areas where negative misconceptions are especially rife and a more positive appreciation would improve our understanding of the world significantly.

## VENTURE CAPITAL DRIVES AMERICAN INNOVATION

The American system of venture capital (VC) is the envy of the world. If you have a new idea but are not sufficiently well established to go public, you can approach venture capitalists. The phrase "venture capital" is used in slightly different ways, but think of it as early-stage funding for small emerging firms with high growth potential, done through a systematic assessment of projects and personnel. America is very good at this process: measures for VC activity in the United States for 2015 range from $58 billion to $77 billion. In that year there were 74 megadeals ($100 million or more invested), with nearly 8,100 rounds of investment closed.[4]

Venture capitalists will fund a lot of risky ideas that banks will not. Let's say a brilliant entrepreneur has a new idea for a web product that has a 2 percent chance of becoming huge but otherwise will fail and cause the company to go bankrupt. Bankers probably won't be interested, because they are simply looking to get their capital back and will not participate in any of the potential upside. Nor is there much collateral they can seize if things go badly. A venture capitalist, on the other hand, will gain from the upside while understanding the long odds. He or she might fund dozens or even hundreds of start-ups, knowing that many will fail but a small number of them will succeed and account for most of the investor's final profit.

But venture capital isn't just about the money. It's also about systematic networks of expertise, so start-up capital is bundled with advice, guidance, mentoring, and monitoring. Venture capital as it is practiced in Silicon Valley is most of all about talent evaluation and, eventually, helping the real talent find the right hires, board members, and business connections. The best venture capitalists have remarkable intuition about other human beings and are in essence connectors and enablers, putting their money into projects to bring together a lot of talent for an extraordinarily intense and fruitful joint creative enterprise. VC brings together a lot of the best sides of the human experience.

The nature of venture capital reflects a more general point about finance: that it is not just a matter of money. Financial activities of many kinds tend to be geographically clustered, whether it is traditional bank lending and deal making in New York or London, VC activity in Silicon Valley or Tel Aviv, or green-lighting movie projects in Hollywood. That clustering comes about because finance is so closely linked to the building of trust relationships. The investors want to meet with, judge, monitor, and advise the people they are dealing with, and that is going to require some degree of physical proximity for the network as a whole. Great financial centers will blossom precisely in those areas that are wonderful connectors of human talent, and New York, London, and Silicon Valley all exhibit this skill in nonfinancial areas as well, whether it be for the arts, entertainment, cuisine, or, in the case of northern California, for programming, management, and prediction. One of the most striking features of venture capital is how scarce it is in the broader world, which shows it rests upon a fragile and difficult to replicate set of auxiliary institutions, most of all strong and trusting networks of mutual business support.

The public most commonly associates venture capital with Silicon Valley and the tech world, and indeed virtually all of the major tech companies have venture capital origins. Still, the venture capital phenomenon is broader: only about 20 percent of VC firms specialize in what might be called information technology companies. Most VC firms are invested in three industries or more, and 39 percent of VC firms describe themselves as generalists without a particular industry focus.[5]

Medicine is another area where venture capital has been important and likely will remain so. About 13 percent of venture capital firms specialize in some form of health care, and this often is combined with information technology. As in the broader tech world, potential medical and biotech innovations have a high fail rate, which tends to put off banks and other traditional lenders. Yet the possible upside is huge, most of all for the broader society. That again suggests equity investment is the way to go, but many biotech projects are too small, too immature, or too hard to explain or demonstrate to go public. Again, venture capital helps fund much of the innovation in this area. If it ever turns out that more cancers are cured or that human beings routinely live to the age of 120, probably we will have venture capital to thank.[6]

Solar power, components for electric cars, and new battery technologies also are attracting attention from venture capital, again with many of the new ideas being quite risky in financial terms. If and when America shifts to a green energy economy, venture capital likely will deserve much of the credit.

According to the National Venture Capital Association, companies that have been backed by venture capital account for 21 percent of U.S. GDP and 11 percent of private-sector jobs. That association is a sector advocate and possibly a biased source; still, most experts agree that venture capital has had an impact far beyond the size of the initial investments. Companies with venture capital origins include Microsoft, Apple, Google, Cisco, eBay, Amazon, Amgen, Adobe, Starbucks, Symantec, and Uber. One estimate is that of the half a million new American businesses that are started every year, only about one thousand receive venture capital funding. Yet over 60 percent of initial public offerings (IPOs) have venture capital origins. Along related lines, it is estimated that ventures receiving VC backing account for about 20 percent of American market capitalization and about 44 percent of the research and development spending of publicly listed American companies.[7]

In other words, even with a low hit rate, venture capital is doing a really good job of finding and funding winners. And when venture capital does fail, most of the time no one comes around asking for a bailout or handout.

At the regional level, it is not just Silicon Valley but also Boston, Brooklyn (which if it were not part of New York City would be America's fourth-largest city), and Austin, Texas, that have had their economies revolutionized by venture capital and the associated investments. If you are wondering why Austin, for instance, has so many good restaurants and such a cool downtown to walk around in, and why the percentage of the population that is well educated has risen so rapidly, venture capital is a big part of the answer. In Brooklyn, venture capital has helped drive gentrification and lower crime rates. Significant parts of Boston are populated by VC-funded operations, often in biotech, and the presence of venture capital has helped MIT and (to a lesser degree) Harvard maintain and extend their pivotal roles as centers of talent.

Most of the world's other major economies have not had much of a venture capital scene until lately. It is only now starting to come into existence in places such as Berlin, Seoul, and Singapore, whereas the United States has had significant venture capital activity since the 1980s, with some of it some going as far back as 1946. Semiconductor firms were benefiting from venture capital as long ago as 1959 (Fairchild Semiconductor), and the early presence of these markets is a major reason Silicon Valley is in the United States and not abroad. The second-largest venture capital market in the world for tech is located in Israel; that a country of about eight million people holds the number-two position is a sign of how backward venture capital remains throughout much of the world and how hard it is to pull off the associated levels of trust and business networking. Of course, the Israeli venture capital market has drawn a lot of its ideas, inspiration, and talent from the United States.[8]

Sometimes you will hear the claim that venture capital is "good finance," as compared with the broader category of "bad finance" or "wasteful finance." But venture capital does not operate in a vacuum, apart from the rest of the American economy. It is integrated into a system of bank backstops and letters of credit, efficient asset management for venture capitalists, orderly initial public offerings, and liquid securities markets, among other features. The successes of venture capital would not be possible without other well-functioning features of the broader American financial system.

Part of the reason we have finance, and venture capital in particular, is that we don't always know in advance which parts of the system are going to pay off. In the early days of venture capital, it was hardly obvious that it was going to succeed on a large scale; in fact, it had a bit of a reputation as a conceit and a money waster. Only a fairly small number of visionaries saw it would help drive innovation in Silicon Valley and later biotech. Furthermore, one of the wonders of venture capital is that the visionaries found more and more resources concentrated in their hands, which in time led to further investment in venture capital because visionaries are not the type of people who stash all of their wealth in T-bills or their checking accounts. Venture capital rewards the winners in a big way, and it gives them a greater say over where the next rounds of capital will be going.

The culture of initial public offerings is connected to venture capital, even though not every IPO has venture capital origins. Nor does every new company long to do an IPO; the advantages of staying private seem to be rising, as reflected in ongoing declines in the number of IPOs. Still, IPOs are at the very least an option for companies to make their founders more liquid, even if the IPO never happens or happens only late in the life of the company—either way, the founders know they have an option to become more liquid, should they need to. In any case, both IPOs and venture capital reflect how American capital markets make it much easier to move, in the words of Peter Thiel, from zero to one.

Of course, shutting down the losers is the flip side of all this new business growth. These days there is less capital for older technologies and much more capital for nursing homes, biotech, start-ups, restaurants, luxury tourism, and other growing endeavors. Venture capital is part of a broader phenomenon whereby bank lending, the bond market, and all the other parts of the American capitalistic system decide which investors will receive additional funds and which will not. This may seem like a trivial function, but a lot of the world's financial systems perform poorly in this regard. Both Japan and significant parts of Western Europe have propped up "zombie banks" or "zombie companies" for years or decades, hindering the flow of capital into new endeavors. The goal behind those policies was to limit economic disruption, but long-term dynamism has suffered. By keeping older, possibly insolvent banks and companies up and running, previous decisions and decision-makers are more likely to stay locked in place, which slows down the marketplace process of creative destruction and the replacement of old economic sectors with new ones, including tech. In sectoral terms, the American economy has adjusted better to a changing world, and part of the credit goes to its relatively dynamic institutions of corporate finance.

## AMERICAN STOCKS HAVE PERFORMED WELL, ENRICHING AMERICANS

One way of boosting returns is to distribute the benefits of equity to a greater and more diverse set of individuals. Since the mid- to late nineteenth century, American stocks have delivered some pretty astonishing returns. It depends on the exact time period under consideration, but by many common measures American equity returns have averaged about 7 percent a year, and that is after adjusting for inflation. To put that in context, a 7 percent annual return means that the value of a portfolio doubles about every ten years. Those same returns may or may not hold over the future, but for the purposes of this discussion let's focus on what we know, and that is the returns from equity holdings from the historical past.[9]

Of course, the 7 percent figure is only an average—most years, stocks bring either more or less than 7 percent. Furthermore, not every American holds a diversified bundle of stocks, and many investors squander some of their gains through excess trading and incurring the associated trading costs. Advisor fraud is a problem too. According to one recent study, 7 percent of active financial advisors have a misconduct conviction or settlement on their record. The median settlement in such misconduct cases is $40,000, only half of advisors involved in such cases are fired, and of those fired, about half find a new job in the financial services sector.[10]

Still, over any thirty-year period in American history, the return on stocks is remarkably high, especially compared with the return on bonds. To make that concrete, if you had bought a representative bundle of stocks right before the crash of 1929, thirty years later, relative to what would have been available on Treasury bills, you would have earned over 6 percent a year on your money.[11] For a comparable thirty-year period, safe government securities tended to yield only about 1 percent a year, which is much less than one could earn in the stock market. With returns of 1 percent, it takes about seventy years for an investor to double his or her money.

The United States is, quite simply, one of the countries that encourages its citizens to invest the most in equities. As of 2015, 55 percent of Americans had money invested in stocks. That is a major benefit from the American financial system, and for ordinary American citizens it is worth hundreds of billions of dollars. Even if you do not personally own many or any equities, there is a good chance your retirement fund or pension fund does. While much of the world has been catching up with the American system in this regard, that global spread of equity ownership is yet another benefit of America's pioneering efforts.[12]

It's not that all Americans have used these returns to squirrel away wealth. In fact, the United States is known for its consistently low rate of household savings, typically running under 5 percent and sometimes under 4 percent. That is a major problem for the United States, but in fact it reflects too little engagement with financial intermediaries, not too much. In any case, high equity returns allow Americans to engage in more consumption.

One reason Americans buy so much equity is that U.S. financial markets have made so many financial assets fairly liquid. American equity markets are considered relatively fair and supportive of liquid trading, more or less on demand, with accurate record keeping. That means an investor can opt for higher-yielding assets without sacrificing much in the way of liquidity, and indeed, helping individuals liquefy their wealth is one of the main functions a financial sector should serve. For instance, cash management accounts and money market funds are easy to obtain and charge relatively low fees. It is also possible to hold stocks and have ready access to those funds. The American system performs well in this regard, as there is a dazzling array of investment products at virtually all levels of risk. Furthermore, Americans can borrow against relatively illiquid forms of wealth, such as homes, cars, and other possessions, with relative ease through a variety of competitive lenders. Banks, investment banks, portfolio managers, and other institutions all have helped make equity investing a legitimate strategy, thereby mobilizing funds in that direction.

When it comes to consumption, arguably the American financial system has succeeded all too well in liquefying wealth. As just mentioned, the American household savings rate is relatively low, compared either with other wealthy countries or America's historical average, and there is a disturbing new trend of individuals borrowing against their retirement savings. If anything, American finance is too responsive to what people want, in this case a lot of new debt. That criticism may be a case of "blaming the waiter for obesity," but it remains one of the most significant and mostly correct charges that can be leveled against American business. American business as a whole is better at talking people into spending money than helping them save money.

Marketers have had a strong influence on American financial markets, mostly for the better. For instance, consider the mutual fund. Its exact history is debated, with examples running back to the seventeenth century or possibly earlier, but it is the American economy that realized the idea on a very broad scale in the 1980s, allowing ordinary investors to invest in diversified stock portfolios at relatively low cost. American financial marketers promoted mutual funds with savvy over the following decades, thereby making Americans feel more comfortable about these largely profitable investments. You could say that Madison Avenue helped Americans boost their wealth. It also seems that the much-maligned marketing activities of professional asset managers increased household participation in equity markets. During the period 1980–2007, the share of household assets in either mutual funds or other marketable securities rose from 45 percent to 66 percent. The percentage of households owning stock rose from 32 percent in 1989 to 51 percent in 2007 and 55 percent in 2015, again with nudging from financial intermediaries along the way.[13]

Note also that the costs of equity investing are coming down over time. For instance, from 1980 to 2007, the average fee on equity mutual funds dropped from about 2 percent to about 1 percent. That was driven largely by the greater use of no-load funds, as investors learned—albeit slowly—that higher-load funds do not offer superior performance overall. I expect this learning process to continue and for fees to fall further, due to competition and the general spread of information.[14]

If you look at the major criticisms of the American financial system, they are intertwined with some more general features of the American culture, such as a willingness to take risks and an openness to new products and ideas. For instance, the subprime crisis wasn't just caused by the banks; rather, it stemmed from a more general American culture of the intense marketing of get-rich-quick schemes, going well beyond banking and real estate. That said, these rather open and optimistic cultural tendencies create a corresponding upside, as reflected in the high returns American citizens have received through equity.

You might think these high equity returns in the United States stem from the performance of American companies and not from

American capital markets, but actually it's both. American equity values have been (generally, not each and every year) high and rising because companies have had relatively high earnings. Still, funds must be mobilized and brought into loan and equity markets and into other channels of funding, such as venture capital. Mutual funds and hedge funds must be willing to take chances, and they need the opportunity to funnel savings into equities and also into relatively new ventures. Pension investors must consider American capital markets to be sufficiently fair and transparent that they are willing to funnel their trillions into American equities.

One issue is whether those high equity returns for American citizens represent net gains or just a reshuffling within the American economy. It could be, for instance, that American citizens are earning 7 percent on some investments, but this cuts into returns that otherwise would accrue to shareholders inside the businesses themselves. Still, if the American financial system redistributes high equity returns away from insiders and to a broader group of citizens, most of us regard that as good.

Furthermore, Americans hold a lot of their equity in foreign concerns. Foreign equities were only 2 percent of the portfolios of U.S. residents in 1980, but by 2007 this had risen to 27.2 percent. Part of that change stems from the aggressive marketing of overseas equities by American brokers and fund managers, as well as the more general growth of foreign and emerging markets. This American overseas investment probably represents a significant net gain to the citizens of the United States.[15]

One way of thinking about this net gain is to consider that domestic U.S. firms invest a good deal overseas, and at fairly high rates of return. The gains from these investments are sometimes called "dark matter," because the gains cannot be observed easily and thus their size is the subject of debate. In economics, the "dark matter hypothesis" first became popular in 2005–2006, when the U.S. trade deficit was unusually large but, contrary to many predictions, the dollar showed no signs of collapsing and most of the time was not even falling. How could this be? Some economists, most notably Ricardo Hausmann and Federico Sturzenegger, suggested a new hypothesis: that America's actual trade deficit might be much lower than measured if we took into account intangible American exports overseas, typically bundled with American investment abroad. To make that more concrete, if there is a McDonald's franchise in Europe, America is also exporting some brand-name capital, some organizational know-how, and some managerial expertise, but these will bring future rather than current returns, unlike exports narrowly measured. The upshot is that America's net foreign position is much better than it looks on paper. And that is why the phrase "dark matter" is used, as a hat tip to a hypothesis in physics that says most of the matter in the universe is essentially invisible to our measuring instruments. Of course, this point about economic dark matter is a restatement of the earlier observation that American capital markets help bring higher rates of return to this country.

I once had a chat with a leading Korean economist, who lamented to me: "We work so much harder than you do to export! But we give it all back by just investing in your T-bills. You Americans earn more by investing in businesses overseas." That is another way of putting the "dark matter" point, and again it reflects the American willingness, and indeed eagerness, to seek out higher-yielding (and riskier) equity-based investments.

There is no general agreement on how large this "dark matter" phenomenon might be. Hausmann and Sturzenegger in their original work suggested a figure as high as 5.6 percent of GDP per year, with an accumulated stock of dark matter as high as 40 percent of GDP (a 2006 estimate). If that is true, rather than foreigners having a net claim of $2.5 trillion on the United States in the form of capital assets (a 2005 estimate), the United States has a net claim of $724 billion on foreigners—a big difference in value.[16]

A lot of subsequent writers have expressed skepticism that dark matter gains could be so high, and the dark matter hypothesis fell out of favor during the financial crisis, when American investments overseas lost a lot of their value and the chaos made a lot of these values yet harder to measure. Now, though, that value has mostly come back, and even the skeptics admit that American investments earn higher rates of return abroad than do foreign investments in the United States. There is also plenty of independent evidence that American corporations are especially well managed, as I discussed in chapter 3.[17]

So how large is the return to the American strategy? One economist, Pierre-Olivier Gourinchas, estimates that since 1973 the overseas assets chosen by Americans have yielded between 2.0 and 3.8 percent more than what foreigners are holding in the United States. These higher returns, in his view, allow America to run a trade deficit of about 2 percent of GDP a year without losing ground in terms of the country's net asset position. In other words, that is about 2 percent of GDP each year as a kind of international free lunch—in absolute terms, about $334 billion a year. That is a pretty big gain to reap from the U.S. financial sector.

In essence, you can think of America as the world's largest and most successful hedge fund. That involves some risks, but it has made us a much wealthier nation.[18]

## AMERICA AS TAX HAVEN AND BANKING HAVEN

Americans typically think of Switzerland, Liechtenstein, or maybe Monaco or Andorra as the tax and banking havens of our time. Those with Asian connections will know about Singapore and Hong Kong in this capacity, or maybe Chinese private banking. But in recent times the United States has proven to be one of the most significant financial havens in the entire world. David Wilson, a partner in a Swiss law firm, stated: "America is the new Switzerland." Hard data are difficult to come by because of the very nature of this enterprise, but possibly the United States is the world's largest offshore financial center.[19]

Without much explicit debate or discussion, American laws evolved to produce an especially high degree of secrecy for some asset holdings in this country. In particular, state governments are often allowed to do what the federal government will not do—in this case, augment provisions for asset secrecy. The American version of asset secrecy involves running money through trusts and shell companies and foundations rather than banks in the narrow sense.

Consider South Dakota, which has only about 850,000 people. The state also is home to more than $226 billion in assets held in trusts, up from $32.8 billion in 2006. If you hold a financial trust in South Dakota, that trust is legally secret provided some basic conditions are met, such as having a local trustee appointed and there being an American director to provide instructions to the trustees. As you might expect, the government of South Dakota openly markets the creation of the trusts on this basis, because the government knows these investments are good for South Dakota's economy. Nevada, Delaware, and Alaska, among other states, offer their versions of the same thing.

A lot of these trusts are shell companies, and it cannot be said that they contribute significantly to the actual economic life on the ground in South Dakota, though they do pay small fees to the state treasury. And since these secret trusts are, well, secret, it cannot be said definitively what the owners are doing with the money. Still, as a matter of common sense, if an investor pulls money out of Argentina or Venezuela and brings it to South Dakota or Delaware, the chance of those funds being invested in the United States rather than abroad is higher. After all, the very act of shifting the funds is a vote of confidence in the United States, and if that money had been moved to, say, Singapore it might have been more likely to have been invested in Asia, given how social and financial networks remain somewhat tied to geographic proximity.

The likely upshot is that America as a tax, bank, and trust haven likely leads to more investment and more job creation for this country. We just don't know how much.

It is also estimated that there are hundreds of billions of foreign dollars held in American banks—about $800 billion, according to one estimate from Boston Consulting Group.[20] This is because of the privileged status of the dollar, the presence of many liquid markets in America, and the relative safety and secrecy of American banks and other financial institutions. It is believed that about half of these deposits come from Latin America. Again, that is the American financial sector at work. Think of it as America being open to refugee money.

You might be wondering how beneficial these institutions really are. Critics portray a heartless, corrupt tax world where tax havens prevent local governments around the world from reaping their fair share of tax revenue, thereby undercutting good governance. But the reality is not so simple. A lot of countries have inadequate civil liberties and highly corrupt regimes, and protecting private money from the depredations of foreign powers is often the right thing to do. It is a pretty common tactic for bad governments to investigate the finances of political opponents and then bring charges as a means of reprisal, with no fair trial at the end of the process. Even if *some* of those charges are justified, this is not in general a political tactic that America should feel bad about discouraging or sometimes disabling altogether. Furthermore, *a lot of the funds in these trusts already have been legally taxed*, and their owners wish to avoid the possibility of future confiscations. If you look at who is sending money out of China, Russia, or Venezuela, very often it is the good guys, not the villains. Do you remember when in 2017 the ruling prince of Saudi Arabia locked Saudi millionaires and billionaires in the Ritz-Carlton and demanded billions of their wealth, refusing to release them until they had paid up? Whichever side of the Saudi dispute you might be on, it shouldn't be much of a surprise to learn that Saudis are major users of confidential offshore financial institutions.

America's status as a tax, bank, and trust haven is definitely good for the United States, and from a broader point of view it might be good for the rest of the globe too. That would be yet another benefit of the American financial system, although we don't know the entire net calculus on this one.

## IS THE FINANCIAL SECTOR OUT OF CONTROL AND TOO BIG?

You might think that all of these gains come at some enormous cost. But contrary to what you might often hear or read, America's financial sector is not, in terms of size, out of control. In fact, for a long time the American financial sector has held pretty steady in terms of the percentage of assets it controls, about 2 percent. In other words, American finance is a fairly regular share of national wealth—at least the parts we can easily measure the value of.

It is true that as the twenty-first century began, the U.S. financial sector ended up exceeding 8 percent of GDP, an all-time high for the country, culminating in the financial crisis. As recently as the 1960s, this figure had stood in the range of about 4 percent of GDP, and so it may seem that the size of finance has been spiraling out of control.[21] But measuring the financial sector in terms of GDP is not the right way to go.

Think of finance as an activity of wealth management, applied to our wealth overall and not just to our flow of current income. For instance, if you open up a brokerage account, typically you are charged management fees based on how much is in the account, not on your yearly income. As noted at the beginning of this section, finance as a share of measurable wealth has been pretty stable. By measurable wealth, I mean bonds, stocks, money market funds, and other forms of value that can be assigned market prices. It does not include the harder to measure value of human capital or the value of the items sitting around your house.

Keep in mind that ratios of national wealth to national income vary over the course of history, and thus the size of the financial sector relative to income will vary too. Let's say a nation experiences domestic peace for many decades on end. The ratio of wealth to income in that country is very likely to rise. Many durable structures, durable companies, and good institutions are put in place, and their value accumulates over time. The wealth-to-income ratio in that society will go up. Measured as a share of GDP, the assets controlled by the financial sector will go up too, and that is a desirable state of affairs. When the financial sector is a higher share of GDP, all other things being equal, that implies some basic things have been going right in that economy. The relatively large size of the financial sector is not causing the good news, but it does reflect it. So commentators who criticize the financial sector for being a high or rising share of GDP are making the wrong comparison. There may be specific reasons parts of the financial sector are too large, such as the repackaging of subprime mortgages, but a larger financial sector relative to GDP is frequently a sign of previous economic success and stability.

It is a possible and indeed plausible response to be disappointed that, in percentage terms, the costs of financial intermediation are not falling but rather sticking at around 2 percent of those forms of intermediable wealth. Why hasn't the financial sector been more innovative and disruptive? After all, the costs of a phone call to Africa have fallen a great deal, so should we not expect comparable progress from banking and finance? I'll return to that issue, but for the time being it is important to establish that America's financial sector is not an out-of-control monster. For the most part it's a pretty boring story of near-constant percentage cost and predictable growth in accord with the underlying wealth of American society.[22]

There is some evidence that employees in the financial sector are paid more than their education and risk taking warrant. Until 1990, workers in finance earned about the same as workers outside of finance, adjusted for their educational backgrounds. By 2006, however, that premium rose to about 50 percent, and for top management it was about 250 percent. About half of that can be attributed to risk bearing, and another fifth follows from the greater size of financial firms. The rest is a mix of special talents for which educational degrees do not serve as a good proxy (ambition and drive?) and unproductive rent-seeking—in what proportions, we do not know.[23]

One likely possibility is that the highest-earning firms enjoy some economies of scale, due to the network effects of bringing together so many smart people. Those firms earn much more, and in turn they share some of those earnings by paying their employees more, most of all top management. Technologies that favor superfirms are also, to some extent, going to favor big finance. Some of these firms earn superior returns by figuring out how to apply new quantitative techniques to market trading and investing.

By the way, the economies of scale that favor some investors and speculators over others also keep down the social costs of finance. For instance, if the top hedge fund manager earned $1 billion in a year, you might think that other individuals not in that field would spend about $1 billion in resources scrambling to get to this spot too, maybe by quitting their engineering studies and doing finance instead. That could become a wasteful drain of resources from the rest of the economy, as too much talent would pursue monopoly profits rather than useful production for consumers. But such clusters of financial talent are difficult to build, just as few local banks try to take on Goldman Sachs and few global cities try to rival New York and London as financial centers. And so the rent-seeking costs and the talent drain costs of the financial sector are much less than the size of the large rewards at the top might indicate.

Furthermore, the best direct evidence we have suggests that, as things stand right now, finance is not draining away America's best talent from science and engineering. Pian Shu, from the Harvard Business School, developed a systematic database of individuals graduating from MIT from 1994 to 2012. She found that those who went into hedge funds and trading jobs had high academic talent, but at school they specialized more in developing their soft skills, as measured by extracurricular activities, than in attaining the highest academic achievements possible. They seemed to be systematically different from those who later went on to be awarded the most patents, a possible measure of scientific success. Furthermore, Shu studied the period of the financial crisis, when the number of jobs in finance contracted significantly. She found no evidence of greater flows of talent into science and engineering. Her overall conclusion: "These results suggest that finance does not attract the most productive scientists and engineers from MIT." That's only a study from a single school, and it should not be regarded as proof for the American economy as a whole. Still, it is far from reflecting the nightmare scenario of finance as draining talent away from other kinds of innovation. If anything, the net flow these days suggests that tech is luring top candidates away from finance.[24]

One of the more startling facts about finance sector pay comes from 2007, when the top five hedge fund managers earned more than all five hundred CEOs from the S&P 500 put together.[25] That's so extreme, it sounds like something must be deeply wrong (though it's possible those numbers are off a bit). How can the people who *produce things* in such huge quantities earn less than just five money manipulators? But if you think about it with a bit of perspective, it's actually not that weird. A lot of the people who bet on horse races—and here I am referring to the big winners—earn much more than the horses and their jockeys do. Let's say that the horses and their jockeys produce a net social entertainment value of $x$ for a given race. It's pretty easy for the winningest bettors to earn more than $x$, if only because they are betting at odds—sometimes heavy odds. That doesn't mean the horses are less important than the bettors, because you couldn't have the bettors without the horses. Nor does it necessarily mean that the winning bettors are being paid too much. It's a pretty normal state of affairs, and it follows from some simple mathematics. To go back to finance sector pay, that discrepancy between hedge fund managers and CEOs doesn't have to indicate a huge social problem, even if you might feel that high pay for the hedge fund leaders isn't always so deserved in a moral sense. Keep in mind that the hedge fund activities themselves (like the horse racing bets) are simple transfers of wealth; they aren't a direct consumption of real resources that makes those resources unavailable to the rest of the economy.

To better understand the size of the financial sector in America, let's look at where most of the growth in that sector came from. From 1980 to 2007, about one-third of the growth in financial sector output came from higher asset management fees in the aggregate. In part, the value of these assets simply was much higher, owing to asset price gains. Furthermore, a greater share of wealth was invested in financial firms with professional management, such as hedge funds and venture capital funds. Those vehicles generally have higher associated fees, and thus the services from the financial sector will register as a higher percentage of GDP. And the fees were paid mostly by one group of wealthy people to another.[26]

In some areas, asset management fees have been falling dramatically, most of all with the advent of relatively low-fee funds at Fidelity and Vanguard. One estimate found that parking assets in Vanguard has saved consumers about $175 billion compared with paying the average active fund fee since 1974. Vanguard also has, by rough estimates, saved investors about $140 billion through lower trading costs. Finally, if you add in how much Vanguard has encouraged or forced other funds to lower their fees too, it is not difficult to come up with a figure of $1 trillion as a financial benefit from Vanguard. You can take that as praise for Vanguard, or an indictment of the previous state of affairs, or perhaps a bit of both. Nonetheless, these figures, even though they are rough estimates, show good progress in lowering fees. But do note the fees are still high: one estimate from 2004 measures various kinds of mutual fund broker fees at $23.8

billion. Since that time indexing and passive investing have grown, but the core problem of excess fees has by no means vanished.[27]

Keep in mind also that mutual fund growth, as it represents a growing part of financial service fees, stems from a fundamental change in the nature of retirement. In the supposed "good old days" (which were in fact not always so wonderful), workers relied more frequently on defined benefit pensions from corporations. Workers would not save as they do today through mutual funds and other intermediaries; rather, their employers would perform that particular kind of saving for them. This did not necessarily show up as explicit financial sector fees, in part because companies were relying on future revenue streams to meet their obligations to their future retired workers. In essence, the financial service of "retirement saving" was supplied within the corporation rather than being attributed to the financial sector per se. Of course, private corporations were not always stable guarantors of future payments, and that is one big reason individual savings have become more important. In any case, that history means that some of the measured growth of the financial sector is an accounting convention that resulted from guarantees being removed from corporations and put into the hands of individuals, who then preferred mutual fund investments to relying on the future solvency of their corporate employers. In other words, the workers substituted a lower-fee service for what was in essence a higher net fee, although now the new (and lower) fee goes on the books of the financial sector in the national income accounts.

Another significant part of the growth of the financial sector is the growth of credit, which accounts for about one-quarter of financial sector growth from 1980 to 2007. That is about equal to the growth in the size of insurance and less than the growth in the size of the securities industry, two other components of financial sector growth. Some of that growth was due to the growth in mortgage loans and bank origination fees and thus was connected rather directly to the financial crisis. Nonetheless, that problem of excess credit growth was far from the dominant source of financial sector growth over those years.[28]

## WHITHER FINTECH?

One of the simplest questions asked about finance is "What has it done for me lately?" What are the innovations of note since, say, the ATM that have improved the life of the average person? Here I'm not talking about abstractions such as "dark matter" but rather actual stuff—devices or institutions that we use every day to make our lives more convenient.

That is a perfectly fair question, and it does seem that after the spread of the ATM in the 1980s, the American financial system experienced a period in which there were few useful innovations on the retail side. This can and should be considered a deficiency. That said, the spell was broken some time ago. PayPal started in 1998, and it gives people an easy way of buying and selling with strangers. Without PayPal, for instance, it would be much harder to use eBay, or harder to send money to perfect strangers, including people you do not trust with your credit card information. PayPal has made my life better for about twenty years now.

Another convenience innovation, now well established, is the ability to pay most bills online. That was not possible in the early or even mid-1990s, and it has saved millions of Americans many hours a year. It also eases record keeping because you can keep track of your finances without having to save, organize, and store all that paper. As part of those advances, taxes can be filed online and tax refunds obtained more quickly, and if need be your tax procrastination can run until the very last moment without your having to pay a late fee or penalty.

More recently, Bitcoin has created an entirely new kind of asset, based on principles that only a decade ago very few people had imagined. It competes with gold as a hedge and unorthodox store of value, and you can use it as a currency to buy (legal) marijuana, a transaction that, because of federal regulations, the regular banking system cannot support. It enables a blockchain as a new medium for recording, storing, and verifying information and common agreement as to who owns what. It remains to be seen how much Bitcoin, along with other cryptocurrencies and more generally the blockchain, will prove transformational. It might not even hold its market value. But that is how innovation usually proceeds. Innovators try lots of new approaches; some are discarded, others take off, and yet others evolve into something more useful with the passage of time. So far Bitcoin and some of the other cryptocurrencies have defied the skeptics. Maybe they will have taken a tumble by the time you are reading this, but nonetheless, they are signs of an active process of dynamic innovation.

Are you frustrated by how the credit card system works? Apple Pay is already accepted by a large number of merchants. Just swipe your system key—or, better yet, your Apple Watch, if you have one. I'm waiting for it to be synced to a scan of my retina; perhaps that is only a few years away. The unfortunate reality is that many of the payment methods used in China are now quicker and more convenient than those used in the United States, but I expect American business to catch up.

There is today plenty of online lending, I would say with mixed results and probably a fair amount of misrepresentation. I think of this as a nascent market, a bit like junk bonds, still going through its teething phase and not quite ready for prime time. But someday it will be, and online lending will be a permanent part of the financial landscape, as is already the case in China.

Some of today's most significant financial innovations are relatively invisible. Consider Stripe, a payments company based in San Francisco, founded by two Irish entrepreneurs, brothers Patrick and John Collison. Among other services, such as making it easier to accept payments over the internet, it supplies back-end information storage to merchants. Stripe solves a problem that many business owners have:

how to accept customer credit cards and then hold and store this information in a secure fashion, given the risks of being hacked or simply experiencing a mishap. Stripe serves as the intermediary, lowering the online security costs faced by firms that don't have much skill in dealing with these issues. In the longer run that means lower prices and better service for customers, including better credit card security and more privacy. Yet this service will never be visible to most retail customers in the same way as an automatic teller machine is. Additionally, Stripe's Atlas project makes it easier to register as an American corporation in Delaware, easing burdens of expense and paperwork, and allowing many entrepreneurs living abroad to enjoy the benefits of the American legal system. It turns out that a finance platform is in fact a useful way to market business services more generally.

Given the ongoing integration of finance and information technology, I don't know many people, whether they are critics of the financial system or not, who expect it to be technologically stagnant twenty years from now. America's financial system is on the verge of doing a lot more for consumers, and in the last fifteen years there has been a decisive swing toward much more beneficial innovation.

## PAX AMERICANA

Possibly the largest benefit from America's role as global financial capital is that it helps sustain America's larger role as world policeman and, to some extent, global hegemon. Just to be clear, arguing American foreign policy is well beyond the scope of this book, and we all should recognize that America has over the course of its history made some disastrous foreign policy decisions, most obviously Vietnam and the second Iraq War. Still, like most Americans—and, I would say, like most liberal-oriented Westerners—I am of the view that America's presence on the global stage has on net been a strong positive. It helped protect Western Europe from communism, led to the eventual fall of the Iron Curtain, has protected South Korea, Japan, and Taiwan, and probably has limited the number of nations looking to build or buy nuclear weapons. The world today is a much freer and wealthier place than it was in, say, 1975, and the United States, for all of its arrogance and errors, has played a fundamental role in that process.

Lecture over.

Okay, so here is the key point (and, in fact, it is based on the recurring theme of finance helping to turn low-return assets into high-return assets): it is very hard for a country to sustain its role on the global stage without being a major financial center. The Soviet Union, for instance, had a major role in the world for decades, but eventually the country ran out of money. It couldn't revitalize its technology or even pay the bills. There are numerous reasons for this, but the country's underdeveloped capital markets were a major problem. Hard currency availability was always a significant constraint for the Soviets, even for the elites and for state-favored projects. The much smaller Great Britain, in contrast, was an effective global hegemon for much of the period from the mid-eighteenth century up through the First World War or even slightly thereafter. (I am not saying that all or even most of their colonialist decisions were good ones.) It is no coincidence that over this same period of time the country was the world's economic and financial leader, and London was the world's financial capital until the rise of New York City. If Great Britain needed to fund a war or an initiative abroad, it was able to raise the money, even during a time when general levels of taxation were quite low and governments were extremely fiscally constrained. Furthermore, the fall of Britain as a world power and center of empire coincides pretty directly with the country losing its capital market heft and having to approach the International Monetary Fund to borrow money in the 1970s.

The United States, by being a major financial center with a global reserve currency, can make (relatively) credible commitments abroad. When need be, America can finance a significant budget deficit; you may recall that when President Reagan "spent the Soviet Union into the ground" on military matters, he did it, for better or worse, largely with borrowed money. Because of the central financial role of New York City and other parts of the country, America has significantly more economic independence than other countries, and that translates into greater international independence. The United States government knows that most of the financial machinery of the country is not at the mercy of foreigners, and to the extent there is interdependence, most of it is with our allies, including Canada, the United Kingdom, and Germany.

In the current struggles between the United States and Russia, a common American threat is that it will cut off Russia from the international banking network, most of all from the wire transfer service SWIFT. That is perhaps what America and its allies would do if Russia were to, say, invade a NATO ally in the Baltics. Russia is highly vulnerable to this move because the country does not have well-developed, top-quality international banking and finance of its own. And the United States can make such a threat, and expect it will receive reasonable support from allies, precisely because it has the central role in the global economy and global finance. The major banks that form the backbone of SWIFT typically see the United States as a major customer; they may even be regulated directly by the federal government.

You sometimes hear that nowadays the Chinese can tell us what to do because they finance such a large part of our budget deficit. But that isn't really true. The U.S. government doesn't release detailed figures on who holds or buys how much of the American debt, but common estimates suggest the Chinese now hold less U.S. debt than the Japanese. In reality the Chinese have diversified away from Treasury debt a great deal over the last decade, but American interest rates have continued to stay relatively low, in part because there are so many other willing buyers for what is the world's most liquid asset market. Along this dimension, the Chinese don't really have much leverage over the United States at all, and if Americans wanted to undertake some kind of action or sanctions against China, China's role in the Treasuries market would not be a significant hindrance.[29]

Again, I am not saying that this greater American freedom and discretion is always used for the better; it is not. I am saying that it would be a worse world overall if that freedom and discretion were to go away, and deep down most of the rest of the world knows this even if they do not want to admit it all of the time. That is one big reason for the widespread foreign angst over Donald Trump and his "America First" orientation, even if it sometimes is only rhetoric.

American policymakers long have understood the logic I am outlining here, even though President Trump is somewhat of a dissenter. As the end of the Second World War approached, the Americans and the British started to think very seriously about the new world order. It was understood that America now had a more permanent role in protecting at least some parts of the world from oppression, and that this needed to be complemented by an international economic order that put America and American finance at the center of the global economy. And so the Bretton Woods talks and the surrounding decisions created an international economic architecture with the U.S. dollar as the central reserve currency and the International Monetary Fund and World Bank as multilateral institutions to back up an overall liberal trade and currency order. Later came the General Agreement on Tariffs and Trade, which morphed into the World Trade Organization. And even after the fixed exchange rates of Bretton Woods broke down in the early 1970s, the world was still a place where the dollar was the central reserve currency and New York City the number-one banking center, today rivaled only by London, which evolved into part of the same broad Anglo-American axis for a liberal world trading order. (Admittedly, now there is some significant post-Brexit and Trump-related fraying at the edges.)

Those economic institutions are important for America's role as global policeman, and important as transmitters of America's soft power and cultural influence. In reality, America doesn't, and indeed cannot, get much done by just threatening to attack or bomb countries, though at times it has tried. Effective diplomacy, coalition building, and beneficial global social change all rely essentially on America's role as a carrier of ideas, source of economic opportunity, and gatekeeper for entry into the world trading order and global finance.

It is hard to put a price tag on these foreign policy benefits, but they shape the world as a whole and in my view very much for the better. Again, this is a subjective judgment on my part, and not one I can support in the confines of this book, but if that were all we got because of the American financial sector it would be worth the price for the world as a whole, many times over.

In reality, we Americans get a lot more from our financial sector than just global influence. We get the world's best venture capital markets, we get to be the global center for tech, we get to profit by hundreds of billions by living in the world's largest and most successful hedge fund, and we get overall a more dynamic economy due to better and more rapid reallocation of capital. Soon enough, fintech may do more for us yet. Again, we're turning lower-return assets into higher-return assets.

To be sure, none of those benefits are free lunches, but if there is one thing that is underrated, it is how much banks and the financial sector do for the American economy, and indeed for the world as a whole.

## ARE AMERICAN BANKS TOO BIG?

Finally, I'd like to mention that some of these benefits, especially the rise of New York City as a financial capital, require some banks to be pretty big, if only to compete on the world stage.

That said, it is hardly the case from a consumer point of view that we are confronted by outrageous monopolists. For instance, the largest American bank by retail deposits, Bank of America, accounts for less than 11 percent of the market. Or if you do the comparison by asset values, JPMorgan Chase is number one, with about 14 percent of the total. Those examples are hardly close to monopoly power. There are ways of measuring market concentration other than retail deposits and asset values, but still America has a large number of banks overall, whether at the national level or in more local and regional markets. Where I live in the D.C./Northern Virginia area, for instance, I frequently see branches of BB&T, Capital One, SunTrust, PNC, Bank of America, Wells Fargo, Citibank, HSBC, and others.[30]

The current fear that banks are too big has an odd historical lineage. In the 1920s, it was commonly believed that American banks were too big, and so regulations were passed limiting their size, most of all by restricting interstate branching. The McFadden Act, passed in 1927, made American banks much smaller. When the Great Depression started, however, a large number of these small banks failed, as they were insufficiently diversified and had a hard time raising capital or otherwise protecting against sudden losses. In Canada there also was a severe depression, but the banking sector was much more concentrated, and so Canada did not see any bank failures at all. And so from 1929 through the 1990s, the dominant refrain was that American banks were too small and insufficiently concentrated (though in the postwar era restrictions on interstate branching were relaxed). In the 1980s, the common claim was that America should try to mimic the more concentrated "universal banking" systems of Germany and Japan, which had banks that were quite large relative to the GDPs of those countries.

The more important point is that the mantra "banks are too small" eventually became an overreaction to a single historical event. Today the mantra "banks are too large" has a similar status—it is an overreaction to a single event. As the experience of the Great Depression shows, having a lot of very small banks is no guarantee against a terrible outcome and in fact may make an economy more vulnerable to systemic risk.

If America were to break up its banks today, a big macroeconomic risk, such as a bursting bubble, would affect a larger number of small banks rather than a smaller number of large banks. That wouldn't necessarily be easier to handle, and in fact it could make crisis management more difficult by requiring the Fed to respond to a greater number of discrete points of danger. That would mean more deals to be done, more bank CEOs to have to call on the phone, more mergers to encourage and oversee, more situations to monitor, and overall, probably, a greater rather than a smaller number of headaches. A world of itty-bitty banks is no remedy for the ability of systemic risk to bring a financial system to its knees, as was illustrated during the Great Depression of the 1930s. So if you're looking for a villain, big banks aren't the right candidate.

# 8.

## CRONY CAPITALISM: HOW MUCH DOES BIG BUSINESS CONTROL THE AMERICAN GOVERNMENT?

OK, so what about business and the government? Doesn't big business control what goes on in Washington? There are indeed numerous government privileges for business; most of those are bad policy, and yet they persist for many years, perhaps indefinitely, as has been pointed out eloquently by Luigi Zingales in his 2012 book *A Capitalism for the People*.

I am against virtually all manifestations of crony capitalism, but I'm also not sure people are getting the basic story right. Business does have some real political pull, but the basic view that big business is pulling the strings in Washington is one of the big myths of our time. On closer inspection, most American political decisions are not in fact shaped by big business, even though business does control numerous pieces of specialist legislation. Voters drive most of the major decisions about the government budget, since entitlement spending consumes so much of the federal budget. In reality, corporations, as they relate to our federal government, are devoting more and more of their time and energy to minimizing legal risk, deciphering complex government regulations, and trying to avoid major economic losses from adverse decisions coming from Washington or state and local governments.

Big business is hardly "America's persecuted minority," to cite Ayn Rand's phrase, but overall the general prevalence of anti-business sentiment has led to significant exaggerations about the political power of business. The influence of big business on American government is often very much overrated. We don't, in fact, live in a plutocracy, and business does not always get its way.

For instance, for years many critics alleged that big business controlled the Republican Party. Yet even though the Republicans nominated Donald Trump to run for president, as of late September 2016 not one Fortune 100 CEO had donated to Trump's campaign, whereas in 2012 about one-third of them had supported Mitt Romney by that point. Why did Trump win the nomination? It is obvious: because the voters supported him to a sufficient degree.

Steven Pearlstein, commonly a critic of big business and former economics columnist of the *Washington Post* (and currently my colleague at George Mason University), wrote in the fall of 2016, "Indeed, one irony of the 2016 election is that populist antipathy toward corporate America seems to be peaking at precisely the moment when corporate influence on government policy is as low as anyone can remember." And Jeffrey Immelt, the former CEO of General Electric, wrote in a 2016 shareholder letter, "The difficult relationship between business and government is the worst I have ever seen it." William Daley, chief of staff in the Obama White House, opined, "Honestly, I don't think big business matters much anymore."[1]

I believe these views are exaggerations, as the relationship between big business and Washington has some inevitable cyclical elements, as perhaps those commentators would themselves admit. For instance, after those statements were issued, the Trump administration responded with a tax plan that was very favorable to business, especially large multinationals, and business interests responded with enthusiastic support. So at the time I am writing this chapter, American policy is *in some ways* especially heedful of business interests, as indeed is *sometimes* the case. If the influence of business is again high by the time you are reading this book, keep in mind that most of my discussion is focused on what is the most typical state of affairs.

Even in 2018, big business is hardly dominating the agenda. America's corporate leaders often promote ideas of fiscal responsibility, free trade and robust trade agreements, predictable government, multilateral foreign policy, higher immigration, and a certain degree of political correctness in government—all ideas that are ailing rather badly right now. Again, you can expect some cyclical ups and downs, but the losses sustained by these causes are a sign that big business is not in charge. The resurgence of interest in doing something about national infrastructure is another example of a business priority surviving in the national debate, but it may or may not happen, and it seems to depend more on the personal priorities of Donald Trump than the strength of the business lobby. Even if a major infrastructure program does break through and become policy, it will have taken decades for this talk to have come to fruition.

For all of his pro-business rhetoric, Trump has been pro-business only in an unpredictable, lurching fashion, and his general tone, manner, and method have been anti-business. As noted, businesspeople like political predictability, and Trump has offered them anything but. Right after his election, a variety of corporations, from Carrier to Ford to Boeing, among others, were the targets of his needling tweets, in part for their outsourcing. Trump attacked Boeing for the high cost of Air Force One, his own presidential plane, and he has repeatedly gone after Jeff Bezos and Amazon on Twitter. Trump has also initiated a series of trade wars and opened up a rhetorical war against America's trade agreements, neglected the details on health care reform, brought many of America's most important foreign alliances into question, and called the media—a big business, of course—"the enemy of the people." Business tends to be pro-immigration, both because it brings in more customers and because it boosts the available labor supply; Trump made opposition to both illegal and legal immigration a defining characteristic of the early days of his administration. Trump also seems to show no sign of recognizing the proper line between business and politics; the ultimate crony capitalist, he uses his office to drum up publicity and business for his Trump hotels and resorts. That may be good for his bottom line, but most of the American business community feels very nervous about this mixing of missions and possible violations of the emoluments clause of the U.S. Constitution.

With Trump, the news comes so fast and furious that this discussion probably will be out of date by the time you are reading it. So much more will have happened, maybe even in the week right after I am writing this. But that constant churn of events is antithetical to the general and largely justifiable business desire for predictability and political stability. Trump in some key regards likes to favor crony businesses, but it is hard to avoid the suspicion that he does not really know how business works, in spite of having spent his whole life in this vocation.

## THE BROADER HISTORY OF BUSINESS INFLUENCE IN GOVERNMENT

There is indeed plenty of crony capitalism in America today. For instance, the Export-Import Bank subsidizes American exports with guaranteed loans or low-interest loans. The biggest American beneficiary is Boeing, by far, and the biggest foreign beneficiaries are large and sometimes state-owned companies, such as Pemex, the national fossil fuel company of the Mexican government. The Small Business Administration subsidizes small business start-ups, the procurement cycle for defense caters to corporate interests, and the sugar and dairy lobbies still pull in outrageous subsidies and price protection programs, mostly at the expense of ordinary American consumers, including low-income consumers. To these anecdotes you could add overpriced defense contracts, legal barriers to entry for laying cable to households, and cozy contractor arrangements in state and local government, among many, many other examples.

The danger, of course, is that competition for consumers will be replaced by competition for political pull. There are thousands of instances of companies lobbying for tariffs, price supports, subsidies, and restrictions on their competition, all for their own self-interest and profits of course. When such lobbying is successful, capitalism becomes about sucking up to power and cultivating the coercive powers of the state to be on one's side, rather than about lowering costs, lowering prices, improving quality, and serving consumers.

The footprint of crony capitalism appears especially prominent these days because of President Trump, who is, as I've said, a preeminent practitioner of the doctrine. Donald Trump spent his career in business and during the primaries boasted of how he paid off politicians for favors and special access. His main businesses, real estate and casinos, typically rely on getting permission from varying levels of government to build and then open something, whether it be apartment blocks, corporate suites, or a new venue for boxing or gambling. The potential for corruption and influence is obvious, and business is the beneficiary. There are also numerous allegations that Trump and his businesses have violated the Foreign Corrupt Practices Act—in other words, they may have bribed foreign governments in their efforts to expand their businesses globally.[2]

All that said, the data just do not support the view that big business is the dominant force shaping American government. For instance, corporations spend about $3 billion a year lobbying the federal government. That sounds like a lot of money, but it is very little in comparison to the approximately $200 billion they spend each year on advertising. To put the $3 billion in perspective, that is about equal to how much General Motors spends on advertisements during a year;

Procter & Gamble is higher yet, spending $4.9 billion a year on advertising. One executive, who is also a former government official, put it this way: "Here's the way these guys look at it. Should I go to Washington and waste my time or go to China and talk to people who can actually do something?"[3]

If corporations have such amazing influence over federal policy, why are they spending only three or four billion dollars on lobbying when they could be investing at a more fervent pace and shifting around the allocation of much, much more government money? Well, corporations aren't actually so much in control.

The *Citizens United* Supreme Court decision of 2010 has contributed to the impression that corporations are all-powerful in American politics. After all, a company, whether for-profit or nonprofit, can now spend money on campaigns and "electioneering communications" without general restrictions. It sounds like big business has been taking over American politics and there are no longer laws to stop it. But in fact *Citizens United* is one reason big business has *lost* influence in Washington. Individuals too can now spend billions of dollars to attempt to advance their intellectual and ideological agendas. While most of these individuals are businesspeople and earned their money through business, being a donor on that scale selects for those businesspeople who have very strong ideological commitments. It doesn't make sense to spend that amount of money to advance narrow business interests, and indeed the political spending of big business proper, through the businesses themselves, never has come close to the level of what individuals are now spending. No matter what you think of the *Citizens United* decision, it seems to have heralded an era in which the influence of ideology is rising and the role and power of mainstream business is diminishing.

Arguably business is more influential through lobbying than through campaign contributions, but even there the numbers are less intimidating than many people might think. As of 2007 (I cannot find more recent exact numbers), the business lobbyists with the biggest

Washington presence were Blue Cross Blue Shield (56 in-house lobbyists plus 30 connections with lobbying firms), Lockheed Martin (31 + 53), and Verizon (21 + 58), and those companies were in fact getting a lot of favors, or sometimes just forbearance, from the federal government. Or if we look at spending, the most prominent lobbying companies are General Electric, Altria, AT&T, and Exxon. But overall, lobbyists are not running the show. The average big company has only 3.4 lobbyists in D.C., and for medium-size companies that same number is only 1.42. For major companies, the average is 13.9, and the vast majority of companies spend less than $250,000 a year on lobbying. Furthermore, a systematic study shows that business lobbying does not increase the chance of favorable legislation being passed for that business, nor do those businesses receive more government contracts; contributions to political action committees (PACs) are ineffective too.[4]

If you are looking for a villain, it is perhaps best to focus on how corporations sometimes help poorly staffed legislators evaluate and draft legislation. But again, national policy isn't exactly geared to making businesses, and particularly big business, entirely happy.

Look at the main features of the federal budget. The two biggest programs are Social Security and Medicare, both of which are extremely popular with the American public. And since the elderly vote at disproportionately high rates, politicians usually compete to defend and extend these programs. Surely lobbying by hospitals and doctors is one major reason Medicare costs so much; for instance, Medicare is prohibited from negotiating to drive down the prices of prescription drugs, and hospitals have forced into federal policy a high-cost model for American health care. That's one of the biggest influences of corporations on the federal budget, but it is very much within a voter-driven context. (I'll discuss Medicaid in a moment.)

Next in line in the federal budget are defense spending and interest on the national debt. Defense spending is bloated by the influence of military contractors on the procurement process, but a lot of the costs the military incurs are labor and pensions, not capital spending. Furthermore, defense spending tends to be politically popular, even when weapons systems are costly. Few politicians get very far by running against defense spending as a major issue. Finally, interest on the debt isn't a corporate issue at all.

Farm subsidies are the clearest and most egregious example of a government policy driven almost completely by corporate special interest groups. But even those subsidies are "only" about $20 billion a year (varying with market conditions), out of a federal budget of more than $4.4 trillion. Another policy area where corporations exert a very strong influence is intellectual property (IP) law. For instance, in international trade treaty negotiations, the United States government always insists on very tough provisions for patent and copyright protection. That is because America exports so much intellectual property and those exporting companies have influence over the treaty process, not because voters demand tough IP law. There is some indirect effect through voters, however, because weaker IP enforcement might lead to a loss of jobs in IP-exporting industries, which would hurt some voters. So even when corporations seem to be in charge, very often there is an indirect voter influence in the background.

Or look at the budgets of state governments. You might think that state governments are easier to push around, more out of the spotlight, less fiscally secure, and thus more likely to do the bidding of business. Yet it is again the wishes of voters that shape most of the budgets. The major categories in a state government budget typically are K-12 education, prisons, roads and infrastructure, Medicaid, and higher education. K-12 spending is popular with voters, and that is not mainly driven by corporations. There is a prison-industrial complex, which has perhaps led to too many private prisons, but the boost in prison expenditures came mainly as a result of voters demanding tougher policies on crime starting in the 1980s. Roads and infrastructure spending, to be sure, is boosted by corporate demand, but if anything, those policies are being neglected these days—hardly a sign of business being in charge. Public support for higher education has little direct connection with corporate desires, although many businesses are happy to be connected to public universities such as the University of Michigan and the University of California, Berkeley. But again, this is mainly about the wishes of voters; furthermore, expenditures in that category have been falling, mostly because it is not an absolute voter priority.

The most controversial expenditure on the state budget list is Medicaid, and that is especially controversial in the red (Republican-leaning) states. There I do see the so-called medical-industrial complex as playing a significant role in pushing for more Medicaid spending, in both the state and federal components of the program. Medicaid is less popular than Medicare because its official purpose is to serve the poor rather than the elderly (obviously the two categories overlap somewhat), and thus it needs an extra push from the medical establishment. Whether or not you agree with the idea of boosting Medicaid spending, in this case the medical establishment actually is helping to realize a priority of the progressive left. In any case, most, but not all, state budgets are determined by what voters want, not by what corporations want. What I've seen during the early Trump years, at least so far, is voters, including Republican voters, deciding they want to keep the Medicaid expansion that was such a big part of Obamacare.

Or consider the regulatory apparatus. You can tell thousands of tales of businesses shaping regulations for their benefit, evading regulations, persuading regulators not to enforce statutes on the books, and so on. Yet businesspeople are almost always very unhappy about the current state of regulation. Most of them feel they are regulated by the government far too much, and indeed there is a lot of independent evidence that regulations, whether or not you favor them on net, do indeed impose fairly high costs on American business. Above and beyond the direct compliance costs they are a significant drain on the attention and energy of CEOs. It is pretty common to find estimates that the regulatory burden involves direct business costs of trillions of dollars a year, and some of this (we don't know how much) eventually gets passed along to consumers. I don't think we have a good grasp of these regulatory costs, but I hardly think of regulation as an area where business is getting its way, and I do believe those regulatory costs are in fact very high. Despite all the deregulatory initiatives of the Trump administration, the overwhelming majority of regulations are still in place and are not going away anytime soon.[5]

## DO THE RICH REALLY RUN EVERYTHING?

There is a common line of argument, stemming from the research of Martin Gilens of Princeton University and Benjamin Page of Northwestern, suggesting that wealthy elites run American policy and that voters have very little influence. But this view mostly has failed to hold up.

The core method of Gilens and Page is to use a database of 1,779 policy issues and then to show that actual policy outcomes are closer to the opinions of elites than to the typical or median voter. That sounds good. But a number of authors have debunked some of Gilens and Page's findings, and I find those debunkings very persuasive. First, rich and middle-class Americans agree on 89.6 percent of all legislation in the data sample. So it's hardly the case that the wealthy, insofar as they are in charge, are acting in gross variance with the views of the middle class. Furthermore, on the remaining pieces of legislation on which the opinions of the wealthy and the middle class differ, those agreement gaps are mostly small. On average they are 10.9 points—something like 43 percent of middle-class individuals might support a bill, but 53.9 of the wealthy would support it, which is hardly a chasm in opinion. And on those bills on which the rich and the middle class do disagree significantly, the rich got what they wanted 53 percent of the time and the middle class won 47 percent of the time. Of course, that is a slight edge to the rich, but the middle class is hardly getting rolled. Finally, when the rich do win, their victories can be labeled "conservative" only slightly more often than they could be identified as "liberal." In sum, the evidence suggests that the middle class is coming pretty close to getting what it wants, in terms of congressional votes, at least (and noting, of course, that the middle class does not always want whatever you might think are the right things).[6]

One thing we do learn from the data is that the poor don't get their way very often, at least not when the poor want something the middle class and wealthy do not want. If only the poor support a bill, the probability of its passing is only 18.6 percent. Now, this may well be a significant problem for American democracy, but to refer back to the original question, it does not show that the federal government is controlled by the wealthy. If anything, it shows that both the middle class and the wealthy do not worry enough about the desires of the poor.

Status quo bias also shapes much of what government does, or does not do. If there is a legislative proposal on the table, the expected probability of change is hardly ever higher than 0.5 percent, or one chance in two hundred. To be sure, some of that gridlock may come from corporate opposition, but that number also suggests a simpler explanation—namely, a lock-in to the status quo, which can happen for a wide variety of reasons, including political and ideological gridlock. And that gridlock means corporations are not so powerful that they can overturn the basic laws of American politics and keep on rewriting the rules in their favor. The more prosaic truth is that virtually all parties find real change hard to pull off in Washington, D.C., and that stems more from checks and balances, the overall complexity of the system, and lack of deep voter involvement in the details than from corporate conspiracies. If corporations were really in charge, politics wouldn't have nearly so much inertia.[7]

Finally, keep in mind that corporate influence on government is by no means always bad. When it comes to the major issues those major companies report lobbying on, taxes, trade, immigration, and copyright are high on the list, consistent with the discussion above. In my view, when it comes to trade and immigration, that lobbying is arguably beneficial, but on copyright it is somewhat less so, and on taxes it is mixed. Corporate lobbyists typically seek a simpler tax system with lower rates. They typically favor trade agreements and freer trade (which is another positive, most of all for exporters in the developing world). Small companies are much more likely to lobby for earmarks and government contracts, possibly a sign of waste or rent-seeking, even if many of those contracts are necessary.[8]

## ARE CORPORATIONS INTRINSICALLY CREATIONS OF PRIVILEGE AND STATE MONOPOLY?

Some commentators regard the very existence of the limited liability corporation as a moral outrage and proof that corporations are creatures of the government. After all, limited liability is a legal stipulation that the shareholders of a corporation cannot be sued for any more than the value of the equity they put into the company. At first glance limited liability seems like a strategy, backed by the law, to allow individuals to escape the consequences of their activities as performed behind the corporate veil. Thomas Jefferson himself was suspicious of the limited liability corporate form.[9]

Nonetheless, such critiques don't stand up. The limited liability form has persisted and (mostly) dominated because of its efficiencies, not because of the law. Consider what the incentives would be if corporations were run on the basis of double liability, which to this day is not against the law as a possible contractual form. It's just that people don't find it a useful way to do business. Under double liability, if a shareholder put in $1 million in equity, he or she would be responsible for $2 million in potential liability. So if the corporation went bankrupt, the legal system could in effect reach into the bank accounts of the shareholders and pull out extra money to send to the creditors or the plaintiffs in a liability suit.

Over time, we would expect fewer wealthy individuals to own companies based on double (or, more broadly, multiple) liability. Alternatively, the would-be shareholders could set up thinly capitalized shell corporations that would own the shares, again protecting most of the wealth held outside the initial company. If somehow those options were banned or restricted, the end result would be that investors could not easily diversify, as they would find it too difficult to monitor the solvency of so many different investments, or to monitor the solvency of the other shareholders across varied investments. In fact, this point about diversification helps explain why non-limited liability in the partnership form works in some select instances where non-diversification is the norm in any case, such as legal partnerships. If most of your wealth will be held in the legal partnership anyway, and the number of partners is relatively small, non-limited liability stands at least some chance of working.

In any case, the most likely outcome from non-limited liability would be highly inefficient ownership structures. Often the very best owners of companies are individuals who have a direct stake in the company, have lots of experience in the sector, have a fair amount of wealth held outside the company, and wish to diversify across many investments. With non-limited liability, we would be discouraging the involvement of those individuals in corporate affairs, to the detriment of quality governance, and forcing most corporate leaders into strange and untenable financial positions. The resulting risk would likely induce corporate stasis and a defensive posture rather than innovation. Again, maybe these wealthy owners would find ways of sheltering their assets from double liability, such as by passing assets to family members, foundations, or other shell corporations. In that case double liability would bring few if any benefits.[10]

In other words, double or other forms of multiple or unlimited liability are inefficient, and they don't contribute much to broader notions of social justice. They have been tried, and most of the time markets evolved toward lower-cost structures, typically involving limited liability in the classic sense.[11]

American history does show extensive experimentation with deviations from limited liability law for corporations, but each time economic pressures induced states to create or move back toward limited liability structures. Up through 1830, for instance, Massachusetts had a joint liability rule, which meant that any single shareholder could be pursued for all of the debts of the firm. New Hampshire, Michigan, Wisconsin, and Pennsylvania all experimented with deviations from limited liability law but rapidly moved back to it. The inability of state governments to finance infrastructure profitably on their own, without bankruptcy, was one big reason for these changes. A breakthrough for the limited liability form came when the state of New York eased the creation of limited liability ventures in a series of legislative and judicial decisions over the 1811–1828 period. California didn't have a limited liability law until 1931, but it had to put one in place once the state started to develop. In all of these cases, the problem was that corporations found it too costly to do business, or they would move to other states. By the time America was undergoing major industrialization, in the latter part of the nineteenth century, the limited liability form was in the ascendant and proving its worth virtually everywhere it was being tried. These days, limited liability corporations bring in about 90 percent of all business receipts in the United States, and some form of limited liability law has spread to just about every wealthy developed nation.[12]

## DO MULTINATIONAL CORPORATIONS RULE THE WORLD?

Finally, while the focus of this book is the United States, I'd like to briefly rebut another (unfortunately) common charge, which is that multinational corporations rule the world. In reality, as the wealthier countries grow even wealthier and more democratic, multinationals have evolved into a relatively vulnerable interest group with only a limited base of domestic support in most of their outposts. Uber, Facebook, and Google have left China; the European Union is pursuing a regulatory war against American tech companies; India limits Walmart at the retail level; and a wide range of emerging economies are, for better or worse, flexing their regulatory muscles and relegating American and other Western multinationals to lower-tier positions in their economies. If anything, we have seen a resurgence of nationalism, mercantilist sentiment, national-level barriers to entry for outsiders, state-owned companies with fundamentally domestic power bases, and a partial retrenchment of globalization. Those developments are all both causes and symptoms. They are causing multinationals to lose some influence and political power, but that they happened is also a sign that multinationals never ruled the world in the first place.

There are plenty of particular cases where multinationals have exercised too much foreign influence of the wrong kind. Take, for instance, how oil companies have interfered in the politics of African states, practiced bribery to ensure concessions, and tolerated or encouraged regime corruption when it was in their business interests. Another example would be foreign companies that court, benefit, or perhaps even bribe—if only indirectly—foreign politicians so that they can continue to pollute. However, these cases do not mean that multinational corporations run the world. For all these examples of corruption, there are numerous examples of multinationals that find foreign environments too difficult or too burdensome to operate in, precisely because matters are not in general arranged to please corporations. If you look, for instance, at the history of Haiti, most American multinationals left some time ago. The problems included poor electricity supply, bad roads, a corrupt port, a bad court system, and high levels of crime. Haiti is hardly a powerful country, but multinationals have not succeeded in running the place.

Overall, you can think of many of the world's poorer countries (and some of the richer ones too) as having very bad governance. That leads to many policies that benefit foreign corporations excessively, and also to many policies that don't create a friendly enough environment for business, including foreign business. That's a better model than to assert that multinationals run the world's poorer countries, even though you can find plenty of outrageous anecdotes of abuse. On the whole, American corporations would rather invest in Canada than in Bhutan or Cameroon, and that is a more telling reality than any collection of anecdotes.

With all that in mind, let's now turn to the question of why we are so untrusting of business, and big business in particular.

## IF BUSINESS IS SO GOOD, WHY IS IT SO DISLIKED?

OK, so now we come to a kind of culminating question. If business does so much good for America, and if so many criticisms of business are overstated, and if business is no more rotten than the ordinary human beings who populate it, why is business so often so unpopular? I think the answers are pretty deeply rooted in human nature: we cannot help judging business by many of the same standards we apply to people. I'd like to lay out why we tend to think of businesses as people, how this skews our judgment, how business encourages and indeed requires this response from us, and finally how popular culture and entertainment cement this entire logic.

If I think back to the 2012 campaign season, one of Mitt Romney's biggest blunders was telling a crowd, "Corporations are people, my friend." That may seem like a small faux pas compared with some more recent utterances of Donald Trump, but at the time it created a firestorm. It was as if the human and the non-human were being seen as one and the same, a sure sign that *somebody's* moral compass was deeply askew, and as if the Republican candidate was so coldhearted and so ensconced in his wealthy lifestyle that he had lost all sight of humanity.

Of course, when considered in the proper context, Romney's point was entirely reasonable and all too commonly neglected. The matter under discussion was tax reform and taxes on corporations. Romney simply was saying that any tax on a corporation, sooner or later, at some level, has to be paid by actual human beings. He was not suggesting that there was no distinction between, say, Bain Capital and his precious grandchildren. The remainder of the exchange went like this: A heckler replied, "No, they're not!" and Romney answered back, "Of course they are. Everything corporations earn ultimately goes to people. Where do you think it goes?"[1]

Romney was right. But for all the outrage spewed at Romney over the gaffe, here's the funny thing: Virtually all of us think of corporations as people to some extent. And *it is the critics of corporations who commit this gaffe most of all.*

At an intellectual level, we all know the differences between *Homo sapiens* and the limited liability corporation. We do not confuse our dear grandmother with Monsanto. But when it comes to the implicit categories we use for processing information about corporations, typically we relate to them as people, we praise or damn them as people, and we can be loyal to them as we (sometimes) are to people. That is partly why we are so quick to conclude that corporations are controlling our politics. We also feel betrayed or abandoned by corporations in the same way that we can have such feelings about people. For better or worse, our default is to transfer at least some of our categories for thinking and feeling about people to thinking and feeling about corporations. We turn corporations into people in our minds, and also in our hearts. In other words, we *anthropomorphize* corporations—we imbue them with human qualities. We think of them as living, conscious beings in their own right, worthy of some of the same moral sentiments we hold and direct toward human beings.

In 2016, the insurance and financial services company MetLife finally ceased its use of the Snoopy character from the *Peanuts* comic strip, but its long history of using Snoopy reflects how companies try to turn themselves into people, or in this cause a lovable dog. Snoopy is arguably the central character of a comic strip series originally centered on Snoopy's owner, a young boy named Charlie Brown. Snoopy is identified as being cuddly, philosophical, benevolent, hip and detached, and understated and enigmatic; he reminds many viewers of their childhood and of the notion that pets accompany you through life and provide a kind of mirror for the expression of your sensibilities.[2]

MetLife used the Snoopy icon for thirty years in print ads and TV commercials, and the company also put Snoopy on the side of its blimps at public events. The company reported that it adopted Snoopy as a symbol in 1985 to seem "more friendly and approachable during a time when insurance companies were seen as cold and distant."

So why did MetLife drop Snoopy? Well, as a symbol, he was no longer quite modern enough. The company's new design uses the colors blue and green to form what they call "the partnership M," while a broad range of secondary colors represents the diversity of the company's customers. Snoopy became too old-fashioned to get customers and clients to identify with the company in exactly the right way. And MetLife's new motto tries to make the company seem all the more personal: "MetLife: Navigating life together." The old motto now feels a little distant and harsh: "Get Met. It Pays."

MetLife surveyed thousands of its customers and concluded that the Snoopy icon didn't show enough leadership, responsibility, and recognition of the hectic nature of modern life, nor did Snoopy prompt customers to think of insurance. Besides, things are now at the point where more than a thousand different brands around the world use Peanuts characters in their marketing one way or another. MetLife + Snoopy didn't feel so special anymore.

In an excellent *New York Times* story by Christine Hauser and Sapna Maheshwari on MetLife's switch away from Snoopy, Esther Lee, MetLife's global chief marketing officer, summed up the general issue: "Corporations are viewed as more approachable these days, Ms. Lee said, and consumers are no longer intimidated by them, she added. 'So many companies are actually reaching them one-on-one, tweeting back and forth with them.'" In other words, companies are getting better all the time at inducing us to think of them as people, so MetLife doesn't need a beagle to create a friendly impression.[3]

One of humanity's key problems is that human beings evolved to make sense of an environment where a lot of the main problems were caused by individual human agency. Our biggest benefactors, and also our biggest threats, were small groups of other people who sought to either aid or harm us with very deliberate, conscious intent. We evolved in groups of status-conscious primates, for whom building the right social alliances was a key to reproductive success and thus important to our well-being. So, for better or worse, we are geared to think in terms of what small groups of socially allied people will do to us and what their intentions are toward us. We are rather less well constructed for thinking about abstract systems, the import of rules, and how the secondary or tertiary consequences of those rules may improve (or harm) human well-being in nonobvious ways.

In other words, people tend to anthropomorphize even when such attributions are inappropriate. Along these lines, we tend to think of corporations as being like people and we tend to judge corporations by the same standards that we use to judge people, whether we seek to do so consciously or not. To some extent we are bound to talk that way, but we need to understand that it can mislead us, and it is a kind of shorthand that has pitfalls and hazards if we take the metaphors too literally or allow them to drag around our emotions too much. It is simply very hard for most people to think about corporations without investing them with the personal attributes of human beings or at least the attributes of those small groups of social allies and enemies we evolved to obsess over.

If you think about it, this personalized conception of the corporation is hardly surprising from an evolutionary perspective. Human beings did not evolve with specific modules for dealing with corporations, but we do have many millennia of experience dealing with other living creatures. Earlier in the history of our species, humans spent most of their time dealing with other people as lone individuals, dealing with families, bands, and clans, and of course dealing with nonhuman animals. Corporations weren't around or even conceived of, and the intentionality of the individual or the small group was and still is a strong mental category. Humans often thought of the weather and other natural forces as embodying personalized spirits and intentions, as reflected in many earlier (and some later) religions. Where do you think the phrase "Mother Nature" comes from? It's not so different from our readiness to see a human face in the surface of the moon. When it comes to our cars, our ships, and our pets, we give them names, talk about their loyalty, and feel abandoned or let down if they disappoint us.

Or consider ancient Greek mythology, where the goddess Gaia is a stand-in for the earth, and she gives birth to her husband, Uranus, who represents the sky. Just about every major aspect of nature was traced back to a god or goddess with intent and a very real human personality, complete with emotions, often on an exaggerated scale. We still give hurricanes and tropical storms human names, and often we christen ships with the names of people. We personify so many objects, if only to make them more vivid before our eyes, because people are our traditional category for organizing the world. The single most influential religion in the Western world, of course, is Christianity, based on the idea of a God personified through Jesus Christ. The Blessed Virgin Mary is a pretty important symbol of the divine too.

The human tendency to anthropomorphize is perhaps nowhere stronger than in young children, and it is no accident that cartoons for young children so frequently turn inanimate objects into thinking, living, feeling, and talking beings. The anthropologist Stewart Guthrie, in his study of anthropomorphism, put it as follows: "Piaget found that the youngest children see virtually all phenomena simultaneously as alive, conscious, and made by humans for human purposes. . . . Their world consists of a 'society of living beings' which humans have produced and in which humans hold first place."[4]

So when modern business corporations came along (mostly after the industrial revolution), with apparently extraordinary powers to change the world, it was no surprise that so many people thought of these corporations in some kind of humanized form. As observers, we are built to anthropomorphize as a natural reaction to change or to the unexplained or to possible menace. We find comfort in the language of conscious planning and intent, and that is one reason people have trouble grasping the operation of a relatively impersonal market order of the sort that characterizes the modern world. People often look for the plan or conspiracy, rather than trying to grasp the subtler concepts of outcomes that are the result of human action but not of human design, as was described by Nobel laureate economist Friedrich A. Hayek.[5]

The penchant for conspiracy theories also reflects the human tendency to anthropomorphize public events and impersonal forces. It is hard to convince the public that assassinations are sometimes just the work of random nuts, and hard for the United States government to convince citizens of other countries that the CIA is not behind every coup d'état or that we didn't really haul away all of the oil in Iraq. When significant events occur, many observers wish to identify and blame the conscious planning of some set of identifiable and supposedly all-powerful villains. And this is not just a matter of being ill-informed or undereducated. Being well educated often does not insulate a person from conspiracy thinking, and in fact some education may encourage conspiracy theorizing. The more facts about the world a person knows, the more readily he or she can spin a semi-plausible conspiracy fable. In the same way, better-educated people do not necessarily have more accurate attitudes toward corporations. Instead, they are better able to construct plausible stories about how companies are failing various moral standards, ruining the economy, or plotting to rip us off—or, by contrast, maybe they have an overly heroic view of corporations. These theories, especially the negative ones, seem all the more plausible because the fear of being cheated often has roots in real-life experience, and that lends credibility to the broader accusations.

Perhaps in part because we cannot do without business, many people hate or resent business and love to criticize it, mock it, and lower its status. Business just *bugs them*. After I explained the premise of this book to one of my colleagues, Bryan Caplan, he shrieked to me: "But, but . . . how can people be ungrateful toward corporations? Corporations give us *everything*! Corporations do *everything* for us!" Of course, he was joking, as he understood full well that people are often pretty critical of corporations. And they are critical precisely because corporations do so much for us. And do so much *to* us.

Does my colleague's outburst remind you of anything? Well, immediately he followed up with this: "Hating corporations is like hating your parents."

Hmm. Your parents too (usually) have done lots and lots for you, but—especially in America—large numbers of people are unhappy with how that all turned out, or at least some parts of it. For all of their gratefulness, they resent what their parents have done *to* them. With parents we don't have a choice until we are older, but when it comes to corporations, most of us have turned over more and more of our lives to external, autonomous, selfish corporate agents—agents who take our wishes into account only insofar as it suits them. That sounds terrible, but in fact most people are moving ever more deeply into the corporate nexus. They love its creativity, they love its normalcy, they love the potential for fulfillment, and they love corporate products as a respite from the craziness of so many other parts of their lives.

## CORPORATIONS CONSPIRE IN OUR DELUSIONS

Here is the clincher to this whole discussion: corporations themselves encourage us to think of them as people, and this is one of their most powerful manipulative tools for drumming up loyalty and sympathy. As with MetLife's use of Snoopy, companies refer to themselves as our friends as a way of cultivating brand loyalty—"You're in good hands with Allstate."

Corporations run ads on TV with benevolent dads, happy families, caring moms, and vaguely interracial couples, designed to appeal to all and to offend no one. The children in such ads should all appear to have bright futures, at least if you buy the indicated product. Google, to sell its Android phone, runs an ad, "Friends Furever," where the video friends in question are cute animals. It's been shared millions of times on social media and in 2015 was named the most viral ad of the year by *AdWeek*. Even when an ad does not show loyalty or friendship per se, often the goal is to have the viewer come away from the ad with feelings of warmth, attentiveness, caring, and deep bonding with others, including of course with the product or corporation in question.

Companies want you to think of them as your friends, so let's consider with some specific examples exactly how they try to make this happen.

Why are companies so active on social media? Well, partly because Facebook and Twitter are effective ways to bring messages to the broader public and to engage in targeted advertising. But companies also use those services because your friends do. Many Facebook users think of it as a way of connecting and staying in touch with friends. And so if you see a business on Facebook, to some extent you might classify that company in the same category as you do your friends. There is a kind of subconscious warmth and familiarity by association. Isn't it nice when your favorite restaurant sends a birthday card with a coupon for a free appetizer?

More and more companies have created what are called "loyalty programs." But note that it is you who should be loyal to them, not vice versa. All those discounts feel great when you get them as a customer, but economists know that very often these are plans for segmenting markets, limiting competition, and boosting corporate profits at customer expense. Consider, for instance, a frequent flyer program or a loyalty program for a hotel chain. Once you have a lot of accumulated miles or points, the companies do not compete for you on an equal basis; they have managed to some degree to divide up the customers among themselves, leading to higher prices in the longer run. What kind of loyalty is that?

You may know that frequent-buyer plans are spreading to more and more parts of the American economy—to my dismay, I might add. I often encounter loyalty programs for buying books in bookstores, groceries in supermarkets, and indeed most of the things I spend my money on these days. I've seen loyalty programs for rental cars, cruise lines, sandwiches, and Amtrak train trips. I'm not saying these arrangements have *no* efficiency features, but overall, as I just explained, they limit competition somewhat and raise prices, all the while exploiting the parts of our character that value loyalty in others and make us want to be loyal ourselves.

It is also common for businesses to encourage salespersons to have direct contact with customers and to behave in such a way that customers develop loyalty to those salespeople and identify them with the company as a whole. In our minds we substitute the salesperson for the corporation, just as religion might use a saint, or more proximately a cleric, to signify a more distantly removed god. The salesperson makes the company more human to customers. And the fact that we want to please that salesperson, to be liked, to impress the salesperson with our judgment and financial resources, only further encourages us to have human-like emotional ties with corporations.

Robert Cialdini, in his classic marketing and persuasion text *Influence*, details just how hard corporations will work to foster our loyalty to them, as if they were people themselves. The Amway Corporation makes and sells household and personal care products, and one of its core strategies has been to give away free samples door-to-door. An Amway representative visits your house and leaves a bag of products, almost like Santa leaving a gift. You're allowed to hold on to them for a while and scrutinize them, and eventually the representative visits your home again and asks you which of the products you would like to buy. The method is to make the customer feel obligated to the representative, just as you might feel an obligation to a friend who brought a gift to your home. Not surprisingly, the sales representatives receive training in how to be personable and act like your friend. Amway wants to make you think of the company as your friend as well, so what better vehicle to create that impression than an articulate, attractive person who leaves gifts and seems to like you—or, better yet, really does like you?[6]

Tupperware goes further yet. Rather than recruiting a professional representative to act as your friend, it uses sales parties that typically are run by one of your *actual* friends. Maybe you're not pressured to buy, but hey, one of your good friends is throwing a party for you. Wouldn't you feel obligated to buy just a little something, as a show of appreciation for that friendship? One woman said, "It's gotten to the point now where I hate to be invited to Tupperware parties."[7]

Sometimes companies are so intent to have their salespeople seem nice that they stop being nice to the salespeople themselves. Consider Trader Joe's, the grocery retailer. It is company policy that the workers on the floor will walk customers to items they cannot locate and accept returns of food items with no questions asked. Those are some pretty friendly gestures, and furthermore the workers are encouraged to smile during those interactions. Yet now it has reached the point where many workers are complaining that they are pressured to show they are happy, and that such pressures are making them unhappy. Here is a November 2016 report from the *New York Times*: "Thomas Nagle, a longtime employee . . . was repeatedly reprimanded because managers judged his smile and demeanor to be insufficiently 'genuine.' He was fired in September for what the managers described as an overly negative attitude."[8]

Remarkably, the personification of fundamentally impersonal experiences can work even when the phoniness is entirely transparent. Ever watch a situation comedy? Typically there is a laugh track in the background, so viewers feel they are watching the show in a friendly, familiar environment, full of shared mirth and bonded affection. Few viewers think these laugh tracks are "real," or that they represent the responses of real audiences or even what real audiences would do if they were there. Instead it is a phony construct, designed to manipulate us, and we go along with this manipulation rather gladly; indeed, we welcome it or even demand it for many of our favorite television shows.

The corporation's presentation of the product as a talking, living, and emoting entity is yet another manipulation. Companies make those products more like people, often through the use of animation in ads, now with more sophisticated digital technologies such as CGI. Do you find a talking or singing raisin more persuasive than a raisin that just sits in the box? The famous Scrubbing Bubbles announce in an ad, "We work hard so you don't have to." An oven mitt tries to attract customers to Arby's, and the Pillsbury Doughboy giggles about dough and other baked products, among many other promotions of this kind.[9]

One study showed that people who are reluctant to trust other humans are more likely to believe talking products than human messengers. When other humans are talking, the low-trust listeners are especially strongly primed to be skeptical: what could be less trustworthy than another human? Untrusting types are especially attuned to the nature and conduct of the messenger, and it is easier to identify a talking human on TV as untrustworthy or shifty, perhaps because of a false smile, suspicious look in the eyes, or a general sense that people on television have an ulterior motive. It is harder to pick up the same cues and clues from a talking dog or an animated product, and so there is the possibility of a higher level of trust.[10]

There is also evidence, admittedly partial, that people are less likely to get rid of an anthropomorphized product than a non-anthropomorphized one once they are done with it. Perhaps they still feel attached to the anthropomorphized product in some way because it might have a greater emotional resonance in their lives. I talk to my satellite radio device in my car to tell it to change the channels, and it talks back to me. I sometimes wonder if this makes me feel just a little more bonded to the product, and the fact that I'll probably never really know is not entirely reassuring.[11]

Some tech products talk to you in real time. Apple's Siri was the pioneer, but Siri has not taken off. Amazon's Alexa, which sits in your home and responds to your commands, is a market leader, and Microsoft's Cortana, Google Home, and other products are vying to have a bigger presence as personal assistants, if that is the right description. At times it feels like you are bringing an actual companion into your home, and it will feel that way all the more as these products improve, as they have been doing at a rapid clip. We might not be so far away from a world where you sit around and talk to them for fun, or maybe instruction, or maybe just to keep yourself busy. It is also pretty easy to imagine a future where many of the elderly do most of their conversing with these artificial devices.

It's a big question for the tech companies how these devices should sound and come across to their users, and whether the voice of a servant should be female or male (usually it is female, at least so far). Siri is a bit saucy and sarcastic, whereas Alexa uses more "hmms" and "ums," perhaps to seem more human. There are nurse avatars on their way, reported to be named "Sophie" and "Molly," and probably they will be more caring in their tone and manner than sardonic. The bottom line is that our ability to identify a corporate product with an actual person is about to take a big leap forward.

As a first-order approximation, I expect many people will develop emotional ties to these products, just as they do to their pets, including to many of their less intelligent pets. The Spike Jonze movie *Her*, released in 2013, is a parable of a man who falls in love with his personal assistant, only to later feel betrayed when he learns she is carrying on intimate conversations and love affairs with many, many other customers as well. The next generation of products stands a good chance of being truly amazing, but that also means we may end up very disappointed in them too, just as we so often feel let down by flesh-and-blood human beings. Counterintuitively, maybe we'll never be as satisfied with our Siris and Alexas as we are with our graham crackers and our paper clips.

By the way, the personification of the business enterprise isn't directed at customers only; it is pointed toward the business's employees as well. Bosses manipulate their workers just as they manipulate their customers, and often using the same tools. In part corporate leaders rely on advertising and public relations campaigns to help convince workers that they are working for an attractive or "cool" enterprise. Lots of employees get a warm glow from reporting that they work at Google or Facebook, especially if their friends and family have been primed by good public relations (and a good underlying reality) that those companies are in fact cool places to work—admittedly, a view that has been somewhat dented over the last few years.

Managers also subject their workers to a steady stream of morale-building and bonding exercises, and go to great lengths to make the company seem "real" to people—for instance, by having the CEO walk around the factory floor or spend lots of time eating in the employees' cafeteria. Managers talk about the company in terms of both a home and a parent. Most of all, they encourage employees to bond with each other, so that workplace peers in part stand in for the company itself. As workers, we are often encouraged to think of our company as a collection of warm, homey, and devoted people, rather than as an abstract legal and institutional set of profit-maximizing proclivities. When a CEO or corporate representative goes on social media, it isn't just to attract and retain customers; it is also to burnish the image of the company with employees and potential employees.

Once again, we see that businesses themselves are backing and boosting the natural human inclination to misidentify a business corporation with a flesh-and-blood human entity. And is this so surprising? I doubt it would be an effective public relations campaign for a business to advertise "This company itself has no thought or emotion of its own. Rely on competition to constrain us!"

## THE DOWNSIDE OF PERSONALIZATION

Thinking of corporations as our friends, however, has its difficulties.

For one thing, our popular culture often tells us that corporations are not our friends. It provides stories of evil big-business executives and establishment figures because we viewers and listeners demand them. For instance, there are far more negative portrayals of business on television and in the movies than positive portrayals. Critics sometimes ascribe this to the high percentage of Democrats in Hollywood, but I think the true explanation runs deeper: stories of business evil, and indeed establishment evil, make for marketable products much more easily than do stories of business success.[12]

Think about the ingredients of a successful movie or television episode. Very often there is an identifiable villain, a conspiracy of sorts, a "good guy," and finally a struggle, leading to the victory of one side over the other, typically with good beating evil. Furthermore, the audience usually includes many more people who identify with the workers rather than with the bosses. So it is common to portray a crusader rooting out corporate evil, and perhaps taking on a corrupt political establishment. For instance, consider the movie *Erin Brockovich*, which was based on a real American environmental activist. In the movie, the smart, beautiful, and spunky main character, portrayed by Julia Roberts, discovers a scandal of evil corporate polluters and, after a considerable struggle, brings them to justice. Very few people who watched that movie know that most of the cinematic account simply was fabricated—for the purpose of making the drama more compelling, of course. The point is not that movies are the dominant force shaping society. Rather, movies are a ready way to observe the biases in the storytelling mode, and to see why presentations of dramatic ideas tend to have anti-corporate biases.

There is another reason it doesn't quite work to think of businesses as our friends. Friendship is based in part on an intrinsic loyalty that transcends the benefit received in any particular time and place. Many friendships also rely on an ongoing exchange of reciprocal benefits, yet without direct consideration each and every time of exactly how much reciprocity is needed. In addition to the self-interested joys of friendly togetherness, friendship is about commonality of vision, a wish to see your own values reflected in another, a sense of potential shared sacrifice, and a (partial) willingness to put the interest of the other person ahead of your own, without always doing a calculation about what you will get back.

A corporation just doesn't fit this mold in the same way. A business may wish to appear to be an embodiment of friendly reciprocity, but it is more like an amoral embodiment of principles that usually but not always work out for the common good. The senior management of the corporation has a legally binding responsibility to maximize shareholder profits, at least subject to the constraints of the law and perhaps other constraints embodied in the company's charter or bylaws. The exact nature of this fiduciary responsibility will vary, but it never says the company ought to be the consumer's friend, at least not above and beyond when such friendship may prove instrumentally valuable to the ends of the company, including profit.

In this setting, companies will almost always disappoint us if we judge them by the standards of friendship, as the companies themselves are trying to trick us into doing. Companies can never quite meet the standards of friendship. They're not even close acquaintances. At best they are a bit like wolves in sheep's clothing, but these wolves bring your food rather than eat you.

We judge companies not only as product suppliers but also as bosses, and here as well, treating companies as people in this role leads us to expect too much. Public policy shows just how much we expect companies to do for us, as if they were friends, parents, spouses, and governments all rolled into one. It depends on the polity and time period, but we have expected companies to provide our health insurance, our disability insurance, parental leave, counselors for mental health issues, and sometimes daycare for our children. And that's on top of the salaries, offices, internet connections, and friendships they supply us with.

The British economist and journalist Tim Harford has raised the possibility that perhaps corporations never can live up to all of those expectations and we ought to give companies a narrower mission and judge them accordingly. Whatever social services and benefits need to be provided, perhaps those ought to be conveyed explicitly through the government or through individual markets. Corporations would then be allowed to focus on what they do best, which is to produce desirable products at a profit. But instead—especially in the United States—we put corporations into the roles of caretaker and nanny state. And then we are never happy, because corporations don't provide health insurance for every worker, and sometimes they lay people off because it is not profitable to keep them on, thereby severing many individuals from a lot of their benefits, and also from their social networks.

I'm not saying that bundling all of those services into companies is necessarily a bad idea, and in any case it may be too late to undo each and every part of what the American system already has wrought. Many commentators, from both left and right, expected that Obamacare would bring a large-scale shedding of health insurance coverage away from companies and toward the Obamacare exchanges, but that hasn't happened, and it suggests that employer-provided health insurance in America may be quite robust, for better or worse. In any case, looking to companies to provide these social welfare functions reflects yet another way we think of corporations as people or as like people in some emotionally resonant manner. Corporations already do so much to take care of us—with varying results in terms of efficacy—that they slip very easily into personified roles as parents, caretakers, and guardians.

We, in our roles as customers, also expect a lot from companies. As one example, we expect them to fix or replace our broken or malfunctioning products for us, even when there is no guarantee or warranty. Few customers have sound or rational expectations about the probable rate of product failure, and what might be an efficient investment of resources in remedying or addressing those failures. If a purchase goes wrong, we expect immediate and full redress, but in fact the best response might simply be to forget about it, and the company knows this even if you don't. Alternatively, many callers who are kept waiting on a help line for ten minutes experience a rise in blood pressure and feel an injustice has been done. The underlying reality is that a lot of companies simply choose to ignore individual complaints because addressing them isn't always worth the labor costs, time, and trouble; often the customer is wrong anyway, or possibly flat-out lying and seeking to scam the company. We could have companies that are more attentive, and most of us desire this, but at the same time we are not prepared to pay the higher prices that would result. It's easy enough to do all your shopping at the luxury level and get much better service and a more favorable returns policy, but that is not the course most customers take. It simply costs too much, and so we get the level of service we pay for. And maybe that is also the level we deserve.

The funny thing is, although it is wrong to think of corporations as people, it is probably also necessary for social cohesion. If the American people are going to support business in the court of public opinion, business must to some extent have a friendly face. Otherwise politics might treat business too harshly, ultimately leading to bad consequences for American private enterprise. Furthermore, consumer loyalty to corporations, even if irrational, is part of what induces better behavior from those corporations. Companies know that if they build up a good public image and stick around with a track record of reliable service, consumers will reward them with a kind of emotional loyalty. Overall, that creates a largely positive business incentive, one that would not be present if all consumers were aware of the somewhat more cynical truth: that corporations should be judged not as friends but as abstract, shark-like legal entities devoted to commercial profit. The more that consumers see their relationships with business as possibly long-term, the more loyally profit-seeking corporations will end up behaving in a socially responsible manner. Societies need their illusions in this regard, and thus it can be dangerous to fully articulate and make publicly known the entire truth about business and the fundamentally dubious nature of their loyalty.

So the trick is this: the public needs to some extent to think of corporations as people just to keep the system running. Workers need to hold similar feelings to maintain workplace cohesion. Yet when it comes to politics and public policy, we need to distance ourselves from such emotional and anthropomorphized attitudes. We need to stop being loyal to corporations for the sake of loyalty and friendship, and we also need to stop being disappointed in corporations all the time, as if we should be judging them by the standards we apply to individual human beings and particularly our friends. Instead, we should view companies more dispassionately, as part of an abstract legal and economic order with certain virtues and also plenty of imperfections. Unfortunately, that is not about to happen anytime soon.

People find it especially difficult to view corporations as part of an abstract, impersonal system of practical good because of what I call the "control premium"—the strong human desire to feel that we are in control of our lives, in control of our future, and also to some limited extent in control of what the people around us might be doing. If we don't feel this level of control, we become anxious and will act to try to reestablish a sense of control. Ideas of this nature are common in psychology and social psychology, but unfortunately they have not yet played a significant role in the discipline of economics.[13]

One reason we like to think of corporations as our friends is that we can feel in greater control that way. I've already discussed just how much we rely on corporations—for our food, for our entertainment, for communicating with our friends and loved ones, and for getting us from one place to another. But for all the talk from economists about consumer sovereignty, it's not clear how much people actually are in control at all. It's true you can choose what to buy at Giant, Safeway, or Whole Foods, but it's hard to step outside the commercial network as a whole, and the nature of that network shapes so many of our choices and thus our lives.

Of course, it is impossible for customers to ponder these philosophical questions in their deepest and subtlest terms all day long, as that would consume way too much of people's mental and emotional energies. So instead people translate their rather bizarre, non-hunter-gatherer modern commercial society into terms that their more primeval selves are familiar with. That is, people carry around a mental picture of being surrounded by people they can trust, if only salespeople, and of being in a familiar environment in which they are exercising their free will as consumers and also as workers. Given the need to get through each day, it is emotionally very hard for people to internalize the true and correct picture of those businesses as partaking in an impersonal order based on mostly selfish, profit-seeking behavior.

You can debate exactly how true or untrue our generally held picture of freedom in modern commercial society is, but I can't help feeling that part of it is a lie. The system offers many formal properties of freedom, such as the immense choice of products and jobs, and the relative lack of imposed coercion on most of these decisions. Still, when you combine pressure for conformity, the scarcity of attention, the stresses of our personal lives, and the need for "ready quick" decision-making heuristics, it's not *exactly* a life of true freedom we are living. It is (more or less) close to the freest life a society is capable of providing us, but it isn't quite free in the metaphysical sense of actually commanding our individual destinies through the exercise of our own free will. At least some of the freedom of contemporary consumer society is an illusion, which we create to make our lives feel bearable and to help us feel more in control—precisely because, to some extent, we are not very much in control at all.

So it's very hard to disassociate from that calming picture of freedom and to tell ourselves the truth about the deeply impersonal nature of the commercial and corporate order surrounding us. We can recognize it, but it's almost impossible to internalize that impersonality at a deep level. It's just not how we are programmed to think and to feel. And that is true even if we are professional economists, trained to analyze these parts of human life. I have found that economists are masters of the art of emotional segregation. While working their "day jobs," the best of them have no trouble thinking of the economy as a highly impersonal order, and analyzing its strengths and weaknesses. But put them into regular, daily commercial situations and they respond viscerally and emotionally just like everyone else. They love companies, they get upset at companies, they are loyal (or disloyal) to products, and they will curse the wait on the help line. Once they move away from their compartmentalized work lives and step into commercial society, they anthropomorphize corporations and products and discard their professional and theoretical sophistication. Shame on us, but that's how people actually are, and you shouldn't hold that against the academic economists too much.

When people feel a potential loss of control, they respond in a variety of ways. Sometimes they break down altogether, although that is the exceptional case. Another option is to act to restore more control, and of course we see that all the time. If you don't like how Home Depot treated you, you'll learn more about carpentry or maybe bring along your more experienced friend to help you out, or you'll figure out how to buy what you want on eBay. Yet another option, and an extremely common one, is to *pretend you have more control than you really do*. Indeed, that is often how we respond to our own embeddedness in a highly commercial, highly corporatized society. Rather than learning to grow our own vegetables, we may try to reassert control by going on a shopping spree, by ignoring our current troubles and moving on to the next decision, or maybe just by turning on the television and watching some (corporatized) shows and perhaps also some engaging advertisements. There's nothing wrong with these responses, and indeed, our sanity requires that we largely ignore or even obliterate the ways in which we don't really control the surrounding commercial environment, at least not on an individual basis.

But even after we accept this thin fiction of autonomy, we, as consumers or workers, are never really quite as much in control as we might like to think. And thus we are perpetually disappointed in corporations. Products that do not work as they should will intrude into our lives. The hospital won't explain the bill it sent us as clearly as we might like. Salespeople won't admit their wrongdoing, the wait on the help line is too long, and every now and then we get food poisoning from the restaurant. Most of us don't respond to these events by pondering the larger benefits of the impersonal corporate order. Rather, we feel a personalized emotional sting, and we walk away from those events frustrated, unhappy, and perhaps resentful. Our friend the corporation has let us down once again, and yet like most friends we're still going to continue to take its benefits somewhat for granted.

In other words, it is hard for us to keep a properly detached attitude about business in the forefront of our minds, even if our views are of the political left or if we think of ourselves as cynics. We deal with business almost every day of our lives: as consumers, as employees, or maybe even as customers. It just would be too stressful to keep so much detached cynicism in the forefront of our minds.

Let's say you walk into a Burger King. Do you really want to think they would be willing to increase your chance of listeriosis if it would boost the company's profits a few million dollars (after adjusting for the risk of a lawsuit and bad publicity)? It is hard to have that thought and enjoy your meal with comfort, and so you suppress the thought. You might at some level know it is true, but another part of you realizes that the risk of listeriosis is in fact quite small, and so you can go ahead and eat without being obsessed with calculating the probability of your pending illness. That is, in practical terms, an OK enough way to proceed in many commercial situations. It will give you a nicer day, and because it lowers your stress level, it may lengthen your life. That's one reason you put a lot of bad thoughts out of your mind. It is hard to live on any other terms. Still, you are not quite facing up to the entire truth.

When you go to see your doctor or take a loved one to the hospital, do you focus on the very high rate of medical errors—resulting in 250,000 deaths a year, by some estimates? Well, some people do; actually, I am one of them. My attitude is "Let's get my father-in-law out of this hospital as quickly as possible, before anything bad happens." And I am glad I am that way. For better or worse, it keeps me away from doctors and hospitals, a luxury that (so far) I can afford. But again, not everyone has the emotional makeup to live with that attitude. A lot of people bring their parents or in-laws to the hospital and simply hope for the best. They may push the doctor or nurse for better treatment, but they don't keep running in their minds a loop of the notion that simply sitting in the hospital is a major risk because of the possibility of contracting an infection or being the subject of a medical error. After all, the original medical emergency that prompted the hospital visit already was a stressful enough situation, and who can handle having to worry about another set of major risks at the same time? Some people can, but many others cannot, and so in our mind's eye most of us proceed with a general image of hospitals as safe, curative, and benign places, just to get through our periodic encounters with the medical establishment.

Think of these phenomena as a more general instantiation of the fact that most of us cannot go around all day obsessed with the reality that someday we are going to die. The characters in classic Russian novels who have this obsession tend not to be very effective or, for that matter, very happy. And so the fog of self-delusion settles down upon us all--or almost all—once again. As a side effect, we also end up holding a lot of delusions, most of them implicit, about business and our commercial suppliers. The end result is that there isn't any single, very meaningful statistic about just how much we trust business; rather, we engage in an extreme compartmentalization of our expectations and a segmentation of our emotions. When it comes to business, we're both loyal and skeptical at the same time.

So where do we go from here, and what should we do? It is fine to remain skeptical about business; indeed, in many particular cases our skepticism forces business to improve. At the same time, we should be much less hostile to business in general, and much more appreciative of its role in improving our lives, whether as consumers or as workers, or possibly as entrepreneurs ourselves. Most of the criticisms of business out there are based on misconceptions of the facts, or sometimes on applying the wrong standards of judgment.

And what, in turn, is the social responsibility of business? I don't think there is a single concrete answer to that question except the following: *the social responsibility of business is to come up with new and better conceptions of the social responsibility of business*, ones that will both boost corporate profits and further other social ends, including prosperity and liberty. You might say the social responsibility of business is to come up with the magic of a vision that will help us trust it more, whether as consumers or as workers. Corporations won't succeed all of the time at this, but American business, by enabling so much wealth creation and by creating so many new opportunities, arguably has outperformed any other set of private institutions in all of world history.

So we really can believe in American business as something that, at its best, represents many of humankind's highest values.

# APPENDIX

## What Is a Firm, Anyway, and Why Do So Many Workers End Up So Frustrated?

Given the arguments of this book, I find it interesting to revisit the economics literature on the nature of the corporation. I've found that over time my views on exactly what a corporation is and what it does have evolved away from the economics mainstream. I'm more likely to think of a corporation as a carrier of reputation and a kind of metaphorical personhood, and less likely to think of a corporation as a means of minimizing transactions costs, as many mainstream economists have suggested.

In a famous 1937 article, "The Nature of the Firm," the economist and Nobel laureate Ronald Coase defined the nature of economic thought about the corporation for many decades to come. In that piece, he described the corporation as essentially a means of reducing transactions costs. It's not always easy to hire the worker you want just by going out into spot labor markets, not to mention get that worker to do your bidding. Or you may extend the size of the firm to ensure the quality of an asset you need for your production plans. In these cases, a company will hire and bring those assets "inside the firm," in the hope that they will be easier to manage and control. That is what Coase meant by lowering transactions costs.

More than three decades later, another Nobel laureate, Oliver Williamson, wrote a series of articles fleshing out similar ideas. Building upon Coase's work, Williamson argued that firm managers, by bypassing spot markets and getting things done within the hierarchical structure of the corporation, would limit problems of opportunism and hold-up behavior. Sometimes it is easier and more effective to give an employee orders rather than trying to write just the right contract with a temporary spot laborer, who may not have the same incentives to keep a good, ongoing, long-term relationship. This research has laid the groundwork for the most fundamental ideas about corporations in economic thought, but while it contains numerous grains of truth, it doesn't describe my own perspective very well.

I agree that sometimes corporations reduce transactions costs, but they don't always, and I am not sure they do on average. Ask yourself a simple question. Let's say you want to buy a work computer for your desk. Which method involves lower transactions costs: going online with Amazon (or driving to Best Buy) or trying to get an order for a new computer through your company's purchasing department? Of course, it depends on the company in question, but most of us already know the likely answer. A lot of markets today involve very, very low transactions costs. The purchasing department may get you a better price if they buy in bulk, but dealing with them probably is more of a pain. Their priorities are not your priorities, paperwork and approval may be required, and your company is probably somewhat or maybe even deeply bureaucratic, especially if it has more than fifty or a hundred employees. Opinions differ on how big a company has to become before deep bureaucratization sets in, but every corporate leader and employee is aware of this phenomenon.

Given this, I don't view lower transactions costs as the *essence* of the corporation, even though companies *do* solve many transaction costs problems. (For instance, my assistant prints out many PDF manuscripts for me, and it would be much tougher to use an Uber-like service to have someone come over each time I need such a service performed.)

Furthermore, I am not sure exactly how to define the scope of the firm in economic (rather than strictly legal) terms. I observe innovative, transactions-cost-reducing contracts being used within firms and also with external partners, and I am not sure where to draw the line between firm and market in terms of the parameters specified by Coase's and Williamson's theories. Drawing the line between firm and market *legally* in terms of liability and the like is much easier, but that reliance on a legal distinction should give us some clues about the best way to think about the nature of the firm—namely, as a carrier of social reputation and legal responsibility.

So in lieu of the Coase and Williamson transactions-costs approach, I typically view a corporation in terms of the following properties:

1. It is a collection of assets, assembled at favorable purchase prices (or at least the prices were favorable for the case of successful corporations).
2. It is a nexus of external and internal reputation and norms.
3. It is a carrier of contractual and legal responsibility.

On top of that, I would add the following as another feature of firms, but not the essential feature:

4. It is a complex bundle of transactionally efficient and sometimes highly transactionally inefficient relationships.

Of course there are selection pressures, so if the inefficiencies are too large, the company will cease to exist. That creates some balance in favor of net efficiency, going back to the core idea of competitive pressures. In this regard, transactions costs are a significant binding constraint on which firms are possible. Thus the Coase and Williamson approaches reflect some truths at the margin, even if they overrate the role of transactions cost reduction in explaining what a firm is.[1]

For much of this book, I have focused on the second feature: the corporation as a carrier of external and internal reputation and norms. People have *opinions about companies*. Prospective workers have such opinions, as do prospective CEOs, financial journalists, government officials, voters, commentators on social media, and just about everyone else. But you also can pick up on some significant hints of the fourth feature of how I view corporations, especially in chapter 3, on CEO pay, and in the chapter on finance.[2]

Still, I wish to push back against the focus on transactions costs in explaining modern business activity. If firms were mainly about lowering transactions costs, they would be loved much more than is the case. Firms do have low enough transactions costs to get the job done, at least compared with the other feasible alternatives. That said, firms do not have especially low or favorable transactions costs, and so we are frustrated with them often, including in our roles as employees. Unless we are working in a very small enterprise, we so often hate the bureaucracies in the companies we work in (even if we enforce comparable bureaucratic strictures when on the other side of the relationship). And we are (partially) right to dislike this bureaucracy so much. Very often those bureaucracies stifle merit, make simple operations complex (for example, by requiring multiple permissions), and fail to reward us when we have done something good (or unjustly elevate those whom we resent). They make it harder for us to rise to the top at the pace we feel we deserve. At the same time, those bureaucracies keep some of the employees from "going off the reservation," or make it harder for the boss to play favorites or for shareholders to use the company for personal purposes. So corporate bureaucracy is necessary. Still, because of bureaucracy, corporate life can be tough and also deeply unfair at times. And that too is "the nature of the firm," to refer back to Ronald Coase's title.

## ACKNOWLEDGMENTS

The author wishes to thank Tim Bartlett, Christina Cacioppo, Bryan Caplan, Natasha Cowen, Teresa Hartnett, Daniel Klein, Ezra Klein, Randall Kroszner, Timothy Lee, Hollis Robbins, Alex Tabarrok, and Dillon Tauzin for useful comments and discussions and assistance. I am especially thankful to Tim Bartlett for his useful and comprehensive edits, and also for seeing this book through the publication process, and Teresa Hartnett for her services as agent. I also have talked to many CEOs and other senior corporate leaders for this project, as well as many workers, but often under impromptu circumstances, and so I will thank them collectively without listing their names. As a disclaimer, I should note that many of the companies discussed in this book have been donors to my university. I sometimes give private lectures for pay, but to the best of my knowledge, I have not done a paid talk at any of the companies listed in this book.

# NOTES

## Chapter 1: A New Pro-Business Manifesto

1. On the poll, see Newport 2018.
2. See Bloom et al. 2012.
3. On productivity gaps, see Syverson 2011; on China and India, see Hsieh and Klenow 2009.
4. In addition to Bloom, Sadun, and Van Reenen 2016, see Pellegrino and Zingales 2017 on these qualities in an international context.
5. Bloom, Sadun, and Van Reenen 2016.
6. On the role of big business in supporting LGBT rights, see, for instance, Surowiecki 2016.
7. See Ehrenfreund 2016; Della Volpe and Jacobs 2016.
8. See Desan and McCarthy 2018. I am presenting the original wording. It was later changed to ". . . the failings of such a system are as clear as those of capitalism itself."
9. On that history, see Segrave 2011.
10. Those numbers are from Gallup 2016.
11. On the wage premium from larger firms, see Cardiff-Hicks, Lafontaine, and Shaw 2014. On big versus small business more generally, including with respect to fraud, see Atkinson and Lind 2018, a very good book on big business.

12. On the right-wing crusade against Big Tech, see, for instance, Grynbaum and Herrman 2018.

13. See https://twitter.com/EdwardGLuce/status/1029760202437001216, August 15, 2018.

14. Friedman 1970. Note that Friedman's article erred in describing the top executives as employees. A better way of describing them would be that the board and the executives are "fiduciaries" and that the top executives have a duty to shareholders. On this, see, for instance, Hart and Zingales 2016, which also surveys some of the subsequent literature. Some of the many other relevant writings on corporate social responsibility are Aguinis and Ghavas 2012, a very useful aggregate survey; Marcaux 2017; Guiso, Sapienza, and Zingales 2013; and Lev, Petrovits, and Radhakrishnan 2010.

15. In passing, I should note that my book *In Praise of Commercial Culture* (2000) covers the history of rock and roll, and my book *An Economist Gets Lunch* (2012) covers some issues surrounding GMOs.

## Chapter 2: Are Businesses More Fraudulent Than the Rest of Us?

1. On dietary supplements, see DaVanzo et al. 2009.

2. See Evershed and Temple 2016, 20, 122.

3. On the survey and related evidence, see Anderson 2016.

4. On the number of daily lies, see DePaulo et al. 1996. On lying to those who are close to us, see DePaulo et al. 2004; DePaulo and Kashy 1998.

5. See Feldman, Forrest, and Happ 2002 for that study.

6. On resumes, see Tomassi 2006; Henle, Dineen, and Duffy 2017.

7. On shoplifting and employee theft, see, for instance, Wahba 2015. On failed drug tests, see Calmes 2016.

8. See Schwitzgebel 2009; Schwitzgebel and Rust 2014.

9. On peers, see Schwitzgebel and Rust 2009; on conference behavior, see Schwitzgebel et al. 2012.

10. See Stephens-Davidowitz 2017, ch. 3.

11. See IRS 2016.

12. The revenue numbers are taken from the Tax Policy Center, http://www.taxpolicycenter.org/statistics/amount-revenue-source. By the way, if you are interested in data on fraudulent accounting moves, see Dyck, Morse, and Zingales 2013, although there is no comparison with private individuals. They conclude that over the period 1996–2004, about one in seven large, publicly traded U.S. firms were engaged in audit-related fraud. Unfortunately, many features of those numbers are inexact. They are based on IRS assumptions about

how much those individuals and companies really do owe. In the case of both taxes, but with special relevance for the corporate tax, the comparison assumes a clear distinction between "tax evasion" and "extreme but legal measures of tax avoidance." As corporations figure out better and better ways to game the tax system, we're seeing that this isn't always such a well-defined difference. Still, there are some rather significant factors militating against the honesty of the filing individual cheaters that I have not included in the calculus. For instance, cheating done on the employment tax was about $81 billion a year during that period, and it mostly took the form of individuals failing to pay self-employment tax rather than corporate misbehavior. Adding that number into the figures would, in relative terms, make individual misbehavior look worse in comparative terms.

13. See Fehr and List 2004.

14. See Henrich 2000, 974.

15. On these results, see Ensminger and Henrich 2014; Henrich et al. 2004; Henrich et al. 2006; Henrich et al. 2010. On the eighteenth-century background, see Hirschman 1992.

16. For a study suggesting that business charity can backfire when the motives are perceived purely in terms of self-interest, see Cassar and Meier 2017.

17. On these results, see Graham et al. 2017. And in fact, the actual history of business in the United States shows strong connections with nonbusiness spheres of life, running in both directions. For instance, Americans have applied their business-based cooperative capabilities to civil society endeavors, such as the organization of charities and political movements, including the environmental movement. Bill Gates carries his Microsoft managerial experience to the public health efforts of the Gates Foundation. To cite some more local and less visible examples, a lot of good CFOs do volunteer work for their churches and help keep their finances in order. American business originally borrowed organizational skills from early American religion, but the expertise has been traded in both directions, so business gives Americans finely honed, market-tested skills for working in teams, whether in the service of God, Mammon, or charity. So much of what runs well in America, even if it does not look like business on the surface, owes its efficacy to the methods and skills of the business enterprise.

18. On all this, see Zak and Knack 2001; Keefer and Knack 1997.

19. The California study is Capps, Carlton, and David 2017. On the hospitals that converted, see Joynt, Orav, and Jha 2014. The older study is McClellan and Staiger 2000, and the 2007 study is Shah et al. 2007. For these references, I am indebted to a blog post by Scott Alexander (Alexander 2016).

20. See Lichtenberg 2013, as well as his work more generally. On life expectancy for HIV-positive individuals, see Cairns 2014.
21. See Brooks and Fritzon 2016; also Hare 1999.

## Chapter 3: Are CEOs Paid Too Much?

1. See, among many other sources, Bloxham 2015; Elson 2003.
2. See, for instance, Walker 2010; Kaplan and Rauh 2013. On pay ratios, see Mishel and Davis 2015, who also survey and endorse many of the most common complaints about CEOs. Bebchuk and Fried 2006 is another well-known source of criticism of CEO pay arrangements in America; for a response to some of their particular complaints, see Core, Guay, and Thomas 2005. On the most recent data, see Stein and McGregor 2018.
3. For one good recent source, see Edmans, Gabaix, and Jenter 2017.
4. See, for instance, Mishel and Davis 2015; Frydman and Saks 2007.
5. See Gabaix and Landier 2008. For a good survey of the discussion on this issue, and CEO pay more generally, see Edmans, Gabaix, and Jenter 2017. On the $31 million figure (in 2014 dollars), see Edmans, Gabaix, and Jenter 2017, 17.
6. Gabaix, Landier, and Sauvagnat 2014, 3–4. For instance, over the years of the Great Recession the declines in CEO pay were roughly proportional to the declines in firm value: "Movements in CEO compensation did indeed closely track movements in firm size: over 2007–2009, average total firm values decreased by 17.4%, equity values by 37.9%, and compensation indices by 27.7%. During 2009–2011, we observe a rebound of firm values by 19%, equity values by 27%, and compensation indices by 22%." Alternatively, across 2014 and 2015, median pay for the CEOs of the largest three hundred publicly traded companies fell 3.8 percent, from $11.2 million to $10.8 million. Of those three hundred CEOs, more than half saw their pay either fall or rise by less than 1 percent for the year. Much of the slowdown was due to weak overall equity returns, and thus slow growth or even shrinkage in the pension values for the CEOs. On CEO pay being static during the first decade of the twenty-first century, see Frydman and Jenter 2010. On the comparison across 2014 and 2015, see Francis and Lublin 2016.
7. On 4 percent, see Bessembinder 2017. On the number of qualified CEO candidates, see Larcker, Donatiello, and Tayan 2017.
8. On the opening point of this paragraph, see Lublin 2017.
9. A 10 percent increase in export capacity for a company is correlated with a 2 percent increase in CEO pay. (And that's after adjusting for the larger size of the company.) That's a sign of just how difficult it is to find globally oriented

talent that can do the other parts of the job, and how much markets will bid for that talent. On this, see Keller and Olney 2017.

10. See Frydman and Jenter 2010. For the numbers on outside hires, see Murphy and Zabojnik 2006.

11. Again, see Frydman and Jenter 2010. On salaries for starting hires, see Falato, Li, and Milbourn 2013. They find that CEOs with stronger credentials are in fact paid more to start and subsequently show stronger performance.

12. On this, see Ales and Sleet 2016.

13. See Kaplan 2012; Kaplan and Rauh 2013.

14. See Kaplan 2012; Kaplan and Rauh 2013.

15. See Kaplan 2012, and note that this ability to create corporate value shows up in the top private equity salaries. According to *New York Times* estimates, Stephen A. Schwarzman, CEO of Blackstone, received just under $800 million in 2015. Most of that was from good deals and his equity share. His base salary was $350,000 and he received no bonus. Also at Blackstone, Hamilton E. James, the president, received $233 million, and the real estate chief, Jonathan D. Gray, was paid $249 million. Other examples of high pay in private equity include $543 million for Leon Black, head of Apollo Global Management, in 2013, and $356 million combined for Henry R. Kravis and George R. Roberts for their work as co-heads of Kohlberg Kravis Roberts in 2015. Note that many private equity top earners founded their firms, and thus they own significant equity shares in the firms' deals. On all this, see Protess and Corkery 2016.

16. See Kaplan 2012.

17. See Frydman and Jenter 2010 on some of these points. On higher salaries for outsiders, see Murphy and Zabojnik 2004.

18. See Song et al. 2015; see also Autor et al. 2017.

19. By the way, superstar firms are also posited as the leading driver of changes in economic inequality in both the United Kingdom and Germany. In those two countries, the big changes are not happening within individual firms, between workers and bosses; rather, the productivity of some firms is outpacing that of their rivals, which are not able to catch up or even keep pace.

20. See Nguyen and Nielsen 2014 and, more generally, Tervio 2008. For the 2.32 percent estimate, see Jenter, Matveyev, and Roth 2016.

21. See Becker and Hvide 2013.

22. See Bennedsen, Pérez-González, and Wolfenzon 2011.

23. For some broader results on CEO replacement data that are consistent with these claims, see Chang, Dasgupta, and Hilary 2010.

24. On worker underpayment, see Isen 2012.

25. For the 68–73 percent estimate, see Nguyen and Nielsen 2014; for the 44–68 percent estimate, see Taylor 2013. In a famous 1990 study, Michael C. Jensen and Kevin J. Murphy found that for large American companies, if a CEO creates $1,000 in shareholder value, that CEO is likely to receive rewards of about $3.25 in return. This 1990 result is now out of date, it did not cover all forms of compensation, it has been revised, and furthermore it covers only gains at the margin rather than the CEO contract as a whole, and thus there are disparities with the results discussed in the text. Since the Jensen and Murphy paper was published, the use of stock options has risen rapidly, bringing CEO incentives closer into line with the shareholder value they create. According to some later estimates, CEOs capture four times more, in percentage terms, of the corporate value they create, or maybe more. For a partial survey of this approach to the problem, see Walker 2010, 10. For some recalculations of the Jensen and Murphy results, see Conyon 2006, Frydman and Saks 2007, and Frydman and Jenter 2010, who discuss the prewar era as well. It is a little-known fact that the current use of high-powered financial incentives for American CEOs still has not reattained the level it held in the pre–Second World War period.

26. See Giertz and Mortenson 2013. Sometimes you hear the claim that the hiring of compensation consultants favors the interests of an entrenched CEO and boosts pay. You can find serious studies on both sides of this issue, but for the time being it is probably best to judge it as a toss-up. It does seem in statistical studies that the composition of the compensation committee does not matter for the level of compensation, although it still could be argued that some directors are cronyist picks in a manner that is not detected by standard measures of who is a crony or close associate. In any case, this criticism has not (yet?) been verified, even though I have heard many CEOs themselves make this charge. It might be true, but I hear it being claimed with a vehemence that the current research doesn't support, at least not yet. See Conyon 2006, 38; Walker 2010, 17–18.

27. Counterintuitively, in some cases it may be desirable for CEO pay to *outpace* increases in the size of the firm. As companies get bigger and CEO pay rises, some CEOs may pursue a strategy of digging in, consuming a lot of perks, securing their position against outside challenges, and turning the firm into a bureaucracy. After all, if you're being paid a few million dollars a year, you probably want to keep that flow of money coming. So what might the board and shareholders consider to keep the CEO on a proper risk-taking track? Well, even higher pay, but with the higher payoffs closely tied to firm performance. Indeed, that has been exactly the form that CEO pay increases have taken. *Very high CEO pay* is in part a response to the incentive problems created by high

CEO pay itself. To many people it seems immoral that CEOs get an extra dose of big pay to counteract their own possible entrenchment and sloth, and maybe it is. But there is an alternative way of assessing the system, based on whether or not it produces better practical results, and from that viewpoint, maybe it does better.

28. See Mauboussin and Callahan 2014 for a survey of the evidence, and also Fama and French 1998. Maksimovic, Phillips, and Yang (2017) estimate that once selection effects are controlled for, going public does not make a company more short-term in orientation.

29. For these numbers, see *Economist* 2017.

30. Mauboussin and Callahan 2014. For a well-done critique of short-termism, but one that does not consider this point about shorter asset life span, see Sampson and Shi 2016.

31. Mauboussin and Callahan 2014.

32. For a related point, see Summers 2017.

33. On research and development, see Davies et al. 2014, 22, and also the discussion in Cowen 2017.

34. On this, see Fried and Wang 2017.

## Chapter 4: Is Work Fun?

1. See Graeber 2018; Moran 2018.

2. See Kahneman et al. 2004.

3. Maestas et al. 2017, 40. This RAND Corporation study, by the way, produced much more favorable results on the quality of American jobs than the surrounding media write-ups might have led an observer to believe.

4. For varying perspectives on these results, see Kuhn, Lalive, and Zweimueller 2007; Tausig 1999; Clark and Oswald 1994. See Paul and Moser 2007 for a survey of results on how being unemployed damages mental health and well-being.

5. McGrattan and Rogerson 2004.

6. See Damaske, Smyth, and Zawadzki 2014 and 2016.

7. See Bernstein 2014.

8. The flow literature is not in every way mainstream psychology, and it is debatable how much one should identify flow with overall human welfare or happiness, as it is hardly the only cognitive or emotional value. Still, the flow concept has had considerable impact on the popular imagination, and it is one interesting perspective on at least some kinds of human satisfaction, including satisfaction through work.

9. See LeFevre 1988; Csikszentmihalyi and LeFevre 1989.

10. On this aspect of the Trump campaign, see Konczal 2016.

11. On friends, see Maestas et al. 2017, 34.

12. I am indebted here to a point from Burkeman 2014.

13. See Lee and Viebeck 2017.

14. On this culture, see Cogan 2017.

15. On compensating differentials, see Hersch 2011. On the ongoing improvement in the quality of the work environment for women, see Kaplan and Schulhofer-Wohl 2018.

16. For two looks at monopsony, see Boal and Ransom 1997; Ashenfelter, Farber, and Ransom 2010. On Walmart, see Bonnanno and Lopez 2009. For a look at why the monopsony model has not won over most economists, most of all as an explanation of medium- to long-run phenomena, see Kuhn 2004. On slow wage growth, see Furman 2018.

17. A starting point here is Kaur, Kremer, and Mullainathan 2015.

18. On this and the preceding few paragraphs, see my related remarks in Cowen 2017b.

19. On these mechanisms, see Freeman, Kruse, and Blasi 2004.

## Chapter 5: How Monopolistic Is American Big Business?

1. For the number on rising retail concentration, see Autor et al. 2017.

2. For the figures, see Frazier 2017.

3. On related points, see Ganapati 2017, who notes, "Non-manufacturing concentration increases over the last twenty years are not correlated with observable price changes, but are correlated with increases in output."

4. See Gutiérrez and Philippon 2017.

5. On the connection between information technology investments in mission-critical systems and industry concentration, see Bessen 2017.

6. For two studies on the economics of hospital consolidation, see Cooper et al. 2015 and Town et al. 2006. For a general popular survey of the issue, see Feyman and Hartley 2016.

7. On the decline in prices for cell phone service, see Leubsdorf 2017. On spectrum privatization, see Skorup 2013.

8. For data on flying, see Cowen 2017c. I draw on the Department of Transportation series on total miles flown and the St. Louis Fed FRED series on inflation-adjusted airline prices, both available online. On the distinction between aggregate concentration ratios and competitiveness in individual re-

gional markets, see Shapiro 2017. I should add that I am personally not happy with the move toward more crowded seats and fewer amenities combined with lower fares. But very often my travel is paid for by third parties, which is not the case for most Americans, and so here the market is telling us that most people really would rather have the money.

9. See Leonhardt 2014; College Board 2016.

## Chapter 6: Are the Big Tech Companies Evil?

1. See Shephard 2018; Manjoo 2017.
2. The list is from Chris 2017.
3. On Alphabet and Google and related ad revenues, see Stambor 2018.
4. On the numbers, see Watts and Rothschild 2017.
5. See Watts and Rothschild 2017.
6. On those estimates, see Allcott and Gentzkower 2017. On polarization, see Boxell, Gentzkow, and Shapiro 2017.
7. See Gentzkow and Shapiro 2014; Boxell, Gentzkow, and Shapiro 2017.
8. I also see Facebook as taking a lot of culture, such as music, out of its broader social context. Since social media allow people to bond so quickly and effectively, we don't, for instance, need music for this end nearly so much anymore. Formerly, young people used music to signal who they were and to which social circles they wanted to belong. If you were a feminist in the late 1990s, you might listen to Indigo Girls and trade Sarah McLachlan CDs and go to Lilith Fair concerts. Today you can use Facebook to show your views with a Planned Parenthood support banner or maybe post something on Instagram. Arguably, the result is that music is less connected to our social attachments, and it doesn't seem to have the cultural force, social influence, or political meaning of earlier times. Pop music has been in the ascendant, and, outside of rap, protest music is less important, even in a time with a highly controversial president (namely, Donald Trump). The above passage draws from Cowen 2017d.
9. On book size, see Lea 2015. Admittedly, these bigger and longer books are of course not always read through, but still this is at variance with the common picture that everything is getting shorter outright.
10. On polemics against the novel, see Cowen 1998, 64.
11. See Alexander 2017.
12. On Shanghai, see Zhen 2017.
13. On the weakness of privacy for medical records, see Caplan 2016.
14. See Farr 2016; Caplan 2016.

## Chapter 7: What Is Wall Street Good for, Anyway?

1. On the roles of banking and finance in boosting growth in nineteenth-century America, see Bodenhorn 2016.
2. On these and many other episodes, see Faust 2016.
3. See Zauzmer 2013.
4. See NVCA 2016; SSTI 2016.
5. Gompers et al. 2016, 12–13. This is based on a survey of 889 institutional venture capitalists at 681 firms.
6. Gompers et al. 2016.
7. See Content First 2009; Kaplan and Lerner 2010; Gompers et al. 2016.
8. Interestingly, some of the earliest venture capital in postwar America came from a Frenchman, Georges Doriot; on his life, see Ante 2008.
9. For a discussion of where the 7 percent estimate comes from, see, for instance, Diamond 1999. Plenty of other estimates are possible—see Brightman 2012—but they are all pretty high.
10. See Egan, Matvos, and Seru 2016.
11. See Backpacker 2015.
12. For the poll results, see McCarthy 2015.
13. Greenwood and Scharfstein 2013, 13–14.
14. See Greenwood and Scharfstein 2007, 9.
15. Greenwood and Scharfstein 2013, 14.
16. See Hausmann and Sturzenegger 2006.
17. Jackson 2013 offers a survey of the subsequent debate on the dark matter effect. Gourinchas 2016 offers the most recent estimate of America's gains from this investment differential. As he put it: "As financial globalization proceeded, U.S. investors concentrated their foreign holdings in risky and/or illiquid securities such as portfolio equity or direct investment, while foreign investors concentrated their U.S. asset purchases in portfolio debt, especially Treasuries and bonds issues by government-affiliated agencies in areas such as housing finance, and cross-border loans." In other words, overall, Americans are more optimistic and more tolerant of risk, and our financial sector helps support those tendencies. Setser 2017 considers whether some of the dark matter effect comes from U.S. multinationals using accounting tricks to switch some of their earnings into lower-taxed foreign affiliates or subsidiaries.
18. By the way, if you've followed the academic literature, you may know that the research on the financial sector and economic growth is in some ways inconclusive. The most plausible specifications show a positive correlation between

finance and growth for lower-income countries and an insignificant relationship for wealthier countries. I interpret this finding in two ways. First, past a certain stage of development the benefits of finance are typically what economists call "one-off" gains rather than increases in the rate of economic growth. But one-off gains are very important, especially if you can reap them for multiple years. For instance, as discussed earlier, the "dark matter" hypothesis means that finance brings Americans a lot of extra consumption each year, but it does not, say, boost the rate of growth from 1 percent to 2 percent. We are considerably better off nonetheless. This is a technical point, overlooked in many discussions, but in fact a lot of beneficial institutions raise consumption or yield other benefits but don't boost growth rates looking forward. Second, wealthier economies naturally grow more slowly, because they cannot engage in catch-up growth. If finance makes an economy wealthier, it also may appear to lower its growth rate, but again that can obscure the very benefits that finance brings. On these points, see Cline 2015. The skeptical paper is Cournede and Denk 2015. For a general survey of finance and growth, see Arcand, Berkes, and Panizza 2015.

19. Scannell and Houlder 2016.
20. Scannell and Houlder 2016.
21. For data on finance as a share of GDP, see Philippon 2011 and 2015.
22. On this, see Philippon 2015.
23. On all this, see Philippon and Reshef 2012.
24. See Shu 2013 and 2016.
25. Kaplan and Rauh 2010, 1006. This paper is in general a very good source on financial sector compensation.
26. Greenwood and Scharfstein 2013.
27. See Balchunas 2016. For the 2004 figures, see Bergstresser, Chalmers, and Tufano 2009. One problem behind high remaining mutual fund fees is that fund trustees often identify more with the interests of management than the interests of investors. See Thomas 2017.
28. For a disaggregated look at this source of financial sector growth, see Antill, Hou, and Sarkar 2014, who show it occurred disproportionately through nonbank credit intermediation.
29. On the decline in Chinese debt holdings, see, for instance, Mullen 2016.
30. For those numbers, see Comoreanu 2017, drawing upon FDIC data.

## Chapter 8: Crony Capitalism

1. These quotations are all from Pearlstein 2016.
2. Luigi Zingales has been one of the most articulate critics of crony capitalism. See, for instance, Zingales 2017.
3. For the estimate on total advertising expenditures, see Statista 2017. For the General Motors comparison, see Austin 2012; see also Drutman 2015, 223. For Coca-Cola, see Zmuda 2014. For the China quotation, see Pearlstein 2016.
4. See Drutman 2015, 83, 86–87, 91. For the study on lobbying, see Cao et al. 2017.
5. For instance, Coffey and McLaughlin 2016 estimate a regulatory burden of about $4 trillion since 1977.
6. See Gilens and Page 2014. On all of the points in response, see Enns 2015; Bashir 2015; Branham, Soroka, and Wlezien 2017; and Matthews 2016.
7. On status quo bias, see Bashir 2015.
8. See Drutman 2015, 92–93.
9. On Jefferson, see Bainbridge and Henderson 2016, 2.
10. One very good statement of the problems with multiple liability, with reference to historical developments, is Halpern, Trebilcock, and Turnbull 1980.
11. There might be some cases where a multiple liability structure makes sense. Here I am thinking of highly leveraged companies that depend a great deal on public trust, such as life insurance companies or some debt-intensive forms of banking. Let's say there was less government regulation in these areas, plus no or fewer bailouts, and in the case of banking no deposit insurance. There is a reasonable chance that a multiple liability corporate form could evolve and persist in these cases. With only limited liability, a life insurance company might take in a lot of premiums, gamble with the money, and not worry if it cannot pay off policies in thirty or forty years' time. The equity holders would get the potential upside from the risk, and the policy holders would bear much of the downside risk. As it stands, insurance and bank regulators typically demand that those companies hold high levels of capital up-front (but without multiple liability), and those capital cushions serve much the same function as multiple liability, arguably with greater efficiency. Partnerships are another corporate form that deviates from the strict limited liability model. For instance, any single one of the partners can be liable for a tort or breach of trust committed by the other partners, provided it is committed within the scope of the business activities of the partnership. Many law firms take this form, and in the older days investment banks, including Goldman Sachs, commonly had the partnership form. Partnerships seem to work well when partners need to monitor

the effort and responsibility put in by other partners, and when the sizes of these ventures are relatively small, thus rendering such monitoring possible. Still, while partnerships succeed in a number of areas, they are hardly pushing out corporate limited liability forms of organization, and to the extent that they are becoming more frequent, it is for tax reasons (the ability to claim pass-through tax rates) rather than their organizational efficiency.

12. On this history, see Osborne 2007, ch. 2, and also Bainbridge and Henderson 2016, specifically 37–38 on New York. For limited liability corporations as substitutes for some of the fiscal failures of state governments, see Wallis 2005. For the 90 percent figure, see Bainbridge and Henderson 2016, 13.

## Chapter 9: If Business Is So Good, Why Is It So Disliked?

1. See Rucker 2011.
2. This and the following information are taken from Hauser and Maheshwari 2006.
3. Hauser and Maheshwari 2006.
4. Guthrie 1993, 107.
5. On the general tendency toward anthropomorphism, see, for instance, Chartrand, Fitzsimons, and Fitzsimons 2008; Guthrie 1993.
6. Cialdini 2007, 28–29.
7. Cialdini 2007, 168–69.
8. See Scheiber 2016.
9. For a look at the history of "smiling" cars and how consumers respond to them by anthropomorphizing the product, see Aggarwal and McGill 2007 and 2012.
10. Touré-Tillery and McGill 2015.
11. The following is based on more speculative evidence, but it may be the case that the personality features of corporate products rub off on us to some extent. For instance, individuals exposed to the Apple brand behaved more creatively relative to control groups (note: that was from a time when Apple was identified with creativity more strongly than might be the case today). Individuals exposed to the Disney brand behaved more honestly. I don't think we should conclude that such lab results always carry over into the real world, but this at least raises the possibility that corporate influence on us is somewhat like the personal influence of human role models, in that we sometimes copy individuals of higher status. Alternatively, some of the priming effects may be motivational. If seeing a brand or corporate image induces us to think that we soon will be interacting with that brand or company in some way, subconsciously we may drum up the motivation to behave in the appropriate manner

for such an interaction. For instance, if a company signals through its ads that it has something to do with smarts, the viewer of the ad might pay closer attention and at least temporarily become smarter because he or she is being primed to expect some kind of interaction with that company. In any case, that would be another way of confusing corporate and human symbols and anthropomorphizing the business corporation. One good source on this is Fitzsimons, Chartrand, and Fitzsimons 2008. On feeling attached to products, see Chandler and Schwartz 2010. On anthropomorphized products more generally, see Cowen 2016.

12. The irony is that American popular culture is itself, for the most part, big business at its core. One of the best arguments against trusting big business is the (largely inaccurate) portrayal of business from popular culture itself. On the brighter side, many of the implicit messages of Hollywood movies and television, once translated to the screen, are not always so anti-business at a deeper level. Most of all, Hollywood movies promote ethics of individualism and heroism, and thus in a broader way they may be conditioning the American public for relatively libertarian attitudes, which de facto can be quite pro-business. And these messages are transmitted in large numbers of uplifting, heroic films that perhaps do not mention business at all. In this sense Hollywood is not wrecking America's intellectual or ideological climate. Unfortunately, however, many of the virtues of business and markets are hard to show on the screen. Adam Smith wrote of "the invisible hand" as a core mechanism through which profit-seeking behavior can cause businesspeople to act in the greater interest of society, yet without their necessarily feeling any benevolence. A balancing of profit and loss goes on behind the scenes, and resources are removed from one set of uses and moved to another. The thing about the invisible hand is that it is, well, invisible. It also requires some level of conceptual understanding, and much of the American public doesn't know enough economics to follow invisible-hand reasoning on the screen. Furthermore, in popular culture, viewers tend to judge individuals by their intentions, and intentions are often easier to show on the screen than the final results of actions. A core economic point, however, is that purely selfish or relatively selfish motivations can bring about good ends, at least in the right institutions. That too is hard to show on the screen because it deals in so many abstracts rather than concretes.

13. For one study of the control premium, see Owens, Grossman, and Fackler 2014.

## Appendix

1. While I have learned a great deal from the writings of Coase and Williamson, my final position is influenced more heavily by Commons, Kreps (the corporation as carrier of reputation), and Rotemberg.

2. You might be tempted to suggest that viewing companies as carriers of social and legal reputation ultimately boils down to transaction-costs-minimizing theories of the firm. To be sure, the firm as a carrier of reputation does minimize transaction costs to some extent, but it also increases transaction costs by making the firm more of a target. I would say the carrier-of-reputation element is not fundamentally a choice a firm makes at the margin, resulting in minimal transaction costs, but rather part of what a firm is required to be (with room for adjustment at the margins), and in this regard it still differs significantly from the Coase and Williamson models.

# SELECTED BIBLIOGRAPHY

Adelino, Manuel, Antoinette Schoar, and Felipe Severino. 2017. "Dynamics of Housing Debt in the Recent Boom and Great Recession." NBER Working Paper No. 23502. National Bureau of Economic Research, Washington, DC.

Aggarwal, Pankaf, and Ann L. McGill. 2007. "Is That Car Smiling at Me? Scheme Congruity as a Basis for Evaluating Anthropomorphized Products." *Journal of Consumer Research* 34 (December): 468–479.

Aggarwal, Pankaf, and Ann L. McGill. 2012. "When Brands Seem Human, Do Humans Act Like Brands? Automatic Behavioral Priming." *Journal of Consumer Research* 39 (August): 307–323.

Aguinas, Herman, and Ante Glavas. 2012. "What We Know and Don't Know About Corporate Social Responsibility: A Review and Research Agenda." *Journal of Management* 38, no. 4 (July): 932–968.

Ales, Laurence, and Christopher Sleet. 2016. "Taxing Top CEO Incomes." *American Economic Review* 106 (11): 3331–3366.

Alexander, Scott. 2016. "Contra Robinson on Schooling." *Slate Star Codex* (blog). December 6, 2016.

Alexander, Scott. 2017. "Silicon Valley: A Reality Check." *Slate Star Codex* (blog), May 11, 2017. http://slatestarcodex.com/2017/05/11/silicon-valley-a-reality-check.

Allcott, Hunt, and Matthew Gentzkower. 2017. "Social Media and Fake News in the 2016 Election." NBER Working Paper No. 23089. National Bureau of Economic Research, Washington, DC.

Anderson, Ryan. 2016. "The Ugly Truth About Online Dating: Are We Sacrificing Love for Convenience?" *Psychology Today*, September 2016. https://www.psychologytoday.com/us/blog/the-mating-game/201609/the-ugly-truth-about-online-dating.

Ante, Spencer. 2008. *Creative Capital: Georges Doriot and the Birth of Venture Capital*. Cambridge, MA: Harvard Business Review Press.

Antill, Samuel, David Hou, and Asani Sarkar. 2014. "Components of U.S. Financial Sector Growth, 1950–2013." *FRBNY Economic Policy Review* 20, no. 2 (December): 59–83.

Arcand, Jean-Louis, Enrico Berkes, and Ugo Panizza. 2015. "Too Much Finance?" *Journal of Economic Growth* 20, no. 2 (June): 105–148.

Ariely, Dan. 2012. *The (Honest) Truth About Dishonesty*. New York: HarperCollins.

Ashenfelter, Orley C., Henry Farber, and Michael R. Ransom. 2010. "Modern Models of Monopsony in Labor Markets." IZA Discussion Paper No. 4915. IZA Institute of Labor Economics, Bonn, Germany.

Atkinson, Robert D., and Michael Lind. 2018. *Big Is Beautiful: Debunking the Myth of Small Business*. Cambridge, MA: MIT Press.

Austin, Christina. 2012. "The Billionaires' Club: Only 36 Companies Have $1,000 Million–Plus Ad Budgets." *Business Insider Australia*, November 12, 2012.

Autor, David, David Dorn, Lawrence F. Katz, Christina Patterson, and John Van Reenen. 2017. "Concentrating on the Fall of the Labor Share." NBER Working Paper No. 23108. National Bureau of Economic Research, Washington, DC.

"Backpacker." 2015. "1929 Was a Great Year to Buy Stocks." Bogleheads.org (blog), May 6, 2015. https://www.bogleheads.org/forum/viewtopic.php?t=165263.

Bainbridge, Stephen M., and M. Todd Henderson. 2016. *Limited Liability: A Legal and Economic Analysis*. Cheltenham, UK: Edward Elgar.

Balchunas, Eric. 2016. "How the Vanguard Effect Adds Up to $1 Trillion." *Bloomberg View*, August 30, 2016.

Ballesteros, Luis, and Michael Useem. 2016. "The Social Value of Corporate Giving and the Economic Costs of Disasters." Wharton School Research Paper No. 84. Wharton School, University of Pennsylvania.

Ballesteros, Luis, Michael Useem, and Tyler Wry. 2017. "Masters of Disasters? An Empirical Analysis of How Societies Benefit from Corporate Disaster Aid." *Academy of Management Journal* 60, no. 5.

Barber, Brad M., Yi-Tsung Lee, Yu-Jane Liu, and Terrance Odean. 2009. "Just How

Much Do Individual Investors Lose by Trading?" *Review of Financial Studies* 22, no. 2.

Barber, Brad M., and Terrance Odean. 2000. "Trading Is Hazardous to Your Wealth: The Common Stock Investment Performance of Individual Investors." *Journal of Finance* 55: 773–806. https://papers.ssrn.com/so13/papers.cfm?abstract_id =1872211.

Barber, Brad M., and Terrance Odean. 2011. "The Behavior of Individual Investors." https://papers.ssrn.com/sol3/papers.cfm?abstract_id=1872211.

Bashir, Omar S. 2015. "Testing Inferences About American Politics: A Review of the 'Oligarchy' Result." *Research and Politics*, October–December 2015: 1–7.

Bebchuk, Lucien, and Jesse Fried. 2006. *Pay Without Performance: The Unfulfilled Promise of Executive Compensation*. Cambridge, MA: Harvard University Press.

Becker, Sascha O., and Hans K. Hvide. 2013. "Do Entrepreneurs Matter?" IZA Discussion Paper No. 7146. IZA Institute of Labor Economics, Bonn, Germany.

Bennedsen, Morten, Francisco Pérez-González, and Daniel Wolfenzon. 2011. "Estimating the Value of the Boss: Evidence from CEO Hospitalization Events." Working Paper, Columbia Business School, 2011.

Bergstresser, Daniel, John M. R. Chalmers, and Peter Tufano. 2009. "Assessing the Costs and Benefits of Brokers in the Mutual Fund Industry." *Review of Financial Studies* 22 (10): 4129–4156.

Bernstein, Elizabeth. 2014. "Work Creates Less Stress Than Home, Penn State Researchers Find." *Wall Street Journal*, June 2, 2014.

Berry, Ken. 2018. "2018 Tax Reform: Pass-Through Income Deduction More Complex Than Thought." CPA Practice Advisor, January 8, 2018. http://www .cpapracticeadvisor.com/news/12389903/2018-tax-reform-pass-through -income-deduction-more-complex-than-thought.

Bessembinder, Hendrik. 2018. "Do Stocks Outperform Treasury Bills?" *Journal of Financial Economics* 129, no. 3 (September).

Bessen, James. 2017. "Information Technology and Industry Concentration." Working Paper, Boston University School of Law, September 2017.

Bloom, Nicholas, Christos Genakos, Raffaella Sadun, and John Van Reenen. 2012. "Management Practices Across Firms and Countries." NBER Working Paper No. 17850. National Bureau of Economic Research, Washington, DC.

Bloom, Nicholas, Raffaella Sadun, and John Van Reenen. 2016. "Management as a Technology?" NBER Working Paper No. 22327. National Bureau of Economic Research, Washington, DC.

Bloxham, Eleanor. 2015. "Here's Why You Should Care About How CEOs Get Paid." *Fortune*, October 20, 2015.

Blumberg, Paul. 1989. *The Predatory Society: Deception in the American Marketplace*. New York: Oxford University Press.

Boal, William M., and Michael R. Ransom. 1997. "Monopsony in the Labor Market." *Journal of Economic Literature* 35, no. 1 (March): 86–112.

Bodenhorn, Howard. 2016. "Two Centuries of Finance and Growth in the United States, 1790–1980." NBER Working Paper No. 22652. National Bureau of Economic Research, Washington, DC.

Bonnanno, Alessandro, and Rigoberto A. Lopez. 2009. "Is Wal-Mart a Monopsony? Evidence from Local Labor Markets." Paper prepared for presentation at the International Association of Agricultural Economists Conference, Beijing, August 16–22, 2009.

Booth, Alison L., and Gylfi Zoega. 2000. "Why Do Firms Invest in General Training? 'Good' Firms and 'Bad' Firms as a Source of Monopsony Power." CEPR Discussion Paper 2536. Center for Economic and Policy Research, Washington, DC.

Bort, Julie. 2014. "The 25 Most Enjoyable Companies to Work For." *Business Insider*, August 22, 2014.

Boxell, Levi, Matthew Gentzkow, and Jesse M. Shapiro. 2017. "Is the Internet Causing Political Polarization? Evidence from Demographics." NBER Working Paper No. 23258. National Bureau of Economic Research, Washington, DC.

Branham, J. Alexander, Stuart N. Soroka, and Christopher Wlezien. 2017. "When Do the Rich Win?" *Political Science Quarterly* 132, no. 1 (Spring).

Brav, Alon, Wei Jiang, Song Ma, and Xuan Tian. 2016. "How Does Hedge Fund Activism Reshape Corporate Innovation?" NBER Working Paper No. 22273. National Bureau of Economic Research, Washington, DC.

Brightman, Christopher J. 2012. "Expected Return." Investment Management Consultants Association, Denver, CO.

Brooks, Nathan, and Katarina Fritzon. 2016. "Psychopathic Personality Characteristics Amongst High Functioning Populations." *Crime Psychology Review* 2 (1): 22–44.

Burkeman, Oliver. 2014. "Why Is Home More Stressful Than Work? Because We're Too Lax About Relaxing." *Guardian*, June 4, 2014.

Burman, Leonard E., Kimberly A. Clausing, and Lydia Austin. 2017. "Is U.S. Corporate Income Double-Taxed?" *National Tax Journal* 70 (3): 675–706.

Cairnes, Gus. 2014. "Life Expectancy Now Considerably Exceeds the Average in Some People with HIV in the US." NAM Aidsmap, January 6, 2014. http://www.aidsmap.com/Life-expectancy-now-considerably-exceeds-the-average-in-some-people-with-HIV-in-the-US/page/2816267.

Calmes, Jackie. 2016. "Hiring Hurdle: Finding Workers Who Can Pass a Drug Test." *New York Times*, May 17, 2016.

Cao, Zhiyan, Guy D. Fernando, Arindam Tripathy, and Arun Upadhyay. 2018. "The Economics of Corporate Lobbying." *Journal of Corporate Finance* 49 (April): 54–80.

Caplan, Art. 2016. "Why Privacy Must Die." *The Health Care Blog*, December 19, 2016. http://thehealthcareblog.com/blog/2016/12/19/goodbye-privacy-we-hardly-knew-ye.

Capps, Cory, Dennis W. Carlton, and Guy David. 2017. "Antitrust Treatment of Nonprofits: Should Hospitals Receive Special Care?" NBER Working Paper No. 23131. National Bureau of Economic Research, Washington, DC.

Cardiff-Hicks, Brianna, Francine Lafontaine, and Kathryn Shaw. 2014. "Do Large Modern Retailers Pay Premium Wages?" NBER Working Paper No. 20313. National Bureau of Economic Research, Washington, DC.

Cassar, Lea, and Stephan Meier. 2017. "Intentions for Doing Good Matter for Doing Well: The (Negative) Signaling Value of Prosocial Incentives." NBER Working Paper No. 24109. National Bureau of Economic Research, Washington, DC.

CBO. 2017. "International Comparisons of Corporate Income Tax Rates," March 8, 2017. Congressional Budget Office, Washington, DC.

Chandler, Jesse, and Norbert Schwarz. 2010. "Use Does Not Wear Ragged the Fabric of Friendship: Thinking of Objects as Alive Makes People Less Willing to Replace Them." *Journal of Consumer Psychology* 20: 138–145.

Chang, Yuk Ying, Sudipto Dasgupta, and Gilles Hilary. 2010. "CEO Ability, Pay, and Firm Performance." *Management Science* 56 (10): 1633–1652.

Chartrand, Tanya L., Grainne M. Fitzsimons, and Gavan J. Fitzsimons. 2008. "Automatic Effects of Anthropomorphized Objects on Behavior." *Social Cognition* 26 (2): 198–209.

Chen, Peter, Loukas Karabarbounis, and Brent Neiman. 2017. "The Global Rise of Corporate Saving." NBER Working Paper No. 23133. National Bureau of Economic Research, Washington, DC.

Cheng, Ing-Haw, Sahil Raina, and Wei Xiong. 2014. "Wall Street and the Housing Bubble." *American Economic Review* 104 (9): 2797–2829.

Chris, Alex. 2017. "Top 10 Search Engines in the World." Reliablesoft.net. Accessed December 6, 2017. https://www.reliablesoft.net/top-10-search-engines-in-the-world/.

Cialdini, Robert B. 2007. *Influence: The Psychology of Persuasion*, rev. ed. New York: Collins Business.

Clark, Andrew E., and Andrew J. Oswald. 1994. "Unhappiness and Unemployment." *Economic Journal* 104, no. 424 (May): 648–659.

Clarke, Conor, and Wojciech Kopczuk. 2016. "Business Income and Business Taxation in the United States Since the 1950s." NBER Working Paper No. 22778. National Bureau of Economic Research, Washington, DC.

Cline, William R. 2015. "Further Statistical Debate on 'Too Much Finance.'" PIIE Working Paper No. 15-16. Peterson Institute for International Economics, Washington, DC.

Coffey, Bentley, and Patrick McLaughlin. 2016. "The Cumulative Cost of Regulations." Mercatus Working Paper. Mercatus Center, George Mason University.

College Board. 2016. *Trends in College Pricing 2016.* Princeton, NJ: College Board.

Comoreanu, Alina. 2017. "Bank Market Share by Deposits and Assets." WalletHub, February 9, 2017. https://wallethub.com/edu/bank-market-share-by-deposits /25587.

Content First. 2009. *Venture Impact: The Economic Importance of Venture Capital–Backed Companies to the U.S. Economy.* Global Insight Report. Arlington, VA: National Venture Capital Association.

Conyon, Martin J. 2006. "Executive Compensation and Incentives." *Academy of Management Perspectives* 20 (1): 25–44.

Cooper, Zack, Stuart V. Craig, Martin Gaynor, and John Van Reenan. 2015. "The Price Ain't Right? Hospital Prices and Health Spending on the Privately Insured." NBER Working Paper No. 21815. National Bureau of Economic Research, Washington, DC.

Core, John E., Wayne R. Guay, and Randall S. Thomas. 2005. "Is U.S. CEO Compensation Inefficient Pay Without Performance?" *Michigan Law Review* 103, no. 6 (May): 1142–1185.

Cournede, Boris, and Oliver Denk. 2015. "Finance and Economic Growth in OECD and G20 Countries." OECD Economics Department Working Paper No. 1223. Organisation for Economic Co-operation and Development, Paris.

Cowen, Tyler. 1998. *In Praise of Commercial Culture.* Cambridge, MA: Harvard University Press.

Cowen, Tyler. 2012. *An Economist Gets Lunch.* New York: Dutton.

Cowen, Tyler. 2016. "When Products Talk." *New Yorker,* June 1, 2016.

Cowen, Tyler. 2017a. *The Complacent Class: The Self-Defeating Quest for the American Dream.* New York: St. Martin's Press.

Cowen, Tyler. 2017b. "Work Isn't So Bad After All." In Elizabeth Anderson, *Pri-*

*vate Government: How Employers Rule Our Lives (and Why We Don't Talk About It)*, 108–117. Princeton, NJ: Princeton University Press.

Cowen, Tyler. 2017c. "The New World of Monopoly? What About Flying?" *Marginal Revolution* (blog), September 2, 2017.

Cowen, Tyler. 2017d. "Facebook's Harm Is Taking Life out of Context." *Bloomberg View*, September 20, 2017.

Cowley, Stacy. 2016a. "'Lions Hunting Zebras': Wells Fargo Employees Targeted People Who Would 'Put Up the Least Resistance.'" *New York Times*, October 21, 2016.

Cowley, Stacy. 2016b. "Scrutiny for Wells Fargo over Ex-Employee Files." *New York Times*, November 4, 2016.

Cowley, Stacy, and Matthew Goldstein. 2016. "Accusations of Fraud at Wells Fargo Spread to Sham Insurance Policies." *New York Times*, December 10, 2016.

Craig, Ben, and John Pencavel. 1992. "The Behavior of Worker Cooperatives: The Plywood Companies of the Pacific Northwest." *American Economic Review* 82, no. 5 (December): 1083–1105.

Csikszentmihalyi, Mihaly, and Judith LeFevre. 1989. "Optimal Experience in Work and Leisure." *Journal of Personality and Social Psychology* 56 (5): 815–822.

Damaske, Sarah, Joshua M. Smyth, and Matthew J. Zawadzki. 2014. "Has Work Replaced Home as a Haven? Re-examining Arlie Hochschild's Time Bind Proposition with Objective Stress Data." *Social Science and Medicine* 115 (August): 130–138.

Damaske, Sarah, Joshua M. Smyth, and Matthew J. Zawadzki. 2016. "Stress at Work: Differential Experiences of High Versus Low SES Workers." *Social Science and Medicine* 156 (May): 125–133.

DaVanzo, Joan E., Steven Heath, Audrey El-Gamil, and Allen Dobson. 2009. "The Economic Contribution of the Dietary Supplement Industry." Dobson DaVanzo & Associates, LLC, May 7, 2009.

Davies, Richard, Andrew G. Haldane, Mette Nielsen, and Silvia Pezzini. 2014. "Measuring the Costs of Short-Termism." *Journal of Financial Stability* 12: 16–25.

Davis, Gerald F. 2016. *The Vanishing American Corporation: Navigating the Hazards of a New Economy*. Oakland, CA: Berrett-Koehler.

Della Volpe, John, and Sonya Jacobs. 2016. "Survey of Young Americans' Attitudes Toward Politics and Public Service." Harvard Public Opinion Project, Harvard University Institute of Politics, April 25, 2016.

DePaulo, Bella M., Matthew E. Ansfield, Susan E. Kirkendol, and Joseph M. Boden. 2004. "Serious Lies." *Basic and Applied Social Psychology* 26 (2–3): 147–167.

DePaulo, Bella M., and Deborah A. Kashy. 1998. "Everyday Lies in Close and Casual Relationships." *Journal of Personality and Social Psychology* 74 (1): 63–79.

DePaulo, Bella M., Deborah A. Kashy, Susan E. Kirkendol, and Melissa M. Wyer. 1996. "Lying in Everyday Life." *Journal of Personality and Social Psychology* 70 (5): 979–995.

Desan, Mathieu, and Michael A. McCarthy. 2018. "A Time to Be Bold." *Jacobin*, July 31, 2018.

Diamond, Peter A. 1998. "What Stock Market Returns to Expect for the Future?" Center for Retirement Research, Boston College.

DiPrete, Thomas A., Gregory M. Eirich, and Matthew Pittinsky. 2010. "Compensation Benchmarking, Leapfrogs, and the Surge in Executive Pay." *American Journal of Sociology* 115, no. 6 (May): 1671–1712.

Drutman, Lee. 2015. *The Business of America Is Lobbying: How Corporations Became Politicized and Politics Became More Corporate.* New York: Oxford University Press.

Dyck, Alexander, Adair Morse, and Luigi Zingales. 2013. "How Pervasive Is Corporate Fraud?" Rotman School of Management Working Paper No. 2222608, February 22, 2013.

*Economist.* 2016. "From Clout to Rout: Why European Companies Have Become a Fading Force in Global Business." *Economist*, July 2, 2016.

*Economist.* 2017. "Corporate Short-Termism Is a Frustratingly Slippery Idea." *Economist*, February 16, 2017.

Edmans, Adam, Xavier Gabaix, and Dirk Jenter. 2017. "Executive Compensation: A Survey of Theory and Evidence." NBER Working Paper No. 23596. National Bureau of Economic Research, Washington, DC.

Egan, Mark, Gregor Matvos, and Amit Seru. 2016. "The Market for Financial Adviser Misconduct." NBER Working Paper No. 22050. National Bureau of Economic Research, Washington, DC.

Ehrenfreund, Max. 2016. "A Majority of Millennials Now Reject Capitalism, Poll Shows." *Washington Post*, April 26, 2016.

Elliehausen, Gregory. 2009. "An Analysis of Consumers' Use of Payday Loans." Monograph No. 41. Financial Services Research Program, George Washington University.

Elson, Charles M. 2003. "What's Wrong with Executive Compensation?" *Harvard Business Review*, January 2003.

Enns, Peter K. 2015. "Relative Policy Support and Coincidental Representation." *Perspectives on Politics* 13 (4): 1053–1064.

Ensminger, Jean, and Joseph Henrich, editors. 2014. *Experimenting with Social Norms: Fairness and Punishment in Cross-Cultural Perspective*. New York: Russell Sage Foundation.

Evershed, Richard, and Nicola Temple. 2016. *Sorting the Beef from the Bull: The Science of Food Fraud Forensics*. London: Bloomsbury Sigma.

Falato, Antonio, Dan Li, and Todd Milbourn. 2015. "Which Skills Matter in the Market for CEOs? Evidence from Pay for CEO Credentials." *Management Science* 61, no. 12 (December): 2845–2869.

Fama, Eugene F., and Kenneth R. French. "Value and Growth: An International Perspective." *Journal of Finance* 53, no. 6 (December): 1975–1999.

Farr, Christina. 2016. "On the Dark Web, Medical Records Are a Hot Commodity." *Fast Company*, July 7, 2016.

Faulkender, Michael, and Jun Yang. 2010. "Inside the Black Box: The Role and Composition of Compensation Peer Groups." *Journal of Financial Economics* 96, no. 2 (May): 257–270.

Faust, Leland. 2016. *A Capitalist's Lament: How Wall Street Is Fleecing You and Ruining America*. New York: Skyhorse Publishing.

Fehr, Ernst, and John A. List. 2004. "The Hidden Costs and Returns of Incentives— Trust and Trustworthiness Among CEOs." *Journal of the European Economic Association* 2, no. 5 (September): 743–771.

Feldman, Robert S., James A. Forrest, and Benjamin R. Happ. 2002. "Self-Presentation and Verbal Deception: Do Self-Presenters Lie More?" *Basic and Applied Social Psychology* 24 (2): 163–170.

Felipe, Jesus, Aahish Mehta, and Changyong Rhee. 2014. "Manufacturing Matters . . . but It's the Jobs That Count." ADB Economics Working Paper No. 420. Asian Development Bank, Mandaluyong, Philippines.

Fitzsimons, Grainne M., Tanya L. Chartrand, and Gavan J. Fitzsimons. 2008. "Automatic Effects of Brand Exposure on Motivated Behavior: How Apple Makes You 'Think Different.'" *Journal of Consumer Research* 35 (June): 21–35.

Foote, Christopher L., Kristopher F. Girardi, and Paul S. Willen. 2017. "Why Did So Many People Make So Many Ex Post Bad Decisions? The Causes of the Foreclosure Crisis." NBER Working Paper No. 18082. National Bureau of Economic Research, Washington, DC.

Foote, Christopher L., Lara Loewenstein, and Paul S. Willen. 2016. "Cross-Sectional Patterns of Mortgage Debt During the Housing Boom: Evidence and Implications." NBER Working Paper No. 22985. National Bureau of Economic Research, Washington, DC.

Foster, Tom. 2017. "The Shelf Life of John Mackey." *Texas Monthly*, June 2017.

Francis, Theo, and Joann S. Lublin. 2016. "CEO Pay Shrank Most Since Financial Crisis." *Wall Street Journal*, April 7, 2016.

Frazier, Mya. 2017. "Dollar General Hits a Gold Mine in Rural America." *Bloomberg Businessweek*, October 11, 2017.

Freeman, Richard B., Douglas Kruse, and Joseph Blasi. 2004. "Monitoring Colleagues at Work: Profit Sharing, Employee Ownership, Broad-Based Stock Options and Workplace Performance in the United States." CEP Discussion Paper No. 647. Centre for Economic Performance, London School of Economics and Political Science.

Fried, Jesse M., and Charles C. Y. Wang. 2017. "Short-Termism and Shareholder Payouts: Getting Corporate Capital Flows Right." Working Paper 17-062. Harvard Business School.

Friedman, Milton. 1970. "The Social Responsibility of Business Is to Increase Its Profits." *New York Times Magazine*, September 13, 1970.

Friedman, Milton, John Mackey, and T. J. Rodgers. 2005. "Rethinking the Social Responsibility of Business." *Reason*, October 2005. http://reason.com/archives/2005/10/01/rethinking-the-social-responsi.

Frydman, Carola, and Dirk Jenter. 2010. "CEO Compensation." *Annual Review of Financial Economics* 2: 75–102.

Frydman, Carola, and Raven E. Saks. 2007. "Executive Compensation: A New View from a Long-Term Perspective, 1936–2005." Working Paper 2007-35. Federal Reserve Board, Washington, DC.

Fuest, Clements, Andreas Peichl, and Sebastian Siegloch. 2018. "Do Higher Corporate Taxes Reduce Wages? Micro Evidence from Germany." *American Economic Review* 108, no. 2 (February): 393–418.

Furman, Jason. 2018. "The Real Reason You're Not Getting a Pay Raise." *Vox*, August 11, 2018.

Gabaix, Xavier, and Augustin Landier. 2008. "Why Has CEO Pay Increased So Much?" *Quarterly Journal of Economics* 121 (1): 49–100.

Gabaix, Xavier, Augustin Landier, and Julien Sauvagnat. 2014. "CEO Pay and Firm Size: An Update After the Crisis." *Economic Journal* 124 (574): F40–F59.

Gallup. 2016. "Confidence in Institutions." Gallup Poll and Report, June 2016. https://news.gallup.com/poll/1597/confidence-institutions.aspx.

Ganapati, Shrat. 2017. "Oligopolies, Prices, and Quantities: Has Industry Concentration Increased Price and Restricted Output?" https//papers.ssrn.com/so13/papers.cfm?abstract_id=3030966.

Gentzkow, Matthew, and Jesse M. Shapiro. 2014. "Ideological Segregation Online and Offline." Chicago Booth Research Paper No. 10-19. Booth School of Business, University of Chicago.

Giertz, Seth H., and Jacob A. Mortensen. 2013. "Recent Income Trends for Top Executives: Evidence from Tax Return Data." *National Tax Journal* 66 (4): 913–938.

Gilens, Martin, and Benjamin I. Page. 2014. "Testing Theories of American Politics: Elites, Interest Groups, and Average Citizens." *Perspectives on Politics* 12, no. 3 (September): 564–581.

Glazer, Amihai. 1978. "The Economics of Repair Markets." Ph.D. dissertation, Department of Economics, Yale University.

Gompers, Paul, William Gornall, Steven N. Kaplan, and Ilya A. Strebulaev. 2016. "How Do Venture Capitalists Make Decisions?" NBER Working Paper No. 22587. National Bureau of Economic Research, Washington, DC.

Gorton, Gary, and Frank Schmid. 2002. "Class Struggle Inside the Firm: A Study of German Codetermination." Working Paper 2000-025B. Federal Reserve Bank of St. Louis.

Gourinchas, Pierre Olivier. 2016. "The Structure of the International Monetary System." Research Summary. National Bureau of Economic Research, Washington, DC.

Gow, Ian D., Steven N. Kaplan, David F. Larcker, and Anastasia A. Zakolyukina. 2016. "CEO Personality and Firm Policies." NBER Working Paper No. 22435. National Bureau of Economic Research, Washington, DC.

Graeber, David. 2018. *Bullshit Jobs: A Theory*. New York: Simon and Schuster.

Graham, John R., Campbell R. Harvey, Jillian Popadak, and Shivaram Rajgopal. 2017. "Corporate Culture: Evidence from the Field." NBER Working Paper No. 23255. National Bureau of Economic Research, Washington, DC.

Gravelle, Jennifer C. 2011. "Corporate Tax Incidence: A Review of Empirical Estimates and Analysis." Congressional Budget Office, Washington, DC.

Green, Francis, Stephen Machin, and Alan Manning. 1996. "The Employer Size-Wage Effect: Can Dynamic Monopsony Provide an Explanation?" *Oxford Economic Papers* 48: 433–455.

Greenwood, Robin, and David Scharfstein. 2013. "The Growth of Finance." *Journal of Economic Perspectives* 27, no. 2 (Spring): 3–28.

Griffin, John, and Jin Xu. 2009. "How Smart Are the Smart Guys? A Unique View from Hedge Fund Stock Holdings." *Review of Financial Studies* 22: 2531–2570.

Grossman, Sanford J., and Oliver D. Hart. 1986. "The Costs and Benefits of Ownership: A Theory of Vertical and Lateral Integration." *Journal of Political Economy* 94, no. 4 (August): 691–719.

Guiso, Luigi, Paola Sapienza, and Luigi Zingales. 2013. "The Value of Corporate Culture." NBER Working Paper No. 19557. National Bureau of Economic Research, Washington, DC.

Guthrie, Stewart. 1993. *Faces in the Clouds: A New Theory of Religion*. Oxford: Oxford University Press.

Gutiérrez, Germán, and Thomas Philippon. 2017. "Declining Competition and Investment in the U.S." NBER Working Paper No. 23583. National Bureau of Economic Research, Washington, DC.

Halpern, Paul, Michael Trebilcock, and Stuart Turnbull. 1980. "An Economic Analysis of Limited Liability in Corporation Law." *University of Toronto Law Journal* 30, no. 2 (Spring): 117–150.

Hare, Robert D. *Without Conscience: The Psychopaths Amongst Us*. New York: Guilford Press.

Hart, Oliver D., and John Moore. 1990. "Property Rights and the Nature of the Firm." *Journal of Political Economy* 98, no. 6 (December): 1119–1158.

Hart, Oliver, and Luigi Zingales. 2016. "Should a Company Pursue Shareholder Value?" Working paper, October 2016.

Hartmann, Thom. 2010. *Unequal Protection: How Corporations Became "People"—and How You Can Fight Back*. San Francisco: Berrett-Koehler.

Hauser, Christine, and Sapna Maheshwari. 2006. "MetLife Grounds Snoopy. Curse You, Red Baron!" *New York Times*, October 20, 2006.

Hausmann, Ricardo, and Federico Sturzenegger. 2006. "U.S. and Global Imbalances: Can Dark Matter Prevent a Big Bang?" Working paper, John F. Kennedy School of Government, Harvard University.

Henle, Christine A., Brian R. Dineen, and Michelle K. Duffy. 2017. "Assessing Intentional Resume Deception: Development and Nomological Network of a Resume Fraud Measure." *Journal of Business and Psychology*, published online December 16, 2017.

Henrich, Joseph. 2000. "Does Culture Matter in Economic Behavior? Ultimatum Game Bargaining Among the Machiguenga of the Peruvian Amazon." *American Economic Review* 90, no. 4 (September): 973–979.

Henrich, Joseph, Robert Boyd, Samuel Bowles, Colin Camerer, Ernst Fehr, and Herbert Gintis, editors. 2004. *Foundations of Human Sociality: Economic Experiments and Ethnographic Evidence from Fifteen Small-Scale Societies*. Oxford: Oxford University Press.

Henrich, Joseph, et al. 2006. "Costly Punishment Across Human Societies." *Science* 312: 1767–1770.

Henrich, Joseph, et al. 2010. "Markets, Religion, Community Size, and the Evolution of Fairness and Punishment." *Science* 327: 1480–1484.

Hirschman, Albert O. 1992. *Rival Views of Market Society and Other Recent Essays.* Cambridge, MA: Harvard University Press.

Hogan, Marin. 2017. "The Powerful Predators on Capitol Hill." *The Cut,* November 9, 2017.

Hsieh, Chang-Tai, and Peter J. Klenow. 2009. "Misallocation and Manufacturing TFP in China and India." *Quarterly Journal of Economics* 124 (4): 1403–1448.

IRS. 2016. *Tax Gap Estimates for Tax Years 2008–2010.* Washington, DC: Internal Revenue Service.

Isen, Adam. 2012. "Dying to Know? Are Workers Paid Their Marginal Product?" Working paper, University of Pennsylvania.

Jackson, James K. 2013. "The United States as a Net Debtor Nation: Overview of the International Investment Position." RL32964. Congressional Research Service, Washington, DC.

Jensen, Michael C., and Kevin J. Murphy. 1990. "Performance Pay and Top-Management Incentives." *Journal of Political Economy* 98: 225–264.

Jenter, Dirk, Egor Matveyev, and Lukas Roth. 2016. "Good and Bad CEOs." Working paper, March 2016.

Joynt, Karen E., E. John Orav, and Ashish K. Jha. 2014. "Association Between Hospital Conversions to For-Profit Status and Clinical and Economic Outcomes." *Journal of the American Medical Association* 312 (16): 1644–1652.

Jylha, Petri, Kalle Rinne, and Matti Suominen. 2018. "Do Hedge Funds Supply or Demand Liquidity?" *Review of Finance* 18 (4): 1259–1298.

Kahle, Kathleen, and René M. Stulz. 2017. "Is the US Public Corporation in Trouble?" *Journal of Economic Perspectives* 31, no. 3 (Summer): 67–88.

Kahneman, Daniel, Alan B. Krueger, David A. Schkade, Norbert Schwarz, and Arthur A. Stone. 2004. "A Survey Method for Characterizing Daily Life Experience: The Day Reconstruction Method." *Science* 306, no. 5702 (December 3): 1776–1780.

Kaplan, Greg, Kurt Mitman, and Giovanni L. Violante. 2017. "The Housing Boom and Bust: Model Meets Evidence." NBER Working Paper No. 23694. National Bureau of Economic Research, Washington, DC.

Kaplan, Greg, and Sam Schulhofer-Wohl. 2018. "The Changing (Dis-)Utility of Work." NBER Working Paper No. 24738. National Bureau of Economic Research, Washington, DC.

Kaplan, Steven N. 2012. "Executive Compensation and Corporate Governance in the U.S.: Perceptions, Facts and Challenges." NBER Working Paper No. 18395. National Bureau of Economic Research, Washington, DC.

Kaplan, Steven N., Mark M. Klebanov, and Morten Sorensen. 2012. "Which CEO Characteristics and Abilities Matter?" *Journal of Finance* 67, no. 3 (June): 973–1007.

Kaplan, Steven N., and Josh Lerner. 2010. "It Ain't Broke: The Past, Present, and Future of Venture Capital." *Journal of Applied Corporate Finance* 22 (2): 36–47.

Kaplan, Steven N., and Joshua Rauh. 2010. "Wall Street and Main Street: What Contributes to the Rise in the Highest Incomes?" *Review of Financial Studies* 23, no. 3 (March): 1004–1050.

Kaplan, Steven N., and Joshua Rauh. 2013. "It's the Market: The Broad-Based Rise in the Return to Top Talent." *Journal of Economic Perspectives* 27, no. 3 (Summer): 35–55.

Kaur, Supreet, Michael Kremer, and Sendhil Mullainathan. 2015. "Self-Control at Work." *Journal of Political Economy* 123, no. 6 (October): 1227–1277.

Keller, Wolfgang, and William W. Olney. 2017. "Globalization and Executive Compensation." NBER Working Paper No. 23384. National Bureau of Economic Research, Washington, DC.

Knack, Stephen, and Philip Keefer. 1997. "Does Social Capital Have an Economic Payoff? A Cross-Country Investigation." *Quarterly Journal of Economics* 112 (4): 1252–1288.

Konczal, Mike. 2016. "Learning from Trump in Retrospect." *The Medium*, December 2, 2016.

Kuhn, Andreas, Rafael Lalive, and Josef Zweimueller. 2009. "The Public Health Costs of Unemployment." *Cahiers de Recherches Economiques du Département d'Econométrie et d'Economie Politique*, University of Lausanne.

Kuhn, Peter. 2004. "Is Monopsony the Right Way to Model Labor Markets? A Review of Alan Manning's *Monopsony in Motion*." *International Journal of the Economics of Business* 11, no. 3 (November): 369–378.

Larcker, David F., Nicholas E. Donatiello, and Brian Tayan. 2017. "CEO Talent: America's Scarcest Resource? 2017 CEO Talent Survey." Stanford Graduate School of Business, Stanford University, September 2017.

Lawrence, Edward C., and Gregory Elliehausen. "A Comparative Analysis of Payday Loan Customers." *Contemporary Economic Policy* 26, no. 2 (April): 299–316.

Lea, Richard. 2015. "The Big Question: Are Books Getting Longer?" *Guardian*, December 10, 2015.

Lee, Michelle Ye Hee, and Elise Viebeck. 2017. "How Congress Plays by Different Rules on Sexual Harassment and Misconduct." *Washington Post*, October 27, 2017.

LeFevre, Judith. 1988. "Flow and the Quality of Experience During Work and Leisure." In *Optimal Experience: Psychological Studies of Flow in Consciousness*, edited by Mihaly Csikszentmihalyi and Isabella Selega Csikszentmihalyi, 307–318. Cambridge: Cambridge University Press.

Leonhardt, David. 2014. "How the Government Exaggerates the Cost of College." *New York Times*, July 29, 2014.

Leubsdorf, Ben. 2017. "How Cell-Phone Plans with Unlimited Data Limited Inflation." *Wall Street Journal*, May 22, 2017.

Lev, Baruch, Christine Petrovits, and Suresh Radhakrishnan. 2010. "Is Doing Good Good for You? How Corporate Charitable Contributions Enhance Revenue Growth." *Strategic Management Journal* 31, no. 2 (February): 182–200.

Levine, Ross. 2014. "In Defense of Wall Street: The Social Productivity of the Financial System." In *The Role of Central Banks in Financial Stability: How Has It Changed?*, edited by Douglas D. Evanoff, Cornelia Holthausen, and Manfred Kremer, 257–259. World Scientific Studies in International Economics 30, Singapore.

Lichtenberg, Frank R. 2013. "The Effect of Pharmaceutical Innovation on Longevity: Patient-Level Evidence from the 1996–2002 Medical Expenditure Panel Survey and Linked Mortality Public-Use Files." *Forum for Health Economics and Policy* 16 (1): 1–33.

Lublin, Joann S. 2017. "Few Can Fill the CEO's Job, Directors Say." *Wall Street Journal*, October 10, 2017.

Maestas, Nicole, Kathleen J. Mullen, David Powell, Till von Wachter, and Jeffrey B. Wenger. 2017. "Working Conditions in the United States: Results of the 2015 American Working Conditions Survey." RAND Corporation, Santa Monica, CA.

Maksimovic, Vojislav, Gordon M. Phillips, and Liu Yang. 2017. "Do Public Firms Respond to Investment Opportunities More Than Private Firms? The Impact of Initial Firm Quality." NBER Working Paper No. 24104. National Bureau of Economic Research, Washington, DC.

Manjoo, Farhad. 2017. "Why Tech Is Starting to Make Me Uneasy." *New York Times*, October 11, 2017.

Marcaux, Alexei. 2017. "The Power and the Limits of Milton Friedman's Arguments Against Corporate Social Responsibility." In *Wealth, Commerce, and Philosophy: Foundational Thinkers and Business Ethics*, edited by Eugene Heath and Byron Kaldis, 339–380. Chicago: University of Chicago Press.

Matthews, Dylan. 2016. "Remember That Study Saying America Is an Oligarchy? 3 Rebuttals Say It's Wrong." *Vox*, May 9, 2016.

Mauboussin, Michael J., and Dan Callahan. 2015. "A Long Look at Short-Termism: Questioning the Premise." *Journal of Applied Corporate Finance* 27 (3): 70–82.

McCarthy, Justin. 2015. "Little Change in Percentage of Americans Who Own Stocks." Gallup, April 22, 2015.

McClellan, Mark B., and Douglas O. Staiger. 2000. "Comparing Hospital Quality at For-Profit and Not-for-Profit Hospitals." In *The Changing Hospital Industry: Comparing For-Profit and Not-for-Profit Institutions*, edited by David M. Cutler, 93–112. Chicago: University of Chicago Press.

McGrattan, Ellen R., and Richard Rogerson. 2004. "Changes in Hours Worked, 1950–2000." *Federal Reserve Bank of Minneapolis Quarterly Review* 28, no. 1 (2004): 14–33.

Melzer, Brian T. 2011. "The Real Costs of Credit Access: Evidence from the Payday Lending Market." *Quarterly Journal of Economics* 126: 517–555.

Mishel, Lawrence, and Alyssa Davis. 2015. "Top CEOs Make 300 Times More Than Typical Workers." Issue Brief No. 399, Economic Policy Institute, June 21, 2015.

Moran, Joe. 2018. "Soiling with Its Poison: The Problem with Employment That Is Insufficiently Rewarding." *Times Literary Supplement*, July 27, 2018.

Mullen, Jethro. 2016. "China Is No Longer the Biggest Foreign Holder of U.S. Debt." CNN Money, December 16, 2016.

Murphy, Kevin J., and Jan Zabojnik. 2004. "CEO Pay and Appointments: A Market-Based Explanation for Recent Trends." *American Economic Review* 95, no. 2 (May): 192–196.

Murphy, Kevin J., and Jan Zabojnik. 2007. "Managerial Capital and the Market for CEOs." Working Paper, April 2007. https://ssrn.com/abstract-984376.

Newport, Frank. 2018. "Democrats More Positive About Socialism Than Capitalism." Gallup, August 13, 2018. https://news.gallup.com/poll/240725/democrats-positive-socialism-capitalism.aspx.

Nguyen, Bang Dang, and Kasper Meisner Nielsen. 2014. "What Death Can Tell: Are Executives Paid for Their Contributions to Firm Value?" *Management Science* 60 (12): 2859–2885.

NVCA. 2016. "$58.8 Billion in Venture Capital Invested Across U.S." Press release, National Venture Capital Association, Washington, DC, January 15, 2016.

Ortega, Josué, and Philipp Hergovich. 2017. "The Strength of Absent Ties: Social Integration via Online Dating." ArXiv working paper, September 14, 2018.

Osborne, Evan. 2007. *The Rise of the Anti-Corporate Movement*. Westport, CT: Praeger.

Owens, David, Zachary Grossman, and Ryan Fackler. 2014. "The Control Premium: A Preference for Payoff Autonomy." *American Economic Journal: Microeconomics* 6, no. 4 (November): 138–161.

Paul, Karsten I., and Klaus Moser. 2009. "Unemployment Impairs Mental Health: Meta-analyses." *Journal of Vocational Behavior* 74: 264–282.

Pearlstein, Steven. 2016. "How Big Business Lost Washington." *Washington Post*, September 2, 2016.

Pellegrino, Bruno, and Luigi Zingales. 2017. "Diagnosing the Italian Disease." NBER Working Paper No. 23964. National Bureau of Economic Research, Washington, DC.

Pfeffer, Jeffrey. 2018. *Dying for a Paycheck: How Modern Management Harms Employee Health and Company Performance—and What We Can Do About It.* New York: HarperCollins.

Philippon, Thomas. 2011. "Has the Finance Industry Become Less Efficient? Or Where Is Wal-Mart When We Need It?" VoxEU, Center for Economic Policy Research, December 2, 2011. https://voxeu.org/article/where-wal-mart-when-we-need-it.

Philippon, Thomas. 2015. "Has the U.S. Finance Industry Become Less Efficient? On the Theory and Measurement of Financial Intermediation." *American Economic Review* 105 (4): 1408–1438.

Philippon, Thomas, and Ariell Reshef. 2012. "Wages and Human Capital in the U.S. Finance Industry, 1909–2006." *Quarterly Journal of Economics* 127, no. 4 (November): 1551–1609.

Phillips, Tim, and Rebecca Clare. 2015. *Game of Thrones on Business: Strategy, Morality and Leadership Lessons from the World's Most Talked-About TV Show.* Oxford: Infinite Ideas.

Protess, Ben, and Michael Corkery. 2016. "Just How Much Do the Top Private Equity Earners Make?" *New York Times*, December 10, 2016.

Roy, William G. 1997. *Socializing Capital: The Rise of the Large Industrial Corporation in America.* Princeton, NJ: Princeton University Press.

Rucker, Philip. 2011. "Mitt Romney Says 'Corporations Are People.'" *Washington Post*, August 11, 2011.

Russell, Karl, and Williams, Josh. 2016. "Meet the Highest-Paid C.E.O.s in 2015." *New York Times*, May 27, 2016.

Sampson, Rachelle C., and Yuan Shi. 2016. "Are US Firms and Markets Becoming More Short-Term Oriented? Evidence of Shifting Firm and Investor Time Horizons, 1980–2013." https://papers.ssrn.com/sol3/papers.cfm?abstract_id=2837524.

Scheiber, Noam. 2016. "At Trader Joe's, Good Cheer May Hide Complaints." *New York Times*, November 3, 2016.

Schizer, David M. 2016. "Between Scylla and Charybdis: Taxing Corporations or Shareholders (or Both)." Columbia Law and Economics Working Paper No. 536.

Schor, Juliet B. 2004. *Born to Buy*. New York: Scribner.

Schwitzgebel, Eric. 2009. "Do Ethicists Steal More Books?" *Philosophical Psychology* 22: 711–725.

Schwitzgebel, Eric, and Joshua Rust. 2009. "The Moral Behavior of Ethicists." *Mind* 118 (October): 1043–1059.

Schwitzgebel, Eric, and Joshua Rust. 2014. "The Moral Behavior of Ethics Professors: Relationships Among Self-Reported Behavior, Expressed Normative Attitude, and Directly Observed Behavior." *Philosophical Psychology* 27 (3): 293–327.

Schwitzgebel, Eric, Joshua Rust, Linus Ta-Lun Huang, Alan Moore, and Justin Coates. 2012. "Ethicists' Courtesy at Philosophy Conferences." *Philosophical Psychology* 25 (3): 331–340.

Segrave, Kerry. 2011. *Vision Aids in America: A Social History of Eyewear and Sight Correction Since 1900*. Jefferson, NC: McFarland.

Setser, Brad. 2017. "Dark Matter: Soon to Be Revealed?" *Follow the Money* (blog), Council on Foreign Relations, February 2, 2017.

Shah, Bimal R., Seth W. Glickman, Li Liang, W. Brian Gibler, E. Magnus Ohman, Charles V. Pollack Jr., Matthew T. Roe, and Eric D. Peterson. 2007. "The Impact of For-Profit Hospital Status on the Care and Outcomes of Patients With Non-ST-Segment Elevation Myocardial Infarction." *Journal of the American College of Cardiology* 50 (15): 1462–1468.

Shapiro, Carl. 2017. "Antitrust in a Time of Populism." Working Paper, University of California, Berkeley, October 24, 2017. http://dx.doi.org/10.2139/ssrn .3058345.

Shephard, Alex. 2018. "Don't Look to Democrats to Regulate Big Tech." *New Republic*, March 13, 2018.

Shu, Pian. 2013. "Career Choice and Skill Development of MIT Graduates: Are the "Best and Brightest" Going into Finance?" Working Paper, Harvard Business School.

Shu, Pian. 2016. "Innovating in Science and Engineering or 'Cashing In' on Wall Street? Evidence on Elite STEM Talent." Working Paper 16-067. Harvard Business School.

Silvergate, Harvey. 2011. *Three Felonies a Day: How the Feds Target the Innocent*. New York: Encounter Books.

Skiba, Paige Marta. 2012. "Regulation of Payday Loans: Misguided?" *Washington and Lee Law Review* 69 (2): 1023–1049.

Skiba, Paige Marta, and Jeremy Tobacman. 2011. "Do Payday Loans Cause Bankruptcy?" Vanderbilt Law and Economics Research Paper No. 11–13, December 1, 2011.

Skiba, Paige Marta, and Jeremy Tobacman. 2008. "Payday Loans, Uncertainty, and Discounting: Explaining Patterns of Borrowing, Repayment, and Default." Vanderbilt Law and Economics Research Paper No. 08–33, August 21, 2008.

Skorup, Brent. 2013. "Reclaiming Federal Spectrum: Proposals and Recommendations." *Columbia Science and Technology Law Review* 15 (Fall): 90–124.

Song, Jae, David J. Price, Faith Guvenen, and Nicholas Bloom. 2015. "Firming Up Inequality." NBER Working Paper No. 21199. National Bureau of Economic Research, Washington, DC.

Sprothen, Vera. 2016. "Trading Tech Accelerates Toward Speed of Light." *Wall Street Journal*, August 7, 2016.

SSTI. 2016. "$77.3B in Total Venture Capital Invested in 2015, Report Finds; VC Trends to Look for in 2016." State Science and Technology Institute, Columbus, Ohio, January 15, 2016.

Stambor, Zak. 2018. "Google's Ad Revenue Jumps Nearly 25% in 2017." DigitalCommerce360, February 1, 2018. https://www.digitalcommerce360.com/2018/02/01/googles-ad-revenue-jumps-nearly-25-in-2017.

Statista. 2017. "Media Advertising Spending in the United States from 2015 to 2021." https://www.statista.com/statistics/272314/advertising-spending-in-the-us (accessed September 29, 2018).

Stein, Jeff, and Jena McGregor. 2018. "CEO Pay Jumps to $19 Million Annually, as Fears Mount over the Wealthy Pocketing Gains." *Washington Post*, August 16, 2018.

Stephens-Davidowitz, Seth. 2017. *Everybody Lies: Big Data, New Data, and What the Internet Can Tell Us About Who We Really Are.* New York: HarperCollins.

Summers, Lawrence H. 2017. "The Jury Is Still Out on Corporate Short-Termism." *Financial Times*, February 9, 2017.

Surowiecki, James. 2016. "The Financial Page: Unlikely Alliances." *New Yorker*, April 25, 2016.

Syverson, Chad. 2011. "What Determines Productivity?" *Journal of Economic Literature* 49(2): 326–365.

Taub, Amanda. 2016. "How Stable Are Democracies? 'Warning Signs Are Flashing Red.'" *New York Times*, November 29, 2016.

Tausig, Mark. 1999. "Work and Mental Health." In *Handbook of the Sociology of Mental Health*, edited by Carol S. Aneshensel and Jo C. Phelan, 255–274. New York: Kluwer.

Taylor, Lucian A. 2013. "CEO Wage Dynamics: Estimates from a Learning Model." *Journal of Financial Economics* 108: 79–98.

Taylor, Timothy. 2014. "Opting Out of the U.S. Corporate Income Tax." *Conversable Economist* (blog), December 22, 2014.

Terviö, Marko. 2008. "The Difference That CEOs Make: An Assignment Model Approach." *American Economic Review* 98, no. 3 (June): 642–668.

Thomas, Landon, Jr. 2017. "Why Are Mutual Fund Fees So High? This Billionaire Knows." *New York Times*, December 30, 2017.

Tomassi, Kate DuBose. 2006. "Most Common Resume Lies." *Forbes*, May 23, 2006.

Touré-Tillery, Maferima, and Ann L. McGill. 2015. "Who or What to Believe: Trust and the Differential Persuasiveness of Human and Anthropomorphized Messengers." *Journal of Marketing* 79 (July): 94–110.

Town, Robert, Douglas Wholey, Roger Feldman, and Lawton R. Burns. 2006. "The Welfare Consequences of Hospital Mergers." NBER Working Paper No. 12244. National Bureau of Economic Research, Washington, DC.

Viscusi, Kip. 1980. "Union, Labor Market Structure, and the Welfare Implications of the Quality of Work." *Journal of Labor Research* 1, no. 1 (Spring): 175–192.

Wahba, Phil. 2015. "Shoplifting, Worker Theft Cost Retailers $32 Billion Last Year." *Fortune*, June 24, 2015.

Wai, Jonathan, and David Lincoln. 2016. "Investigating the Right Tail of Wealth: Education, Cognitive Ability, Giving, Network Power, Gender, Ethnicity, Leadership, and Other Characteristics." *Intelligence* 54: 1–32.

Walker, David I. 2012. "The Law and Economics of Executive Compensation: Theory and Evidence," in *Research Handbook on the Economics of Corporate Law*, edited by Claire A. Hill and Brett H. McDonnell. Cheltenham, UK: Edward Elgar, 2012.

Wallis, John Joseph. 2005. "Constitutions, Corporations, and Corruption: American States and Constitutional Change, 1842 to 1852." *Journal of Economic History* 65, no. 1 (March): 211–256.

Warren, Geoff. 2014. "Long-Term Investing: What Determines Business Horizon?" CIFR Paper No. 39. Center for International Finance and Regulation, University of Melbourne.

Watts, Duncan J., and David M. Rothschild. 2017. "Don't Blame the Election on Fake News. Blame It on the Media." *Columbia Journalism Review*, December 5, 2017.

Weeks, Miles. 2016. "Legendary Hedge Fund Wants to Use Atomic Clocks to Beat High-Speed Traders." *Bloomberg News*, July 7, 2016.

Yang, Stephanie. 2018. "Elizabeth Warren Maintains a Hard Line on the Big Banks." *Wall Street Journal*, June 1, 2018.

Younkins, Edward. 1998. "Cinema and the Capitalist Hero." Foundation for Economic Education, Atlanta, June 1, 1998.

Zak, Paul J., and Stephen Knack. 2001. "Trust and Growth." *Economic Journal* 111, no. 470 (April): 295–321.

Zauzmer, Julie M. 2013. "Where We Stand: The Class of 2013 Senior Survey." *Harvard Crimson*, May 28, 2013.

Zhen, Liu. 2017. "Shanghai Adopts Facial Recognition System to Name, Shame Jaywalkers." *South China Morning Post*, July 3, 2017.

Zingales, Luigi. 2012. *A Capitalism for the People: Recapturing the Lost Genius of American Prosperity*. New York: Basic Books.

Zingales, Luigi. 2017. "Towards a Political Theory of the Firm." *Journal of Economic Perspectives* 31, no. 3 (Summer): 113–130.

Zinman, Jonathan. 2008. "Restricting Consumer Credit Access: Household Survey Evidence on Effects Around the Oregon Rate Cap." Working Paper, Dartmouth College, December 2008.

Zmuda, Natalie. 2014. "Coca-Cola Maintains Marketing Spending Amid Sluggish Demand." *Advertising Age*, July 22, 2014.

Zuluaga, Diego. 2016. "Why Corporation Tax Should Be Scrapped." IEA Discussion Paper No. 74. Institute of Economic Affairs, London.

# INDEX